Studies in Development Economics and Policy

General Editor: **Anthony Shorrocks**

UNU WORLD INSTITUTE FOR DEVELOPMENT ECONOMICS RESEARCH (UNU-WIDER) was established by the United Nations University as its first research and training centre and started work in Helsinki, Finland, in 1985. The purpose of the Institute is to undertake applied research and policy analysis on structural changes affecting the developing and transitional economies, to provide a forum for the advocacy of policies leading to robust, equitable and environmentally sustainable growth, and to promote capacity strengthening and training in the field of economic and social policy-making. Its work is carried out by staff researchers and visiting scholars in Helsinki and through networks of collaborating scholars and institutions around the world.

UNU World Institute for Development Economics Research (UNU-WIDER)
Katajanokanlaituri 6B, FIN-00160 Helsinki, Finland

Titles include:

Tony Addison and Alan Roe (*editors*)
FISCAL POLICY FOR DEVELOPMENT
Poverty, Reconstruction and Growth

Tony Addison, Henrik Hansen and Finn Tarp (*editors*)
DEBT RELIEF FOR POOR COUNTRIES

George J. Borjas and Jeff Crisp (*editors*)
POVERTY, INTERNATIONAL MIGRATION AND ASYLUM

Ricardo Ffrench-Davis and Stephany Griffith-Jones (*editors*)
FROM CAPITAL SURGES TO DROUGHT
Seeking Stability for Emerging Economies

David Fielding (*editor*)
MACROECONOMIC POLICY IN THE FRANC ZONE

Basudeb Guha-Khasnobis and Ravi Kanbur (*editors*)
INFORMAL LABOUR MARKETS AND DEVELOPMENT

Basudeb Guha-Khasnobis (*editor*)
THE WTO, DEVELOPING COUNTRIES AND THE DOHA DEVELOPMENT AGENDA
Prospects and Challenges for Trade-led Growth

Aiguo Lu and Manuel F. Montes (*editors*)
POVERTY, INCOME DISTRIBUTION AND WELL-BEING IN ASIA DURING THE TRANSITION

Mark McGillivray (*editor*)
INEQUALITY, POVERTY AND WELL-BEING

Robert J. McIntyre and Bruno Dallago (*editors*)
SMALL AND MEDIUM ENTERPRISES IN TRANSITIONAL ECONOMIES

Vladimir Mikhalev (*editor*)
INEQUALITY AND SOCIAL STRUCTURE DURING THE TRANSITION

E. Wayne Nafziger and Raimo Väyrynen (*editors*)
THE PREVENTION OF HUMANITARIAN EMERGENCIES

Matthew Odedokun (*editor*)
EXTERNAL FINANCE FOR PRIVATE SECTOR DEVELOPMENT
Appraisals and Issues

Laixiang Sun (*editor*)
OWNERSHIP AND GOVERNANCE OF ENTERPRISES
Recent Innovative Developments

UNU-WIDER (*editors*)
WIDER PERSPECTIVES ON GLOBAL DEVELOPMENT

THE EXPERT GROUP ON DEVELOPMENT ISSUES (EGDI) consists of a number of international experts in development-related academic fields along with Swedish policy-makers. The main task of EGDI is to contribute to an increased understanding of global development and an improved effectiveness of development policies. The group initiates and produces studies of importance to the international development debate. EGDI is funded by the Swedish Ministry for Foreign Affairs. The research interests of the group, as well as approaches taken in EGDI studies, provide important perspectives on the Swedish policy for global development.

EGDI Secretariat, Ministry for Foreign Affairs
SE-103 39 Stockholm, Sweden

Studies in Development Economics and Policy
Series Standing Order ISBN 0–333–96424–1
(*outside North America only*)

You can receive future titles in this series as they are published by placing a standing order. Please contact your bookseller or, in case of difficulty, write to us at the address below with your name and address, the title of the series and the ISBN quoted above.

Customer Services Department, Macmillan Distribution Ltd, Houndmills, Basingstoke, Hampshire RG21 6XS, England

---

Informal Labour Markets and Development

Edited by

Basudeb Guha-Khasnobis

and

Ravi Kanbur

palgrave
macmillan

First published 2006 by
PALGRAVE MACMILLAN
Houndmills, Basingstoke, Hampshire RG21 6XS and
175 Fifth Avenue, New York, N.Y. 10010
Companies and representatives throughout the world

PALGRAVE MACMILLAN is the global academic imprint of the Palgrave Macmillan division of St. Martin's Press, LLC and of Palgrave Macmillan Ltd. Macmillan® is a registered trademark in the United States, United Kingdom and other countries. Palgrave is a registered trademark in the European Union and other countries.

ISBN-13: 978-1-4039-8755-6
ISBN-10: 1-4039-8755-6

This book is printed on paper suitable for recycling and made from fully managed and sustained forest sources.

A catalogue record for this book is available for the British Library.

Library of Congress Cataloging-in-Publication Data
Informal labour markets and development / edited by Basudeb Guha-Khasnobis and Ravi Kanbur.
p.cm.
Conference papers.
Includes bibliographical references and index.
ISBN 1-4039-8755-6 (cloth)
1. Informal sector (Economics)—Developing countries—Congresses. 2. Labor market—Developing countries—Congresses. 3. Structural adjustment (Economic policy)—Developing countries—Congresses. I. Guha-Khasnobis, Basudeb. II. Kanbur, S. M. Ravi. III. World Institute for Development Economics Research. IV. Sweden. Expert Group on Development Issues.
HD2346.5.I528 2006
331.109172'4—dc22 2006043200

10 9 8 7 6 5 4 3 2 1
15 14 13 12 11 10 09 08 07 06

Printed and bound in Great Britain by
Antony Rowe Ltd, Chippenham and Eastbourne

Contents

List of Figures

List of Tables

Foreword

This volume brings together a significant new collection of papers on informal labour markets in developing countries. The papers were originally presented at a conference organized in Helsinki in September 2004 by the World Institute for Development Economics Research of the United Nations University (UNU-WIDER) in collaboration with the Expert Group on Development Issues (EGDI) at the Swedish Ministry for Foreign Affairs.

Informal labour markets are unregulated, allowing them a free hand to adjust and evolve. At the same time these markets are unprotected, leaving workers more vulnerable to negative shocks. By examining the critical role of informal labour markets in allowing countries to adjust successfully to the forces of globalization, this volume brings to the fore a number of problems associated with the expansion of informal employment, such as poor working conditions, the lack of worker protection, and the proliferation of urban slums. The theoretical and empirical case studies from Africa, Asia, Central Europe and Latin America facilitate comparisons across developing countries from diverse geographical areas. The wealth of empirical information contained in these chapters, and in the literature more widely, can be used to develop guiding principles for intervention that are based on ground level reality.

ANTHONY SHORROCKS
Director, UNU-WIDER

ANNIKA SÖDER
Chairperson, EGDI
State Secretary for International Development Cooperation

Acknowledgements

The editors are grateful to Adam Swallow and Janis Vehmaan-Kreula of UNU-WIDER for their tireless commitment in preparing the final manuscript. They would also like to thank the staff of the Expert Group on Development Issues (EGDI) at the Swedish Ministry for Foreign Affairs, especially Ingrid Widlund and Torgny Holmgren.

UNU-WIDER acknowledges the financial contributions to the research programme by the governments of Denmark (Royal Ministry of Foreign Affairs), Finland (Ministry for Foreign Affairs), Norway (Royal Ministry of Foreign Affairs), Sweden (Swedish International Development Cooperation Agency – Sida) and the United Kingdom (Department for International Development – DfID).

Notes on the Contributors

Christopher Adam is Reader in Development Economics at the University of Oxford, UK. His research is concerned principally with the macroeconomics of low-income countries, particularly those of sub-Saharan Africa, in particular with macroeconomics and the political economy of 'scaling up' of aid.

João Pedro W. de Azevedo is a research associate from the Brazilian Institute of Applied Economic Research (IPEA) and a fellow from the Policy Studies Institute in the UK. He has consulted with the World Bank, UNESCO, UNDP and the IADB on the evaluation and design of social programmes.

Indraneel Dasgupta is Reader, School of Economics, at the University of Nottingham, UK. His research interests lie primarily in the areas of microeconomic theory, development economics and public economics, on which he is published in numerous journals.

Ralitza Dimova is a Lecturer at the Economics and Finance department of Brunel's Business School, Brunel University, Uxbridge and a Research Affiliate at Caisse Nationale d'Assurance Vieillesse in Paris. Her areas of interest are labour economics, intergenerational transfers and economic development.

Abiodun O. Folawewo obtained his MSc and PhD from the University of Ibadan, Nigeria and is currently a lecturer at the Department of Economics, University of the West Indies, Mona, Kingston, Jamaica. His current research interests are in the areas of macroeconomic policy, labour and development economics.

Ira N. Gang is Professor of Economics at Rutgers University and is a fellow of the Migration Research Group at HWWA/HWWI – Hamburg, IZA – Bonn, and the William Davidson Institute – Ann Arbor. His areas of interest are development and transition economics, labour economics and political economy.

Michael Grimm is Professor of Economics at the University of Göttingen, Germany and, in addition, is a research associate at the

Development Economics Research Institute DIAL in Paris and the German Institute for Economic Research (DIW) in Berlin. He works mainly on problems related to income distribution and poverty, with a regional focus on West Africa, and teaches development economics, econometrics and welfare economics.

Basudeb Guha-Khasnobis and has been since 2002, a Research Fellow and Project Director at UNU-WIDER, Helsinki, Finland. Previous appointments include positions with IGIDR (Mumbai), the EXIM Bank of India (Bangalore) ICRIER (New Delhi), and that of a research consultant for several international organizations. He is the editor of *The WTO, Developing Countries and the Doha Development Agenda* (Palgrave Macmillan, 2004).

Isabel Günther is a Research Fellow and teaching assistant at the Department of Economics of the University of Göttingen, Germany. Her major research and teaching areas are poverty and inequality analysis, microeconomics of development and development finance, with a special interest in sub-Saharan Africa.

Ravi Kanbur is the T.H. Lee Professor of World Affairs, International Professor of Applied Economics and Management, Professor of Economics at Cornell University and a member of the Expert Group on Development Issues (EGDI) of the Swedish Ministry for Foreign Affairs. He has taught previously at Oxford, Cambridge, Princeton, Essex and Warwick Universities, and has served on the staff of the World Bank, including the position of Chief Economist for Africa.

John S. Landon-Lane is Assistant Professor of Economics at Rutgers University. His areas of interest are Bayesian econometrics, applied macroeconomics and economic growth.

Dibyendu S. Maiti is Research Officer of the Reserve Bank of India Endowment at the Centre for Studies in Social Sciences, Calcutta, India. Currently, he is engaged in research on the informal sector and the industrial economics of developing economies. He received an Indo-China Cultural Exchange Fellowship in 2005.

Sugata Marjit is Reserve Bank of India Professor at the Centre for Studies in Social Sciences, Calcutta, and Professor of Economics at the City University of Hong Kong. His research interests include international trade, economic development and public economics, in which he is published in both journals and books. He edits the *India Macroeconomics Annual* and has recently been awarded the VKRV Rao National Prize in Social Sciences.

Arup Mitra is Professor at the Institute of Economic Growth, Delhi, India, and presently Visiting Research Fellow at the Institute of Developing Economies, Japan. He has also been Ford Foundation Post-Doctoral Research Fellow at Northwestern University, USA. His research interests include urban development, labour and welfare, and industrial growth and productivity – themes on which he has written several publications.

Sam O. Olofin is Professor of Economics and Director of the Centre for Econometric and Allied Research (CEAR), University of Ibadan, Nigeria. His current research interests are in macroeconomic policy, applied econometrics and international economics.

Anushree Sinha is a Senior Fellow and Chief Economist at NCAER, New Delhi, India, and has carried out development research at the universities of Oxford and Pennsylvania. Presently, she is involved in macro analysis of the Indian and African informal sector and gender.

Eduardo Sojo coordinates the Cabinet of the President of Mexico in economic and social areas, and heads the Office for Public Policies in the presidential office. He has held several positions in federal and state governments, including Chief of Staff to the governor of the State of Guanajuato and Director for Economic and Employment Surveys at the National Institute for Statistics (INEGI).

Tulus Tambunan is currently a lecturer and researcher at the Faculty of Economics, University of Trisakti, Jakarta, Indonesia. His main research areas are poverty and income distribution, economic growth and the development of small and medium-sized enterprises, and the informal sector.

Roberto Villarreal heads the Unit for Social and Regional policies at the Office for Public Policies, in the presidential office of Mexico. Previously, he served in the federal government in areas of social development, public finance, industry and technology.

Guanghua Wan is a Senior Research Fellow, Programme and Project Director at UNU-WIDER, Helsinki, Finland. He has taught at the University of New England and University of Sydney, and has published extensively on the Chinese economy, particularly in the areas of poverty and inequality, rural development and economic growth.

Yuchun Zhu is an Associate Professor at the College of Economics and Management, Northwest A&F University, Yangling, China. She has written over forty papers and five books on the Chinese agricultural economy.

List of Abbreviations and Acronyms

ADB	Asian Development Bank
AusAID	Australian Agency for International Development
BAPPENAS	National Planning Agency (Indonesia)
BFG	Bourguignon, Fournier and Gurgand (2001)
BIHS	Bulgarian Integrated Household Surveys
BPS	Central Bureau of Statistics (Indonesia)
CEAR	Centre for Econometric and Allied Research (Nigeria)
CEE	Central and East European
CGE	Computable General Equilibrium
CPI	Consumer Price Index
CRS	Constant Returns to Scale
CSO	Central Statistical Organisation
DDA	Delhi Development Authority
DfID	Department for International Development (UK)
DIW	German Institute for Economic Research
DMEs	Directory-Manufacturing Enterprises
EGDI	Expert Group on Development Issues
ENCE	Brazilian National School of Statistics
EU	European Union
FOMC	First Order Markov Chain
FOS	Federal Office of Statistics (Nigeria)
IBGE	Brazilian National Office of Statistics
IIA	Independence of Irrelevant Alternatives
i.i.d.	independently identically distributed
ILO	International Labour Organization
IMF	International Monetary Fund
INEGI	National Institute for Statistics Geography and Informatics (Mexico)
INSD	Institut National de la Statistique et de la Démographie (Burkina Faso)
IPEA	Institute of Applied Economic Research (Brazil)
IUDP	Integrated Urban Development Programme
IV	Instrumental Variable
LDC	less developed countries

LSMS	Living Standards Measurement Study, World Bank
MMTC	Minerals and Material Trading Corporation
MNCs	multinational corporations
NBS	National Bureau of Statistics (China)
NCAER	National Council of Applied Economic Research (India)
NDMEs	non-directory manufacturing enterprises
NSS	national sample survey
NSSO	National Sample Survey Organisation (India)
OECD	Organisation for Economic Cooperation and Development
OGL	Open General Licence
OLS	Ordinary Least Square
OPK	Special Market Operation (SSN programme, Indonesia)
QRs	quantitative restrictions
SAM	social accounting matrix
SAP	Structural Adjustment Programme
SEEUY	Self-Employment for Educated Unemployed Youth
SEPUP	Self-Employment Programme for the Urban Poor
Sida	Swedish International Development Cooperation Agency
SMERU	Social Monitoring and Early Response Unit (Indonesia)
SMEs	small and medium enterprises
SOEs	state-owned enterprises
SSA	sub-Saharan Africa
SSN	social safety net
SUSENAS	Survei Sosial Ekonomi Nasional (National Socio-Economic Household Survey, Indonesia)
TVEs	town and village enterprises
UNDP	United Nations Development Programme
UN-HABITAT	United Nations Human Settlements Programme
UNU	United Nations University
WIDER	World Institute for Development Economics Research of the UNU
WIEGO	Women in Informal Employment: Globalizing and Organizing
WTO	World Trade Organization

1
Introduction: Informal Labour Markets and Development

Basudeb Guha-Khasnobis and Ravi Kanbur

The majority of the poor in developing countries depend on the informal sector for their livelihoods. Understanding the informal sector – in particular, informal employment – is therefore crucial for the success of economic development and poverty reduction strategies. Its persistence and expansion over time and across countries prove that the informal sector is not a transitory phenomenon in the development process, waiting to be absorbed by the formal sector. Rather, it is now fairly well recognized that formal and informal sectors will cohabit, and are very much interlinked in subtle and complicated ways. This volume introduces a significant new collection of papers on informal labour markets in developing countries. The papers were originally presented at a major conference organized in Helsinki by the Expert Group on Development Issues (EGDI) at the Swedish Ministry of Foreign Affairs, and the World Institute for Development Economics Research (UNU-WIDER) in September 2004. We have divided the volume into two parts. Part I, *Economic Reform and Informal Labour Markets*, addresses the new dimension added to the complexity of informal labour markets by the recent waves of economic reforms in many developing countries. As the urban informal labour market has been the subject of special policy concern, Part II, *Survival Strategies of the Urban Poor*, focuses on informal employment in the main cities of selected developing countries.

In most cases, certain operational criteria, such as lack of social security coverage, leave entitlements and written contracts, are used to define informal employment. Common additional characteristics include a low level of earnings, unstable working conditions, lack of affiliation to labour organizations and the illegal or quasi-legal nature of the work performed. These common operational criteria were used to identify informal employment in the different chapters of this volume.

In Part I, we attempt to explore the transforming relationship between the formal and informal sectors during liberalization as well as transition. Informal wages are the relevant earning index of the substantial majority of the workforce in a developing economy. Marjit and Maiti (Chapter 2) establish in theory that the impact of deregulatory policies on this index will be positive, provided capital is allowed to flow into the informal sector. They also find empirical support for this proposition after analyzing survey-based data on India during its phase of liberalization. As export markets expanded in India, the informal rural industries showed increasing dynamics of technology adoption and growth, leading to a reorganization of the informal–formal relationship in production. It was difficult for smaller units to survive independently. Rather, it was profitable for them to tie up with larger units with better access to capital and information regarding markets and policies. Marjit and Maiti observe that an increasing amount of working capital went to this newly emerging class of *tied* artisans and, simultaneously, there was a decline in capital formation in the formal sector. Thus, far from absorbing informal activities, the formal sector actually relied upon the informal sector in order to increase its competitiveness and profits.

Unsurprisingly, therefore, high and sustained growth rates are not necessarily accompanied by a corresponding growth in formal employment. Sinha and Adam (Chapter 3) explain this apparent phenomenon of 'jobless growth' in India with the help of a Computable General Equilibrium model. Their simulations imply that official statistics may correctly record the number of 'registered' workers declining, but they fail to record the strong growth of 'unregistered' workers in the economy. Growth in the economy is actually supported by a huge force of 'unregistered' or informal workers. Sinha and Adam vindicate the findings of Marjit and Maiti while concluding that, in the face of strong competition, the formal sector of India reacted by outsourcing to the informal sector and retrenching formal workers to replace them with informal workers. However, though there is less unemployment than actually shown in official records, most of the informal workers suffer from substandard living conditions, as reflected by the fall in their real wages in the simulations. Therefore, even though the informal sector facilitates successful adjustment during globalization and, hence, should be allowed to function in its own way, there is reason to argue that certain elements of formality should probably be introduced into these markets to prevent any exploitation implied by falling real wages, at least for some of the workers.

Union-mandated formal wage contracts tend to protect workers from such exploitation by ensuring that they receive fair pay. However,

Dasgupta and Marjit (Chapter 4) show that if the state is forced (for political reasons) to maintain industrial employment despite import liberalization (for example, through cheaper credit to firms), evasion of formal contracts by employers will increase due to a rise in the formal–informal wage gap. This outcome is generated by institutional delays in the punishment of employers' evasion of formal contracts. Greater contract evasion will entail greater diversion of resources to conflict resolution between employers and unions. To moderate such waste, the state must attenuate its role as the enforcer of contracts between unions and employers.

The role of the state also comes to the fore in the case of the township and village enterprises (TVEs) in China. TVEs can be considered as an informal sector because they are mostly composed of marginal activities and remain largely unregulated. One particular aspect of TVE development is its role in job creation. Wan and Zhu (Chapter 5) estimated labour absorption elasticities for east, central and west China, as well as for China as a whole. They found that the labour absorption capacity of TVEs is quite large, with the elasticity averaging 1.6. That is, every 1 per cent increase in output could induce a 1.6 per cent increase in employment. Using this estimate, the growth rate of over 10 per cent in recent years could have produced a 16 per cent increase in TVE employment every year. That means a doubling of the labour force in TVEs every five years. This did not happen in reality because TVEs in China are becoming more and more capital intensive. In order to reap the full benefit of the labour absorption capacity of the informal sector, this point should be borne in mind by policymakers when making decisions about TVE-related government policies.

The relative expansion of the informal sector is also a hallmark of countries in transition. Dimova, Gang and Landon-Lane (Chapter 6) report that in Bulgaria, the private sector is composed of two very different groups of labourers; those who obtain formal private sector jobs and those who obtain informal private sector jobs. The cause of the co-existence of the formal and informal sectors appears to be the side effects of deliberate government policy. Government policy *vis-à-vis* extra taxes, protective labour legislation, support for unions, payoffs, and a variety of other measures ensures, 'artificially', that the formal private sector will be a high cost sector. The political economy of transition led to policy inertia during the first half of the 1990s. A banking crisis struck in the period December 1996–January 1997. Rapid privatization of state-owned enterprises followed. Between 1995 and 1997, the informal sector grew both absolutely and relatively to the private sector, while the public sector shrank in absolute and relative terms. Overall, the pattern of the transition is one of movement out of formal employment into informal employment. The crisis caused a large reduction in the size of the public sector, and displaced workers could not find jobs in the formal private sector. Hence, they were forced to find work in the informal private sector. Also, the economic crisis forced people who were initially out of the labour force to rejoin the labour force, mostly in the informal sector.

The informal sector thrives mainly in the proximity of its formal counterpart and, hence, it is largely an urban phenomenon. In Part II, Azevedo (Chapter 7) presents empirical evidence on the determinants of labour market earnings for males and females in the slums of Rio de Janeiro, using data from a survey of 21,704 households spread over 51 slums. A main finding is the substantially lower returns to education for the residents of the slums of Rio de Janeiro when compared with the existing empirical evidence from other developing countries. There are significant neighbourhood effects in the city of Rio de Janeiro – the workers from slums closer to more affluent areas of the city had greater earnings, particularly in the case of males.

There is a substantial earning differential between formal entrepreneurs and formal wage-earners, as well as informal entrepreneurs and informal wage-earners. Entrepreneurs (both formal and informal) form the only occupational category in which the probability of entering increases with age, suggesting that this is an important segment for the older population (those above 40 years of age). Formal education has a positive effect on the probability of becoming a formal wage earner, playing a minor role in entrepreneurial choice, and informal wage earnings.

Mitra (Chapter 8) highlights the role of networks in accessing jobs in the urban labour market. Based on a survey of around 800 households in selected slums of Delhi, three types of network are identified. These operate through kinship bonds, caste and ethnicity bonds, and formal channels such as NGOs and employment exchanges. Variations in networks are noted across occupations. Given the differences in the nature of economic activities performed in different parts of the city, factors such as networks and the urge to reside near the contact person and the workplace make the urban labour market highly segmented. Hence, certain pockets within the city tend to become crowded by the growth of slums. Also, interspatial variations in terms of activities/occupations make slum population in the city a heterogeneous set, and thus their problems and needs vary substantially from one location to another, even within the city. Therefore, any uniform policy for clusters located in different zones may not be able effectively to tackle the problems of slum dwellers in the city. Government measures need to recognize these informal mechanisms, which low-income households have developed over the years to cope with uncertainties pertaining to jobs, housing, expenditure and other requirements of life, so that they become complementary to each other. Though possibilities of graduation from the informal to the formal sector are quite limited, as evident from our analysis, within the informal sector, workers are able to experience upward occupational mobility through their own initiatives and willingness to help each other. Planners, therefore, must understand the role of social capital in the context of economic gains and mobility of the informal sector workers and the poor.

It is important for policymakers to ascertain whether pro-poor growth policies have to address the informal sector specifically and in any particular way, or whether the informal sector evolves as does the rest of the economy and therefore good growth policies are also good informal sector policies. Grimm and Gunther (Chapter 9) argue that linkages between the formal and informal sector can exist on a macro- as well as on a micro-level, and analyze both levels for urban areas in Burkina Faso. In this country, macro- or inter-household linkages between the formal and informal economy are somewhat weak, and it is the performance of the whole economy in general that matters most for the informal sector. In contrast, micro- or intra-household linkages between informal and formal labour earnings seem more important, and an understanding of them appears extremely useful when thinking about poverty-reduction strategies. However, this study has also shown that the linkage coefficient for both inter- as well as intra-household linkages is less than one and, hence, good formal growth policies may not be enough for sufficient informal sectoral growth. Also, according to the findings, formal sector growth policies will be more beneficial for workers in the informal sector who are linked to the formal sector via intra-household linkages, and less beneficial to workers in the informal sector who are only linked to the formal sector via the market. As a result, pure 'informal' households might be left out of the overall economic growth. Thus, for poverty analysis, it may be more useful to think in terms of a dichotomy of 'formal and informal' households than of informal and formal wage-earners.

The informal labour market is not synonymous with an unskilled labour market. Olofin and Folawewo (Chapter 10) examine the nature of skill requirements in the urban informal sector of south-western Nigeria. The importance of education, tenure and experience variables in the empirical exercise of earnings determination shows that a high level of skill is critical in the informal sector. From a policy point of view, this is an indication that skill requirements in the informal sector, in respect of wage employment, may not be different from what obtains in the formal sector. At the same time, however, the informal labour market also propagates a social malaise; child labour. Tambunan (Chapter 11), in his survey of poor households in Jakarta, notes how these families turn to the child labour market to cope with poverty. The lack of rural development drives people to the city of Jakarta. Without inadequate infrastructure, the city wilts under the pressure of such influx, leading to fast deterioration in the living conditions of the poor, aggravating their poverty, and forcing them to send their children to work.

In Mexico approximately four million individuals originally in *extreme* poverty registered real income gains during 2000–02 and entered into *moderate* poverty, which is mostly concentrated in urban areas. Sojo and Villarreal (Chapter 12) argue that the social and demographic characteristics, as well as the economic needs of the moderate poor differ markedly from individuals in deeper levels of poverty. The moderate poor are somewhat forced to depend on informal occupation, due to certain structural factors that impede their participation in the formal sector. Opening up the formal sector for the moderate poor requires updating certain laws and regulations, and the provision of education, training, financial services, technical and administrative assistance for entrepreneurs and so on. The combination of all these policy changes should lead to improving income and social protection for the moderate poor, and integrating sectors that can benefit from trading with each other in order to increase competitiveness of the Mexican economy as a whole.

A key policy question is whether informal labour markets should be formalized. The experience gathered from this volume suggests that it is quite impossible to answer it with a *yes* or a *no*. There are several positives associated with informal labour markets: (a) they play a crucial role in developing and transitional countries in facilitating successful adjustment to the forces of globalization and reforms; (b) they provide means for survival to the vast majority of poor and very poor workers in a society; and (c) they facilitate the unlocking of entrepreneurial potential which could become lost in the mesh of formality. At the same time, there are concerns: (a) informal workers are vulnerable to certain forms of exploitation; and (b) being largely an urban phenomenon, the growth of informal labour markets exacerbates problems associated with slums, congestion, urban health and environment. Policy should aim at balancing these pros and cons, and identify the areas where formal intervention is required and to what degree.

Part I
Economic Reform and Informal Labour Markets

2

Globalization, Reform and the Informal Sector

Sugata Marjit and Dibyendu S. Maiti

Introduction

It is well recognized that a substantial part of economic action in the developing world takes place in the informal sector, which hosts unregistered or officially unrecorded activities. Accordingly, the amount of informal employment is also substantial. Agenor (1996) and references therein suggest that the share of informal employment may be as high as 70–80 per cent in many developing countries. For example, in India the proportion is a high as 90 per cent when agriculture is included as a part of the informal sector. 'Informal' is sometimes interpreted as 'illegal'. Strictly speaking, officially unrecorded transactions are not legal because no taxes or licence fees are paid, or because they flout existing labour laws by paying lower wages and ignoring the usual fringe benefits paid to unionized labour in the organized sector. There are also criminal activities, such as smuggling, extortion, theft and so on. All of these, in a sense, are 'informal'. At the outset of this study, we define 'informal' as being essentially the non-criminal production of goods and services that utilizes unorganized workers at a market-determined wage with no restrictions on profitable retrenchment. Such a characterization allows us to focus on the economic conditions of the majority of the workforce in a typical developing country.

Deregulation, economic reform and increasing global exposure should have some impact on informal activities, wages and employment. The way production is organized between the formal and informal segments should also be affected. Unfortunately, empirical evidence on the interaction between the formal and informal sections is quite limited and scattered. However, there is a growing literature that deals with the informal sector of a relatively open, deregulated developing country. In this chapter, we cannot cover all possible dimensions of the problem but, instead, we make an attempt to highlight two specific issues.

The second section of this chapter deals with the issue of reform and informal wages. Is it true that a downsized formal segment depresses the informal wage by pushing laid-off workers from the formal sector into the informal? This is a concern of many who believe that increasing competition will lead to unemployment in the formal sector and to sliding wages in the informal sector. We look at a sketch of a model drawn from some recent papers in this area and conclude that informal wages and employment can go up even when displaced workers crowd into the informal sector. Recent papers by Kar and Marjit (2001), Wuyts (2001), Marjit and Beladi (2002), Marjit (2003) and Marjit *et al.* (2004) provide the building blocks. Empirical support for the theoretical conclusions is gathered from the national sample survey (NSS) data on informal manufacturing in India collected during various rounds in the pre- and post-liberalization periods. There seems to be ample evidence substantiating our theoretical claim. This part of the analysis is concerned with the general equilibrium structure, conceptualizing the formal and the informal as aggregates. We show that a contraction in the formal sector does not imply impoverishment for the existing set of informal workers just because some of the formal workers are forced to find jobs in the informal sector. If reforms are here to stay, capital will tend to move towards the informal sector over the longer run, and that in turn will increase the informal wage along with employment.

However, earlier discussion does not reflect on the changes in the organizational pattern for conducting formal and informal activities as markets expand and trade opens up. This is what we take up next. Informal artisans are integral parts of any traditional production system. Often they are tied to intermediaries, vendors, cooperatives and the like for marketing their items. Does reform or a process of widening of markets through trade alter such relationships? This is discussed in the third section, which is based on fieldwork and primary data.

We look at the operation of the formal/informal segments in the small or cottage industries of rural West Bengal, a province in eastern India. Following its increased exposure to international trade, essentially through expanding export markets, the nature of the formal/informal production structure is undergoing major transformation. There is a clear trend showing the breakdown of independent entrepreneurship of marginal producers who are becoming the tied suppliers to larger, formal units. This possibly corroborates the famous conjecture that the division of labour is determined by the extent of the market. We undertake an analysis of the operation, dynamics and organizational change in the rural industries undergoing rapid transformation through trade and expansion of markets.

One common element that characterizes both of the issues that we take up is a noticeable shift of allocation of complementary inputs to the informal sector. In our analysis of informal wage in India, we note that an upswing in accumulation takes place in informal manufacturing exactly when a clear downtrend is observed in organized manufacturing. In our field study on formal/informal interaction in rural India, we notice that allocation of working capital to the informal segment has been on the rise. Small, relatively poor, independent artisans can hardly keep stocks of expensive inputs, particularly in the quantities required by expanded markets. This forms part of the working capital that is being provided by the merchants and formal producers to tied artisans. Increasing investment by merchants and formal producers is clearly an outcome of the need of an expanding market when the capital market does not function properly.

Economic reform and informal wages

This section highlights the impact of typical deregulatory policy on informal wages and employment in a small, open developing economy. We have a model consisting of four goods. X is produced in the formal sector, with organized labour earning a fixed wage $\bar{w}$ and capital. This is an import-competing manufacturing good. Y is an exportable manufacturing good produced in the informal sector, with labour earning a market-determined wage $w(\bar{w} > w)$ and capital. Z is a non-traded informal good produced using labour and capital, and A is the agricultural product produced with informal labour and land. Workers must find a job either in the formal or the informal sector. Those who cannot be employed at $\bar{w}$ move to the informal segment and become absorbed in Y, Z or A. Such a 'full employment' interpretation of the labour market is consistent with the analyses of dual labour markets in the less developed countries (LDCs), as given in Carruth and Oswald (1981), Agenor and Montiel (1996), Marjit *et al.* (2000), Marjit and Beladi (2002), Marjit (2003) and Marjit and Acharyya (2003). We have a standard neoclassical general equilibrium set-up where each sector operates within competitive markets, constant returns to scale (CRS) and diminishing marginal productivity. The following equations constitute competitive equilibrium and the full-employment condition symbols used have standard interpretation from Jones (1965; 1971):

$$\bar{w}a_{LX} + ra_{KX} = P_X(1 + t) \tag{2.1}$$

$$wa_{LY} + ra_{KY} = P_Y \tag{2.2}$$

$$wa_{LZ} + ra_{KZ} = P_Z \tag{2.3}$$

$$wa_{LA} + Ra_{TA} = P_A \tag{2.4}$$

$$a_{KX}X + a_{KY}Y + a_{KZ}Z = \bar{K} \tag{2.5}$$

$$a_{LX}X + a_{LY}Y + a_{LZ}Z + a_{LA}A = \bar{L} \tag{2.6}$$

$$a_{TA}A = T \tag{2.7}$$

$$D_Z(P_Z,(1 + t),\Omega) = Z \tag{2.8}$$

We chose $P_X = P_Y = P_A = 1$ for this 'small' economy; t is the tariff rate, X is the imported good, and Y and A are the exported goods. P_Z is determined internally.

Given t, (2.1)–(2.4) determine r, w, P_Z and R and hence the factor proportions. This also determines aggregate factor income 'Ω'. Then (2.7) and (2.8) determine A and Z and (2.5) and (2.6) determine X and Y. This completes the determination of the general equilibrium.

Suppose liberal trade policy leads to a decline in t. What would be the implication with regard to informal wages and employment?

A decline in t must reduce r, increase w and reduce R, the rental rate in agriculture. The usual output response will be a contraction in X. As a_{LX} declines with a rise in $\bar{w}/r$, formal employment will fall and informal employment will rise. One could trace the full general equilibrium implications of a decline in t. This is unnecessary for our purpose. A decline in R will increase a_{TA} and reduce A, and employment in agriculture and in the non-traded sector will rise.

This is the case where a reduction in formal employment, and the subsequent movement of displaced workers into the informal segment, raises informal wages. The clue to such a result lies in capital mobility.

For example, if capital cannot move between X and (Y, Z), a drop in t will reduce r, displacing workers but not allowing formal sector capital to move into the informal segment. This implies that the capital–labour ratio in the informal sector will fall, trading to a drop in w. Several variations of this type of structure have been attempted recently in Kar and Marjit (2001), Marjit and Beladi (2002) and Marjit *et al.* (2004), among others. The core result suggests that sufficiently limited capital mobility between the formal and informal sectors lends credibility to the conventional wisdom that more workers in the informal sector means lower wages, otherwise not.

Tables 2.1 and 2.2 provide some statistical evidence from the NSS data for non-directory manufacturing enterprises (NDMEs) in India. This is the

Table 2.1 Annual growth rates of real informal wage for states and union territories in India

States	1984/5 to 1989/90	1989/90 to 1994/5	1994/5 to 1999/00	1999/00 to 2000/1	Post reform average
Andhra Pradesh	−14.94	38.38	0.35	5.54	14.76
Assam	−12.59	9.41	0.50	19.95	9.95
Bihar	−12.48	9.26	−0.91	37.42	15.26
Gujarat	−8.02	5.86	3.76	9.47	6.36
Haryana	−15.42	23.39	−4.12	33.07	17.45
Himachal Pradesh	−11.52	−0.34	3.51	24.56	9.24
Karnataka	−12.82	21.55	7.02	13.44	14.00
Kerala	−14.90	12.56	2.69	21.21	12.15
Madhya Pradesh	−12.61	22.41	1.46	13.12	12.33
Maharashtra	−6.40	9.75	5.25	11.29	8.76
Orissa	−13.16	22.79	−2.39	33.19	17.86
Punjab	−15.14	12.20	−1.07	44.06	18.40
Rajasthan	−15.50	32.53	−1.34	33.04	21.41
Tamil Nadu	−10.11	6.41	14.13	11.49	10.68
Tripura	−14.31	14.90	−5.46	45.37	18.27
Uttar Pradesh	−13.20	18.00	−1.59	26.79	14.40
West Bengal	−11.26	11.41	−7.26	15.30	6.49
Andaman and Nichobar Islands		14.63	3.20	2.91	6.91
Chandigarh		19.21	5.50	12.47	12.39
Dadra and Nagar Haveli		9.83	−4.02	37.77	14.53
Delhi		13.27	20.39	12.11	15.26
Laksha Deep		−0.21	9.93	7.83	5.85
Pondicherry		20.77	−3.97	−18.56	−0.58
Goa		20.50	0.95	23.75	15.07
Jharkhand		20.71	2.84	33.64	19.06
Manipur		24.91	−4.19	26.83	15.85
Meghalaya		18.92	−5.29	33.58	15.73
Mizoram		19.93	−6.93	24.70	12.56
Nagaland		15.63	−1.96	25.16	12.94
Sikkim		28.81	−0.01	42.16	23.65

Sources: NSS reports on unorganized sector in India (various years) and own calculations.

Table 2.2 Annual growth rate (%) of real fixed capital stocks of formal and real fixed assets of informal sector

	Formal sector's real capital stocks			Informal sector's real fixed assets		
	1984/5 to 1989/90	1989/90 to 1994/5	1994/5 to 1999/2000	1984/5 to 1989/90	1989/90 to 1994/5	1994/5 to 1999/2000
Andhra Pradesh	15.77	19.77	−3.37	−7.80	−0.96	36.85
Assam	9.33	2.02	0.46	−6.84	−4.35	23.34
Bihar	−8.0	13.44	−23.06	−16.84	−8.67	36.85
Gujarat	−8.0	51.96	22.51	−3.72	4.87	13.12
Haryana	7.46	4.07	13.82	−2.33	2.71	33.11
Himachal Pradesh	2.75	5.78	3.56	16.64	−12.21	75.33
Karnataka	7.92	9.04	28.46	−6.78	−2.63	25.52
Kerala	5.52	0.52	4.19	−18.85	−2.30	50.75
Madhya Pradesh	4.17	7.56	−9.0	−6.15	−2.45	41.77
Maharashtra	11.56	6.26	7.3	0.80	8.50	34.06
Orissa	33.51	8.49	−9.64	−11.33	12.11	13.38
Punjab	9.34	4.02	−6.37	−12.22	−3.63	26.21
Rajasthan	3.31	12.34	10.46	−8.27	0.42	52.60
Tamil Nadu	15.58	15.06	1.91	−4.04	3.84	18.82
Tripura	90.03	−8.77	−18.81	−3.16	−0.01	40.32
Uttar Pradesh	7.59	10.75	−0.79	−7.97	−0.19	35.92
West Bengal	8.21	14.74	−8.9	−4.83	−2.77	53.23
Andaman and Nichobar Islands		29.23	−11.42		−2.27	95.83
Chandigarh		17.0	20.57		32.90	27.56
Dadra and Nagar Haveli		34.27	103.3		−5.65	141.11
Delhi		64.83	−13.28		−3.47	60.09
Pondicherry		34.43	13.71		−15.85	185.73
Goa		4.97	68.22		−8.17	102.01
Jharkhand		3.47	24.63		13.51	22.22
Manipur		408.76	−19.12		3.05	65.99
Meghalaya		−23.89	2.68		15.75	−9.61
Nagaland		24.34	−11.90		−10.65	115.01

Sources: Economic and Political Weekly Research Foundation (2000) and NSS (various years).

typical representative sample of the informal sector. Tables 2.1 and 2.2 show the increase in real informal wages across the states of India over the pre- and post-liberalization period, along with the growth of real fixed assets.

Table 2.2 also shows the decline in the rate of capital formation in organized manufacturing over the sample period. More detailed econometric analysis is available in Marjit *et al.* (2004). While the overall rate of unemployment, measured in terms of organized employment, has not improved during the reform period, the informal sector has possibly grown, with improved real incomes for the average informal worker.

One caveat should be relevant here. Real wages of agricultural labourers have experienced upswings and downturns, and at the time of writing had recently declined. One needs to explore in detail how informal wages for manufacturing and agriculture are actually related. Although they should have a positive correlation, there might be a host of factors that affects them differently. This should be an important agenda for future research.

Export market and production organization in rural formal and informal industries

This section deals with a micro-level analysis of informalization based on primary data from rural West Bengal, a major province in eastern India. India began liberalizing its economy in the mid-1980s and, since 1991, the process has been vigorously stepped up through the reduction of taxes, opening up to foreign trade and investment, and promoting other deregulatory policies.

Now, the questions are: how is the formal/informal reorganization of production responding to liberalization policies and to increasing market exposure, and to what extent? What are the reasons behind the increasing division of formal/informal productions? This section seeks to analyse the formal/informal division of production organization; essentially being a micro-statistical exercise to gain some first-hand experience of the process.

Important policy changes have taken place through the opening-up of trade (reduction in tariffs and interest rates and so on) and through the uncapping of investment limits of production units in small-scale and cottage industries. In spite of growing competition from large-scale industries and multinational corporations (MNCs), these policies have, to some extent, created favourable conditions for the development of small-scale and rural industries, adding national and overseas demand for crafts and aesthetic value-oriented goods (handmade goods). As a consequence, units having access to sufficient capital and marketing outlets have expanded at a good pace. On the other hand, due to organizational differences and structural backwardness, large sections of other producing units have now become linked to the *mahajans*, traders or master enterprises, to channel products to the national and overseas markets.

The division of informal and formal production units arises because of comparative production costs in the formal structure, such as wages, and administrative and transaction costs. As demand grows, specialization in the production process becomes more intensified to match diversified consumer demands. These specialized labourers engaged in the manufacturing activities of a factory should receive a formal wage rate and other amenities according to the Factory Act and other laws; otherwise, trade union activities become a threat. Thus, these wage costs are saved if the production process performed by the specialized labour force is fragmented to the informal sector.

Current theories of firm organization cannot explain the existence of informal production organization (such as subcontracting on a relatively low scale). They establish the superiority of a firm over the non-firm organization such as the putting out system[1] (Coase, 1937; Knight, 1946; Alchian and Demsetz, 1972; Williamson *et al.*, 1975) but, in practice, different forms of non-firm organizations have developed for reducing transaction costs or for tackling the constraints of organizational design. Through subcontracting, master enterprises or traders save administrative as well as supervision costs. Moreover, entrepreneurs in rural or remote areas face information gaps regarding markets and technology. Thus, to bridge these gaps, intermediaries have evolved to gather information on market sources, product design, types of product, and so on. Artisans with limited capital and traditionally-based skills become dependent on these intermediaries for information in exchange for a part of the profits. The artisans save the opportunity costs of their working capital. Furthermore, the surplus rural masses are forced to search for alternative employment due to the residual factor, and thus get involved in small-scale and cottage industries informally at the household level (Maiti, 2004).

As markets increase, the scale of operations has to expand, necessitating investment in capacity-building. Small local entrepreneurs are far more capital-constrained than businessmen and traders. Therefore, it is natural that the degree of tying-up increases with the expansion of the export market. This is related, in a different context, to a paper by Marjit and Roychowdhury (2004), which suggests that an expansion of market size usually leads to 'buy-outs' of existing joint ventures.

Database and methodology

Owing to the limitations of secondary data, a detailed primary survey was needed. The state of West Bengal was chosen purposely because of its significant growth in rural industries, crafts heritage and high density population. The districts of West Bengal have various diverse types of crafts and rural industries in the different cultural blocks, regions and villages. Keeping limitations of data availability in mind, the present study had adopted multistage stratified random sampling.

In stage 1, sample districts and industries are selected. Districts are divided into two strata by the degree of rural industrial advancement or backwardness on the basis of the percentage share of total workers[2] engaged in rural manufacturing, processing and repairing units. A district having more than 8 per cent of its workers in rural industries is considered relatively advanced; less than 8 per cent is considered backward (Table 2.3). This cut-off point was arrived at so that an equal number of districts are located above and below this benchmark. Two sample districts are

Table 2.3 Socioeconomic characteristics for sample districts, 2001–02

	Nadia	**Midnapore***	**Bankura**	**Purulia**
Area (sq. km)	3,927	14,081	6,882	6,259
Inhabited village (number)	1,248	10,474	3,565	2,456
Population (million)	4.60	9.64	3.19	2.54
Density (per sq. km)	981	686	464	405
% of total state population	5.74	12.02	3.98	3.16
% of total state land area	4.42	15.87	7.75	7.05
% of SC population, 1991	29.01	16.34	31.37	19.35
% of ST population, 1991	2.35	8.28	10.34	19.23
Net area sown (hectare)**	306.9	859.9	383.3	335.8
	(78.6)	(65.0)	(55.7)	(53.9)
Rural literacy rate	62.32	74.42	62.44	53.82
Male literacy	68.70	84.76	76.27	72.82
Female literacy	55.50	63.63	47.92	33.91
Road length (sq. km)	0.25	0.14	0.16	0.13
Road density (sq. km/lakh popu.)	942.82	1,699.24	341.47	783.35
Food-grain productivity (kg/hr.)	2,429	2,305	2,499	1728
Cropping Intensity	242	164	145	104
Agriculture wage rate (Rs, male)	56.00	57.48	55.02	47.48
Rural industrial workers (%), 1991	12.2	9.61	7.23	7.13
Rural non-agricultural workers (%)	46.2	35.7	30.3	28.3
Rural poverty (1999–2000)	28.35	19.83	58.62	78.72
Per capita monthly consumption (Rs)	458.29	490.20	353.28	280.15

Note: * Midnapore has recently been divided into East Midnapore and West Midnapore (2001). Our sample is located in East Midnapore, a relatively well developed area. At the time of the study, data for East Midnapore are not available.
** Figures in parentheses indicate the percentage share.
Source: Government of West Bengal (2001–02a; 2001–02b).

drawn from each stratum based on random sampling without replacement: Nadia and Midnapore from the advanced strata of the sample districts, while Bankura and Purulia constitute the backward strata. With the help of district-level officers and knowledgeable individuals, we prepare a list of units for each district (at the various administrative levels of local governance) consisting of two groups of industries; that is, industries common to all sample districts, and industries that are specific to a certain district. Two industries from the common group of handicrafts and one district-specific industry from each sample district are randomly selected. Our selection of common handicrafts includes handlooming and the brassware industry, while the district-specific industries include clay works in Nadia, hornware in Midnapore, conchshells in Bankura and lac works in Purulia (Table 2.4).

In stage 2, sample blocks of sample industries from the sample districts are drawn. A list of blocks according to type of industry is prepared for each sample district with the help of the local administrative departments. Because not all the blocks in the districts are equally important with respect to rural industries, a sample block for each industry is drawn randomly (see Table 2.4).

In stage 3, sample villages or a cluster[3] of villages from each sample block are drawn. So, a sample village or cluster of villages is randomly selected to represent each industry (see Table 2.4).

In stage 4, sample artisans/units have been selected, mindful of the respective production organization. After preparing an organization-wide list of producing units from each sample village or cluster of villages, 15 units from each production organization are randomly selected. If only one production organization exists in a cluster, 30 units are selected. From the above sample design, 356 units or proprietor households, representing independent (149 units), tied (162 units) and cooperative (45 units) production units, are selected for detailed survey for the financial year April 2001 to March 2002 (see Table 2.4).

Production stages and formal–informal division

Among the total surveyed units, the following informal characteristics are observed as dominant: non-registration (see Table 2.5), non-maintenance of accounts, male domination of entrepreneurship, backwardness regarding formal education and training, household premises units, dependence on other subsidiary activities, caste dominance of industrial activities, and so on (Maiti, 2004). The survey revealed that several distinct stages are adopted in the production process to produce use-value as well as

Table 2.4 Number of sample artisans/units according to sample design

	Stage 1	Stage 2	Stage 3	Stage 4			
Districts	Sample industry	Sample block	Village selection	Sample units/artisans under production organizations			
				Independent	Tied	Cooperative	All
Nadia	Handloom	Santipur	Fulia	12	15	15	72
	Brassware	Krishnagang	Matiari	12	15	0	27
	Clay works	Krishnagar-I	Sadhanpara	20	0	0	20
Midnapur	Handloom	Nilkunthi	Tamluk-I	15	15	0	30
	Brassware	Mahishadal	Ektarpur	3	15	0	18
	Hornware	Panskura-II	Baishnabchawk	12	7	15	34
Bankura	Handloom	Bankura-I	Kenjakura	15	15	15	45
	Brassware	Bankura-I	Mogra	0	30	0	30
	Conchshell	Indpur	Hatagram	15	15	0	30
Purulia	Handloom	Purulia	Nuagarh	15	15	0	30
	Brassware	Manbazar	Gopalnagar	0	20	0	20
	Lac works	Balarampur	Balarampur	30	0	0	30
Total				149 (41.85)	162 (45.51)	45 (12.64)	356 (100)

Source: Field surveys.

Table 2.5 Number of registered units

Industry	Registered	Not registered	All
Handloom, advanced region	22 (30.6)	50 (69.4)	72 (100)
Handloom, backward region	15 (20.0)	60 (80.0)	75 (100)
Brassware, advanced region	8 (17.8)	37 (82.2)	45 (100)
Brassware, backward region	0 (0.0)	50 (100.0)	50 (100)
Clay works	5 (25.0)	15 (75.0)	20 (100)
Hornware	7 (20.5)	27 (79.5)	34 (100)
Conchshell	6 (20.0)	24 (80.0)	30 (100)
Lac works	21 (70.0)	9 (30.0)	30 (100)
Total	84 (23.6)	272 (76.4)	356 (100)

Note: Figures given in parentheses represent percentage share.
Source: Field surveys.

aesthetic value of the industries, but these stages vary with the types of products and forms of production organization. Due to an extensive division of labour in the production process, specialization increases when artisans perform certain phases of the work in their own households or in workshops tied to master enterprises or *mahajans*.

Diverse types of technology and human skill are used in the production process across rural industries, along with traditional techniques. A detailed division of labour is established more intensively with technological development, irrespective of region. Production stages are vertically disintegrated among the producing units. Tied units also become specialized in certain types of work: the master producer or *mahajan*, on a contractual basis, assigns them a part or the whole task of particular products. The instruments/tools of production are owned/possessed by the artisan and the traders (or middleman engaged by them), or the formal producer/master enterprises mostly advance capital/raw materials on credit. The artisans make the product according to the design and order from them. When the artisans supply the finished products, they instantly receive payment for the value of *bani*[4] and, in some cases, compensation for transport. Mostly, they are under tight control[5] because they receive raw materials from the shops of *mahajans* or formal producers' factories without any compensation for transport.

A general notion on rural manufacturing activities is that it would operate on a small scale. However, workshops or factories that hire workers are simultaneously observed along with household units. A few of the relatively larger units hire more artisans on a daily rate basis. At the household production level, household labourers are unpaid. But the

Table 2.6 Characteristics of production organizations

Production organization	**Characteristics**
Independent unit	Possesses own fixed capital and working capital; has control over production process, types of products, sources of raw materials and marketing
Tied unit	Possesses own fixed capital, but is controlled by a master enterprise or contractor, *mahajans*, middleman who is supplied raw materials
Unit/artisan under cooperative	Possesses own fixed capital and is controlled by cooperative society

outsourcing system is different from the one that existed in Europe during the textile manufacturing phase of capitalist development. Obviously, artisans own the means of production, but also bear the losses for damage to production or raw materials; in very few cases does the *mahajan* or trader bear a proportion of the damage. Thus, these units, although seemingly independent, are in truth reliant on the formal sector for survival and, as such, are designated as tied units.

On the other hand, cooperative artisans are akin to the tied production units, but they benefit from society in terms of loans, bonuses, training, coverage of damages and so on, and enjoy certain democratic rights, according to rules. A certain proportion of the surplus is expended for administrative, managerial and marketing purposes, as the organization takes responsibility for marketing the items produced by its artisans.

Hence, it is evident that different forms of production organizations exist in rural industries; namely, units that are independent, tied or cooperative (see Table 2.6). Moreover, units are differentiated by size, defined by the labour used. Overall, of the independent units, 51.7 per cent (77 units) operate with the help of unpaid household labour, while 27.5 per cent (41 units) operate with hired workers in addition to household labour. The remaining 20.8 per cent (consisting of 31 units) run their production based solely on hired help. These are basically directory-manufacturing enterprises (DMEs) or formal producers. Strikingly, 13 per cent of the tied units and 15.6 per cent of the cooperative units utilize hired workers to some extent in their activities to supplement household labour. The remaining 87 per cent of the tied production units and 84.4 per cent of the cooperatives are operated entirely by household members. Looking at all the organizations, 72 per cent of the units rely on household labour, and 19.3 per cent of them employ hired

Table 2.7 Number of units of different production organizations combining all industries

Strata	Organization			
	Independent	Tied	Cooperative	Total
Solely on hired workers	31 (20.8)	0 (0.0)	0 (0.0)	31 (8.7)
Both household and hired workers	41 (27.5)	21 (13.0)	7 (15.6)	69 (19.3)
Solely on household workers	77 (51.7)	141 (87.0)	38 (84.4)	256 (72.0)
All	149 (100.0)	162 (100.0)	45 (100.0)	356 (100.0)

Note: Figure in parenthesis indicates the percentage.
Source: Field surveys.

labour jointly with household. The remaining 8.7 per cent of the units, operating as DMEs, are solely reliant on hired labour. One point that should also be noted is that a significant share of production units in rural areas are household-dominated, while a considerable number of independent units have switched over to factory production, which is dependent entirely on hired labour; tied and cooperative units also hire labourers (see Table 2.7).

Organizational change

As a result of liberalization (1991–2001), significant organizational change has taken place regarding the division of formal and informal production organizations. It can be observed that, out of a fixed set of 356 sample units, the share of independent units declined from 44.38 per cent in 1991 to 41.85 per cent in 2001. The most significant decline is observed in the case of cooperative units, dropping from 34.56 per cent to 12.64 per cent during the same period, while the share of tied units increased dramatically from 21.07 per cent to 45.51 per cent. Among these transformation processes, the tendency towards tiedness, subcontracting or the putting out system is dominant (Table 2.8).

Marketing channels

The essential precondition for growth of an industry, however small, is the demand for its products, which in turn is contingent on the behaviour of three types of market: local, national and export. While local demand for products of rural industries is insufficient because of the low

Table 2.8 Organizational change of industries during 10 years after economic liberalization, 1991–2001

Organization	**1991**	**2001**
Independent	158 (44.38)	149 (41.85)
Tied	75 (21.07)	162 (45.51)
Cooperative	123 (34.56)	45 (12.64)
Total	356 (100.00)	356 (100.00)

Note: Figure in parenthesis indicates the percentage.
Source: Field surveys.

purchasing power of the rural masses, demand in the national and export markets is expanding; the markets for products and raw materials have widened.

For example, in India, the Minerals and Material Trading Corporation (MMTC) supplied foreign scrap to local artisans but following the introduction of the Open General Licence (OGL), any individual can import material directly from abroad, and the MMTC discontinued its foreign scrap operations. Earlier, artisans were also able to import material through the *mahajans* or master enterprises but, due to paucity of funds, the big merchants and traders eventually captured the import market. Thus, most artisans have become reliant for raw materials on the formal producers or *mahajans*, who control prices, quality and frequency of supply. The *mahajans'* intervention and the artisans' persistent dependence on them have forced artisans to work on the *bani* (making charge) system.

In the conchshell, lac and hornware industries, producers in the remote rural areas are directly linked to important cities and towns through traders or formal producers. For instance, raw material for the conchshell industry comes from the coastal towns of southern India, and traders from different towns come to buy the final product. Some hornware industry units transact directly with export merchants or marketing agencies that deal with Japan, Germany and so on. Similarly, an upswing in the lac market is totally dependent on export markets. Markets are expanding because of the aesthetic appreciation of the products and cheap labour costs. A few artisans in the handlooming industries at Phulia are engaged in the production of clothing specifically for the Japanese market. Brassware artisans in Matiari have fairly good marketing channels in the national and export markets. See Figure 2.1 for a schematic representation of formal and informal marketing channels of independent producers for final products.

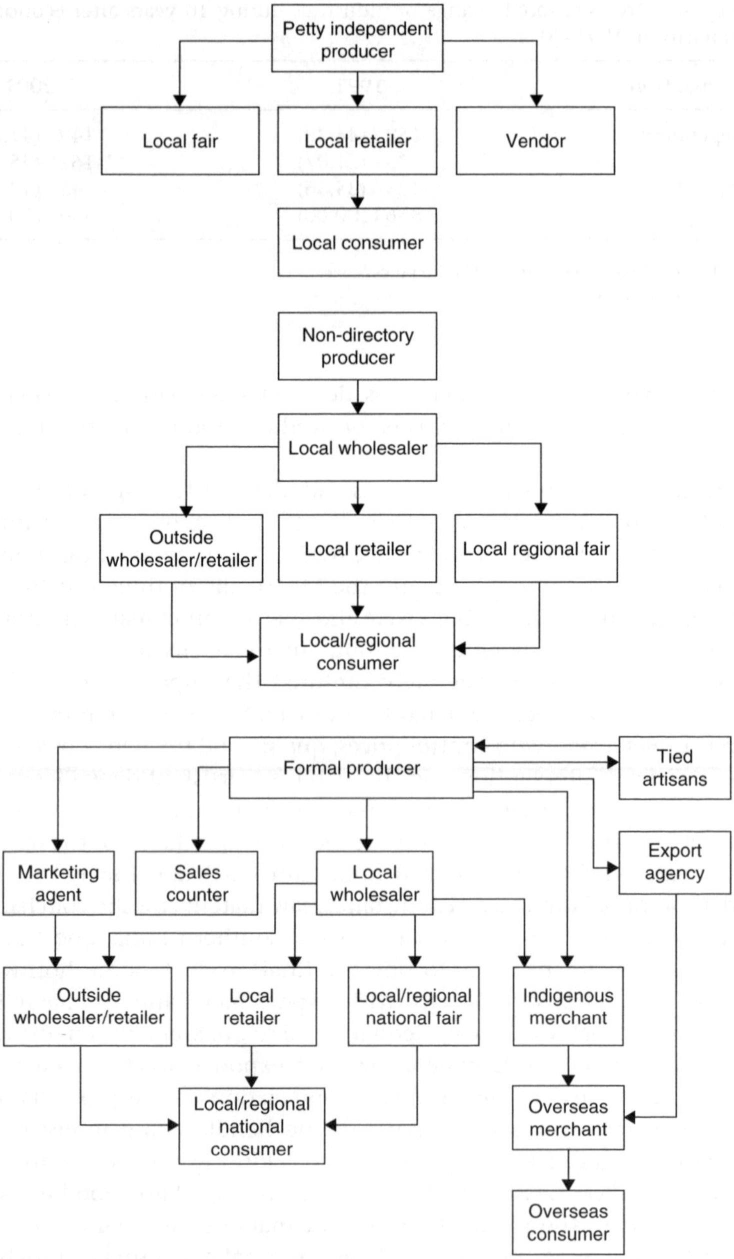

Figure 2.1 Schematic representation of formal and informal marketing channels of the independent producers for final products

Previously, cooperatives functioned by organizing the artisans and marketing their products through different government and non-governmental agencies (such as Manjusha, Tantuja and Bangashree). Recently, however, these activities have declined as a result of the government's reduction of assistance, grants and incentives to the cooperatives. Mismanagement and corruption also exhibit inefficiency within these organizations. Furthermore, artisans within the cooperative unit are paid long after the delivery of their products, inducing artisans to seek loans from the *mahajans* or work from master enterprises, who subsequently control the artisan producers.

As noted earlier, master enterprises, traders or the *mahajan*–middleman nexus expropriate a part of the value added. The ultimate surplus to the tied artisans is sufficient to cover their subsistence living only, and they are unable to invest more fixed capital in increasing the size of their manufacturing unit. Although this arrangement/channel at least ensures them subsistence living, they are forced to remain in the grip of the master enterprise or *mahajan*, who exploit their skills. Independent artisans, on the other hand, purchase raw materials from wholesalers (either within or outside the district). The small-scale independent artisans also procure raw materials from vendors.

The form marketing takes varies across organizations. Major forms of marketing are mainly selling door-to-door, supplying a fixed seller, own sales counter, local traders, trader (or middlemen engaged by them), formal producer, wholesale traders, exporting agency, own salesman, cooperative societies, marketing societies, fairs and so on. It has been noted that the small-scale, independent artisans, who suffer from a lack of working capital and proper marketing knowledge, are restricted to local level markets (vendor and local retailer). The higher the capital, the more diversified the market channel. While small independent artisans who have no retail outlets of their own can sell their products to the wholesalers with better market connections, craftsmen with shops can benefit from the diversified market channels by selling their products directly to the consumer, the local wholesalers, and even to indigenous merchants. Therefore, the formal or directory units have the advantage of diversified marketing channels, whereas the small units are forced to rely on local markets. If the artisans wish to avail themselves of the external markets, they become tied to master enterprises (the formal producers) and traders. Obviously, markets have expanded and consequently the process of fragmentation and tiedness has increased.

Conclusion

This chapter is an attempt to outline the various trends in research on the state of the informal sector in a reforming developing country. We argue that deregulation is likely to improve the conditions of informal workers, provided that capital is allowed to flow to the informal sector. We developed a simple, yet revealing, theoretical structure to argue that the real informal wage can rise equally well in comparison with informal employment provided investment expands in this sector. Our evidence from the informal manufacturing sector in India shows that the real informal wage has gone up across states during the post-reform period; this is also the period over which unorganized manufacturing demonstrates a clear growth in capital formation, proxied by growth in fixed assets. Incidentally, this is also the phase when the organized sector shows a declining trend in capital formation.

As export markets expand, the informal rural industries exhibit increasing dynamics of tying, adoption of technology and growth. This is demonstrated through a first-hand field-based survey. We can argue, based on this evidence, that there is a clear reorganization of the informal/formal relationship in production. It is difficult for smaller units to survive independently. However, at the same time, it is increasingly profitable to be tied up with larger units with better access to capital and information regarding markets and policies. In fact, in both of the analyses we see a clear trend of capital allocation being routed to the informal segment. In informal manufacturing across the states of India, this process parallels a deceleration in formal manufacturing whereas, in the case of our example from the rural sector, we observe that an increasing amount of working capital is provided to the newly emerging tied artisans. A major finding seems to be a breakdown of government-run cooperatives. This has to do with the expansion of individual opportunities and inefficient governance. We plan to develop these findings into a proper theoretical framework in future.

Notes

This is a condensed version of Marjit and Maiti (2005). The authors are indebted to Basudeb Guha-Khasnobis and Ravi Kanbur for helpful suggestions.

1 Firms can be perceived as lumps of butter coagulating in a pail of buttermilk with a long-term transaction, the factory owner having a hierarchical system of monitoring resource-direction. With a price mechanism, a series of transactions is required to decide the true price, while these transaction costs are

saved within the firm. 'The main reason why it is profitable to establish a firm would seem to be that there is a cost of using the price mechanism' (Coase, 1937). 'When a "putting out" system was used ... inputs were organized largely through market negotiation' (Alchian and Demsetz, 1972).

2 Details from Census of India (1991).

3 Cluster means the combination of a few villages in which a particular type of industrial activity dominates. Selection of one particular village could not provide a sizeable number of sample units.

4 *Bani* is the payment received by tied artisans from their master for a particular type of manufacturing work where raw materials are supplied by the master.

5 See Government of West Bengal (1975).

References

Agenor, P. (1996) 'The Labour Market and Economic Adjustment', *IMF Staff Papers*, 32: 261–335.

Agenor, P. and P. Montiel (1996) *Development Macroeconomics* (Princeton, NJ: Princeton University Press).

Alchian, A. and H. Demsetz (1972) 'Production, Information Costs, and Economic Organization', *American Economic Review*, 61 (5): 777–95.

Carruth, A. and A.J. Oswald (1981) 'The Determination of Union and Non-Union Wage Rates', *European Economic Review*, 16 (2/3): 285–302.

Census of India (1991) *Primary Census Abstract* (New Delhi: Government of India).

Coase, R. (1937) 'The Nature of Firm', *Economica*, 4 (November): 386–405.

Economic and Political Weekly Research Foundation (2000) 'Annual Survey of Industries, 1973–74 to 1997–98: A Data Base on the Industrial Sector in India', (Mumbai: Sameeskha Trust).

Government of India (various years) *Annual Survey of Industries* (Delhi: Ministry of Statistics and Programme Implementation).

Government of West Bengal (1975) 'Report on the Enquiry into the Existing Working Conditions of the Workers of Bell Metal and Brass Metal Industry' (Kolkata: Information and Public Relation Department, Government of West Bengal).

Government of West Bengal (2001–02a) 'Economic Review of West Bengal' (Kolkata: Government of West Bengal).

Government of West Bengal (2001–02b) 'District Census Handbook for Nadia, Midnapore, Bankura, and Purulia' (Kolkata: Government of West Bengal).

IMF (International Monetary Fund) (2002) *International Financial Statistics Yearbook 2002* (Washington, DC: IMF).

Jones, R.W. (1965) 'The Structure of Simple General Equilibrium Model', *Journal of Political Economy*, 73 (December): 557–72.

Jones, R.W. (1971) 'A Three Factor Model in Theory, Trade and History', in J. Bhagwati, R.W. Jones, R.A. Mundell and J. Vancek (eds), *Trade, Balance of Payment and Growth* (Amsterdam: North-Holland).

Kar, S. and S. Marjit (2001) 'Informal Sector in General Equilibrium: Welfare Effects of Trade Policy Reforms', *International Review of Economics and Finance*, 10 (3): 289–300.

Knight, F.H. (1946) *Risk, Uncertainty and Profit* (Boston: Houghton Mifflin).
Maiti, D.S. (2004) 'Production Organisation and Dynamics of Rural Industrial Growth: A Study with Special Reference to Some Manufacturing Industries of West Bengal', unpublished PhD thesis (Midnapore, India: Vidyasagar University).
Marjit, S. (2003) 'Economic Reform and Informal Wage: A General Equilibrium Analysis', *Journal of Development Economics*, 72 (1): 371–8.
Marjit, S. and R. Acharyya (2003) *International Trade, Wage Inequality and The Developing Economy: A General Equilibrium Approach* (New York: Springer Verlag).
Marjit, S. and H. Beladi (2002) 'The Stopler–Samuelson Theorem in a Wage Difference Framework', *Japanese Economic Review*, 53 (2): 177–81.
Marjit, S., U. Broll and S. Sengupta (2000) 'Trade and Wage Gap in Poor Countries – The Role of Informal Sector', in A. Bose, D. Ray and A. Sarkar (eds), *Macro, Trade and Institutions* (Oxford: Oxford University Press).
Marjit, S., S. Kar and P. Sarkar (2004) 'Capital Mobility and Informal Wage in a Small Economy: Two Examples', *South Asia Economic Journal*, 5 (2): 261–6.
Marjit, S. and D.S. Maiti (2005) 'Globalization, Economic Reform and the Informal Sector', WIDER Research Paper 2005/12 (Helsinki: UNU-WIDER).
Marjit, S. and P. Roychowdhury (2004) 'Asymmetric Capacity Costs and Joint Venture Buyouts', *Journal of Economic Behaviour and Organisation*, 54 (3): 425–38.
NSS (various years) National Sample Survey, 1989–90, (45th Round), 1993–94 (50th Round), 1994–95 (51st Round), 2000–01 (56th Round), *Survey of Unorganized Manufacture* (Delhi: Department of Statistics, Government of India).
Williamson, O., M. Wachter and J. Harris (1975) 'Understanding the Employment Relation: The Analysis of Idiosyncratic Exchange', *Bell Journal of Economics*, 6 (1): 250–78.
Wuyts, M. (2001) 'Informal Economy, Wage Goods and Accumulation under Structural Adjustment Theoretical Reflections based on the Tanzanian Experience', *Cambridge Journal of Economics*, 25 (3): 417–38.

3
Trade Reforms and Informalization: Getting Behind Jobless Growth in India

Anushree Sinha and Christopher Adam

Introduction

This chapter examines the impact of trade reforms on the informal economy in India, particularly on how such reforms have shaped the distribution of employment in the formal and informal sectors. In recent decades, many developing countries, including India, have opened up their markets and introduced trade reforms as major elements in outward-oriented development strategies. In the 1990s, India put in place reforms aimed at enhancing growth.[1] Prior to liberalization, India maintained import duties that were among the highest in the world; for many items, tariff rates exceeded 200 per cent (Chadha *et al.*, 2001), with effective protection rates often even higher (Pandey, 2004). Since 1991, the maximum tariff rate has been gradually brought down, reaching 25 per cent in 2003–04 and 15 per cent in 2005–06. Trade policy reforms have also involved the removal of the extensive array of quantitative restrictions (QRs) on imports.

Much of the debate on Indian economic performance has focused on the aggregate efficiency and growth consequences of trade reforms (for example, see Srinivasan, 1998; Kelkar, 2004). But running parallel to this debate has been a growing concern about so-called 'jobless growth', which in turn has focused attention on how reforms have shaped patterns of employment and how, in particular, the informal economy has evolved in response to the changing competitive environment facing the formal sector. This concern reflects a growing recognition of the importance of the informal sector, not simply as a source of employment and growth, but also in political and social terms. Most research in this latter area has, however, focused on the microeconomics of informality.

In this chapter, we seek to bridge this 'micro–macro' gap in order to develop a macroeconomic, general equilibrium perspective on the transmission from trade reforms to the informal sector. We do so by adapting a standard computable general equilibrium (CGE) model to introduce aspects of the Indian informal economy. Notions of informality are diverse and highly contested and, clearly, the full richness of informality cannot readily be incorporated in formal models, particularly since these are not well suited to reflecting the fact that informality is not only a matter of degree rather an intrinsic state in its own right, but is also endogenous to changing economic conditions (see, for example, Adam and Harriss-White, 2005).

Notwithstanding these concerns, we focus on four key aspects of informality. First, we allow for differentiated goods, so that formal and informal varieties of goods circulate side-by-side. Second, we allow for different technologies, reflecting the stylized fact that production in informal sectors tends to be much more labour-intensive than in corresponding formal sectors. Third, we allow for a distinction between formal and informal factors of production, labour and capital. There are many aspects of the distinction between formal and informal employment that may be relevant (for example, the security of employment, non-wage benefits, employer pension contributions and so on). Here, we subsume these into the simplified idea that formal sector employees are able to resist reductions in real (consumption) wages. Finally, we assume that formal and informal sectors relate differently to the state, with the latter being able to avoid the payment of direct taxes on factor incomes.[2]

The following section provides a brief review of the general literature on the informal sector and the incorporation of perspectives on informality in CGE models. We then go on to describe our model and the calibration data. The subsequent section discusses our simulation results and the final section presents our conclusion.

Modelling informality

The term 'informal sector' was popularized through the International Labour Organization's report on Kenya (ILO, 1972). However, it has still remained an ambiguous term for researchers and policy-makers. Generally the term is used to refer to unregulated economic activities. Paradoxically, while it is widely recognized that this sector provides livelihoods for the majority of people in low-income countries, including India, systematic estimates of the size and contribution of this sector are rare. One of the reasons for this is the difficulty in collecting data on the informal economy. Generally, informal activities are carried on without a fixed location or in places that are not easily visible to the authorities, such as small workshops or residences. In India, official statistics use the term 'unorganized sector' in their reports. This sector comprises all those enterprises that are not registered or regulated, or whose accounts are not maintained regularly. While using national statistics, the term 'unorganized sector' is used synonymously with 'informal sector'. Following this definition, the informal sector in India contributes more than 60 per cent of GDP and covers about 87 per cent of the workforce (Sinha *et al.*, 2003).

There is ample evidence in literature regarding increase in informal employment following adjustment and liberalization episodes (for example, see Wahba and Moktar, 2000). More recently, Nagraj (2004) reports that between 1995–96 and 2001–02 approximately 1.3 million formal sector workers in India (13 per cent of the workforce) lost their jobs. The loss in jobs, however, has not been reflected in the Indian Labour Bureau's data. This could be partly due to underreporting, but there is also a case for acknowledging the growth in employment on a casual basis. It is now agreed by most employment analysts (Nagraj, 2004) that some of the laid off workers are absorbed by the expanding informal sector. This is corroborated by the rising phenomenon of subcontracting, both in productions of goods and services. However, if employment reappears in the informal sector, under informal contracts, this occurs under different labour arrangements, often including degraded work conditions, weaker (or no) legal protection, and lower real wages.

Modelling informality in CGE models

CGE models provide a useful approach to analyzing the interaction between formal and informal sectors in response to trade-policy reforms. In their conventional usage, CGE models are flexible price models and are used to examine the impact of relative price changes on resource allocations (of goods and factors) across a range of economic agents. Thus, in addition to providing insights into the economy-wide general equilibrium effects of policy changes, CGE models allow key inter-industry linkages to be examined. The CGE structure is relatively well suited to handling aspects of informality. The standard model distinguishes between different commodities, different markets (both goods and factor) and different activities (that is, production processes). Informality can be defined in terms of all three of these dimensions. This can be done in a variety of ways. For example, Gibson and Kelley (1994) differentiate between production processes based on profitability while Portes *et al.* (1989) look at the informal sector only in terms of segmented labour market theories. Another stylized fact associated with the informal sector involves its relationship with the state. The popularity of this theme is mainly due to the work by De Soto (1986), though the legal status of the informal sector has remained a matter of debate for longer than this.

The model and social accounting matrix

The model used in this chapter is an extension of a standard multi-sector real CGE model described in more detail in Sinha and Adam (2004) and which incorporates informal goods and factor markets, and identifies 'informal households' (that is, those whose income derives overwhelmingly from the sale of labour, or provision of capital, to informal activities). The model identifies 10 production sectors spanning the rural and urban economies, five of which are informal and five formal. Basic agriculture and the construction sectors are assumed to be informal (in the sense that they employ only informal factors of production and do not engage directly in international trade), while the capital goods sector and government services are exclusively formal. In the remainder of the economy, which consists of agro-processing, manufactured goods and other services, both formal and informal varieties of the (aggregate) good are produced under different technologies, and in each case the formal variety may use informal factors of production. We classify households at two levels, first between 'rural' and 'urban' households, where rural corresponds to the agricultural and agro-processing sectors, and then in terms of the principal source of factor incomes. The full sectoral classifications are given in Appendix I.

The social accounting matrix (SAM) used in the model is constructed for India by Sinha *et al.* (2004), which has taken the informal sector into account. Information on the informal sector is based on the NSSO survey administered in India by the CSO during 1999–2000. To determine intermediate consumption in the informal sector, same shares are reproduced as those in the formal sector, using similar methodology to that adopted by Fortin *et al.* (1997). As is standard in this type of CGE model, it is assumed that the Indian economy was in equilibrium in the benchmark year (1999–2000).

We have used two versions of the model for simulation exercises carried out in this work. The first assumes full employment and perfect competition in the labour markets. Hence, full employment is maintained through reallocations from contracting to expanding sectors, or movements in real wages, or a combination of both. The second version of the model allows for wage rigidity amongst regular labour employed only in the formal sub-sector, but maintains the assumption that wages are fully flexible in the 'informal' labour market. The wage dualism has been explained by the existence of labour market segmentation that creates entry barriers to higher wage jobs (regular wage-earners) in the formal sector. This segmentation may result from higher efficiency wages in the formal sector, or from the presence of trade unions in the formal sector that succeed in setting wage rates for higher wage jobs. This dualism is also consistent with institutional constraints such as government-set wage rates and other labour market regulations, as long as they are enforced only for formalized employment.

Simulation experiments and macroeconomic characteristics

The model described above is used to conduct a comparative static analysis of trade reforms in India under a range of assumptions about the experiments. Our measure of trade reform combines: (i) the effect of a 60 per cent reduction in import tariffs across the board for all products; and (ii) a corresponding reduction in QRs (where they exist). In the tables presented below, we report the effect of the explicit tariff reduction separately from the combined liberalization. Table 3.1 reports the structure of baseline imports and the level of protection (tariffs and QRs) for India. The QRs are expressed as tariff-equivalent values on different items of consumption. These are determined residually from information on notional tariff rates and domestic and world prices to ensure that the following (model-based) identity is satisfied: $P_M = E(1 + t)(1 + QR)P_M^W$ where for each of the imported items, P_M is import price, t is the tax rate, QR is the quantitative restriction, E is nominal exchange rate and P_M^W is the world price of the good.

In each case, we assume that the authorities seek to implement fiscal-neutral trade liberalization. We run each experiment under two alternative labour market closures, the first where both formal and informal labour markets are fully competitive, and the second where there is (downward)

Table 3.1 India: imports and trade barriers (1999–2000)

	Imports (% GDP)	**Nominal protection rate (tariff + QR)**
Agriculture	2.35	40.00
Agro-processing	1.78	76.71
Other manufactured goods	79.94	61.78
Capital goods	15.93	94.97
Total	100.00	66.47

Notes:
1 Tariff and QR rate computed as proportion of cif value of imports.
2 Nominal rate of protection as percentage of excess of domestic price over world market price due to protection measures.
Sources: Import data: Government of India (various issues); tariff and QR data (Sinha *et al*., 2004).

wage rigidity in the formal labour market. To neutralize the revenue effects of a 60 per cent reduction both in tariff and QRs, indirect taxes (which are levied only on the formal sector) are increased by approximately 20 per cent with flexible wages and by 24 per cent with formal wage rigidity, from a baseline average effective indirect tax rate of 12.5 per cent.

The model is simulated in a purely comparative static fashion in which all factors are in fixed supply (in aggregate for labour, and both in aggregate and inter-sectorally for capital). While households and the rest of the world save, they do so in fixed proportions, while the revenue neutrality assumption ensures that the fiscal deficit is also held constant. Hence, investment has no impact on the net capital stock in each sector. Changes in production in the economy therefore reflect inter-sectoral movements in labour in response to changes in relative goods prices facing firms. The model, therefore, does not provide any insight into the growth dynamics of the Indian economy. And finally, by assuming a closed private capital account, no foreign official borrowing and no official reserve accumulation, aggregate net exports are held constant throughout the four simulations.

Our simulations are based on an extensive analysis on a range of assumptions about the characteristics of demand and production. Specifically, we evaluated the simulated responses for alternative assumptions about the willingness of consumers to substitute between imports and domestically produced goods, and for producers to switch supply between domestic and export markets. Altering these behavioural parameters has important quantitative consequences for the simulation results but does not alter the fundamental qualitative insights from the model. However, to focus the discussion on a manageable set of simulation results, we report the results for a central representative case only. We assume the price elasticity of substitution between domestic goods, both formal and informal, and imports to be relatively low at 0.50 (implying a relatively sluggish response to demand to change in prices) and where producers have a slightly higher elasticity of transformation at 0.75.

Results

Tariff reduction

The starting point for this discussion, a revenue-neutral tariff reduction, is entirely conventional. Let us consider our first simulation. As tariff rates decline, two things happen to shift relative prices (Table 3.2).

First, the domestic price of imports declines which, all other things being equal, leads to an appreciation in the import real exchange rate and a corresponding increase in import demands. This appreciation is

Table 3.2 Percentage change in relative prices (an increase implies a depreciation)

	Flexible labour markets		**Real wage rigidity in formal sector**	
	Tariffs reduced by 60%	**Tariffs and QRs reduced by 60%**	**Tariffs reduced by 60%**	**Tariffs and QRs reduced by 60%**
Import real exchange rate PM/PD	**Simulation 1**	**Simulation 2**	**Simulation 3**	**Simulation 4**
Agriculture	−0.51	−21.95	1.61	−14.48
Agro-processing (formal)	−8.58	−16.69	−7.67	−14.89
Agro-processing (informal)	−8.65	−14.73	−4.83	−11.22
Manufactured goods (formal)	−1.25	−22.99	−1.54	−24.85
Manufactured goods (informal)	−1.94	−22.05	−1.42	−21.76
Capital goods	−6.34	−35.60	−7.15	−38.48
Construction	0.00	0.00	0.00	0.00
Other services (formal)	3.55	9.66	2.61	7.99
Other services (informal)	0.33	6.67	1.40	9.99
Government services	0.00	0.00	0.00	0.00
Weighted average	**−4.56**	**−22.37**	**−4.50**	**−23.04**
Export real exchange rate PX/PD				
Agriculture	−0.51	2.69	1.61	12.52
Agro-processing (formal)	−0.22	5.08	0.77	7.35
Agro-processing (informal)	−0.29	4.41	3.87	8.70
Manufactured goods (formal)	2.12	14.93	1.82	12.16
Manufactured goods (informal)	1.40	16.45	1.94	16.88
Capital goods	3.44	23.84	2.54	18.29
Construction	0.00	0.00	0.00	0.00
Other services (formal)	3.54	9.66	2.61	7.99
Other services (informal)	0.32	6.67	1.40	9.99
Government services	0.00	0.00	0.00	0.00
Weighted average	**1.91**	**11.10**	**2.13**	**11.44**
CONSUMER PRICE INDEX	**−1.517**	**−7.79**	**−1.43**	**−8.24**

strongest for those commodities with the highest initial tariff. However, this effect is compounded by the change in domestic goods prices. In the simulations reported here, the price of domestic goods declines on average, offsetting to some extent the effect of the decline in import prices.[3] This means, for example, that where the import share is negligible, such as in the services sectors, the domestic price effect dominates so that the real exchange rate actually depreciates.

Since export prices remain constant throughout these experiments,[4] the effect of movements in domestic prices can be seen directly from the export real exchange rates in the bottom half of Table 3.2. Thus, in particular, we notice that the manufacturing firms enjoy a favourable move in their internal real exchange rate. As suggested by classical Lerner-symmetry principles, production for the export market is therefore more attractive following import tariff liberalization.

The resource allocation consequences of these shifts in relative prices can be seen in Table 3.3.

The first point to notice is that the economy becomes more open with the liberalization-induced surge in imports (which rise in total by just over 2 per cent); this is accompanied by a corresponding export surge required to finance increased import demand in the absence of other balance of payments flows. Secondly, the rise in imports is heavily concentrated in agro-processed goods (from a small base) and manufactured and capital goods (from a somewhat higher base). This surge is financed in part by a decline in service sector imports and in part from strong manufactured exports.

These net trade effects lead to an inter-sectoral rebalancing of production in the domestic economy, away from the formal sector and towards the informal sector on average (Table 3.4). As is common in full-employment models of this type, the aggregate effects of trade liberalization are positive but their size is relatively modest, not least because of the offsetting adjustment to the domestic tax structure which renders the reforms revenue neutral. Much greater effects are seen when we consider the removal of QRs on imports.

Reducing QRs

Our second simulation considers the combined effect of reducing QRs on imports alongside a tariff reduction. In general, this induces much larger responses in the economy for two reasons. The first is that in terms of relative prices, QRs have the same distortionary effect as (equivalent) tariffs. In this sense, their removal serves simply to magnify the effect of the cut in tariffs. But, more importantly, the benefits of QRs accrue to the capital-owning households and they experience a loss of income when

Table 3.3 Trade volumes (percentage change over baseline)

	Base US $bn	Flexible labour markets		Real wage rigidity in formal sector	
		Tariffs reduced by 60%	Tariffs and QRs reduced by 60%	Tariffs reduced by 60%	Tariffs and QRs reduced by 60%
IMPORTS		**Simulation 1**	**Simulation 2**	**Simulation 3**	**Simulation 4**
Agriculture	88	0.13	13.37	−0.78	6.29
Agro-processing (formal)	42	9.72	23.34	9.35	21.79
Agro-processing (informal)	34	9.96	18.07	−5.62	15.63
Manufactured goods (formal)	1536	2.78	13.97	2.97	16.77
Manufactured goods (informal)	720	2.90	13.01	3.01	16.07
Capital goods (formal)	200	3.12	14.54	3.91	22.91
Construction (informal)					
Other services (formal)	370	−2.72	−5.32	−2.41	−4.81
Other services (informal)	228	0.07	−3.19	−0.17	−2.91
Government services (formal)1					
TOTAL	**3218**	**2.10**	**10.51**	**2.09**	**12.88**
TOTAL IMPORTS BY FORMAL SECTOR	**2148**	**2.00**	**10.88**	**2.26**	**13.73**
TOTAL IMPORTS BY INFORMAL SECTOR	**1070**	**2.30**	**9.74**	**1.75**	**11.20**
EXPORTS					
Agriculture	304	−0.51	2.17	1.22	7.39
Agro-processing (formal)	151	0.81	5.17	1.14	5.45
Agro-processing (informal)	119	0.43	4.63	−5.99	6.72
Manufactured goods (formal)	1245	2.05	9.55	2.11	10.78

(*Continued*)

Table 3.3 (*Continued*)

	Base US $bn	Flexible labour markets		Real wage rigidity in formal sector	
		Tariffs reduced by 60%	Tariffs and QRs reduced by 60%	Tariffs reduced by 60%	Tariffs and QRs reduced by 60%
EXPORTS		**Simulation 1**	**Simulation 2**	**Simulation 3**	**Simulation 4**
Manufactured goods (informal)	562	1.46	8.51	2.35	12.53
Capital goods (formal)	145	2.37	7.90	2.02	9.34
Construction (informal)					
Other services (formal)	1446	1.60	6.24	0.78	4.79
Other services (informal)	894	0.48	4.94	1.57	9.36
Government services (formal)					
TOTAL	**4866**	**1.34**	**6.84**	**1.36**	**8.43**
TOTAL EXPORTS BY FORMAL SECTOR	**2988**	**1.79**	**7.65**	**1.41**	**7.54**
TOTAL EXPORTS BY INFORMAL SECTOR	**1878**	**0.61**	**5.55**	**1.27**	**9.83**

Table 3.4 Gross domestic output (percentage change from baseline)

VARIABLES	Base Rbn	Flexible labour markets		Real wage rigidity in formal sector	
		Tariffs reduced by 60%	Tariffs and QRs reduced by 60%	Tariffs reduced by 60%	Tariffs and QRs reduced by 60%
TOTAL DOMESTIC OUTPUT BY SECTOR					
Agriculture	5763	−0.13	0.20	0.04	−1.47
Agro-processing (formal)	902	0.43	1.43	0.41	0.97
Agro-processing (informal)	654	0.39	1.26	−9.58	1.12
Other manufacturing goods (formal)	5675	0.52	0.28	0.66	2.14
Other manufacturing goods (informal)	2470	0.35	−0.51	0.80	2.62
Capital goods (formal)	1254	−0.06	−7.19	0.21	−2.89
Construction (informal)	2355	1.65	−4.29	2.65	5.64
Other services (formal)	8359	−0.81	−0.29	−1.00	−0.62
Other services (informal)	5056	0.25	0.37	0.60	2.42
Government services (formal)	3679	0.00	0.00	0.00	0.00
TOTAL	**36167**	**0.06**	**−0.43**	**0.02**	**0.79**
TOTAL DOMESTIC OUTPUT BY SECTOR FORMAL	**19871**	**−0.17**	**−0.42**	**−0.19**	**0.23**
TOTAL DOMESTIC OUTPUT BY SECTOR INFORMAL	**16296**	**0.34**	**−0.45**	**0.28**	**1.49**

QRs are reduced. Unlike the pure tariff reduction case, this loss of income is not offset by some other source of quasi-rent. Since the quasi-rents are assumed to be relatively concentrated (across goods and households), their removal adds an important distributional heft to the results.

The initial QRs on other manufactured goods are high, and for capital goods are the highest amongst all sectors. Consequently, imports of capital goods rise very sharply, whereas exports have a more moderate increase leading to a decline in domestic production of capital goods (Table 3.4).

This has implications for the construction sector, which has a strong connection with the capital goods sector and therefore experiences a compression in its output. In this simulation, the contraction of the construction sector leads to overall decline in informal sector output together with a decline in formal sector output. Differential impacts of the simulations on different sectors highlight interesting findings. For agriculture trade, reforms in isolation are modestly output-enhancing but, when this is coupled with QR reduction (simulation 2), the positive effect is enhanced. Further, due to lower domestic prices, real consumption wages for both types of labour increase in this simulation (see Table 3.5).

This stands in contrast to the pure tariff reduction case where real consumption wages for regular workers fell. To examine these important factor market effects, we now turn to the labour market.

Labour-market rigidities

We first consider the case where labour markets are assumed to be fully flexible. The decline in the demand for labour in the formal sector leads to a decline in formal sector real wages (Table 3.5). At the same time, though demand for casual labour declines in formal sectors, it rises by more in informal sectors, hence the real wages of casual labour rise.

In the last two simulations, we examine the impact of the same two experiments under the assumption that wages in the formal sector are sticky downwards and so there may be formal incipient unemployment in equilibrium. This unemployment is hidden, however, since unemployed formal sector workers are assumed to join the informal sector. In our third simulation, the demand for regular labour declines (see Table 3.5), leading to retrenchment of skilled labour at prevailing wages. With nominal wages preserved in the formal sector, the decline in consumer prices results in a *rise* in real formal sector consumption wages. However, as shown in Table 3.5, the decline in demand for regular labour is reflected in an increase in the supply of informal labour as labour laid off from the formal sector becomes informalized. This increased supply of informal labour serves to drive down average real wages in the informal sector *despite the decline in the CPI*. This result is magnified in our fourth simulation.

What these last two simulations show is that when regular labour market rigidities are in place, the 'cost' of wage adjustment is overwhelmingly borne by casual workers (the old and the new entrants to this market).

Finally, we consider how these changes map into household incomes (which give a reasonable proxy for welfare in this model). As noted earlier, we define households in terms of their primary factor income source. By denying the possibility of mixed-income or diversified households, the model arguably overstates the impact of reforms on household incomes, but nonetheless the insights remain valid. Two key features stand out from Table 3.6.

The first is that aggregate income increases in all cases. Secondly, however, the distribution of income gains and losses depends closely on the nature of the reform and the manner in which labour markets are assumed to function. For a simple fiscally-neutral tariff reduction in the presence of flexible labour markets, income gains accrue pretty evenly across different households, with only regular wage-earners experiencing a decline. Here, it is rural households, those dependent on casual labour, and capitalist households that stand to gain most from a simple tariff reduction. If, however, QRs are simultaneously removed, income effects are skewed very strongly away from those who previously enjoyed the quasi-rents, towards those now enjoying the effects of lower consumer prices for previously protected goods. Hence, wage-earners benefit at the expense of capitalists and within wage-earners, it is again the informal, casual-worker households who benefit the most. Once we allow for labour-market rigidities, however, the pattern changes, less so between capital-based and employment-based households, but between regular and casual workers. By enjoying some labour-market power, households continuing to sell regular labour to the formal sector capture a larger share of the aggregate income gain at the expense of casual-labour households who face a sharp drop in their real wages.

Conclusion

In this chapter, we have used a CGE model to examine the impact of trade reforms on the notion of informalization and the related issues of casualization of labour. We have examined one specific set of mechanisms, which explains the apparent phenomenon of 'jobless growth' in India. The existing official statistics reflect that there has been a decline in employment during this period of reforms. As the simulations show, however, though official statistics may correctly record the number of 'registered' workers declining, they fail to record the strong growth of 'unregistered' workers in the economy. Growth in the economy is actually supported by a huge force of 'unregistered' or informal workers. The formal sector is faced with strong competition and they react by outsourcing to the informal sub-sector and retrenching formal workers to replace them by informal workers. Therefore, though there is less unemployment than actually shown in official records, most informal workers suffer substandard living conditions, as reflected by the fall in their real wages in our simulations.

Table 3.5 Employment and real wages (percentage change from baseline)

Variables	Base (millions)	Flexible labour markets		Real wage rigidity in formal sector	
		Tariffs reduced by 60%	Tariffs and QRs reduced by 60%	Tariffs reduced by 60%	Tariffs and QRs reduced by 60%
Employment by sector and skill (millions)		**Simulation 1**	**Simulation 2**	**Simulation 3**	**Simulation 4**
Casual labour	**196.5**	0.00	0.00	0.18	0.24
Agriculture	137.8	−0.26	0.41	0.08	−2.93
Agro-processing (formal)	0.9	−0.53	1.63	2.17	9.03
Agro-processing (informal)	3.2	1.27	4.12	−27.14	3.58
Manufactured goods (formal)	7.3	−0.45	−1.38	2.91	13.34
Manufactured goods (informal)	9.7	1.06	−1.88	2.51	8.23
Capital goods (formal)	0.3	−3.43	−23.56	2.06	0.38
Construction (informal)	9.5	2.20	−5.67	3.52	7.57
Other services (formal)	2.0	−5.53	−4.01	−1.78	7.63
Other services (informal)	21.2	0.80	1.15	1.86	7.69
Government services (formal)	4.6	0.00	0.00	0.00	0.00
Regular labour	**41.7**	0.00	0.00	−0.87	−1.15
Agriculture					
Agro-processing (formal)	1.0	2.97	6.68	0.63	−1.43
Agro-processing (informal)					
Manufactured goods (formal)	7.5	3.39	2.78	1.45	2.12
Manufactured goods (informal)					
Capital goods (formal)	1.1	0.21	−20.66	0.51	−9.99

Construction (informal)					
Other services (formal)	15.0	−1.96	−0.36	−3.28	−3.48
Other services (informal)					
Government services (formal)	17.1	0.00	0.00	0.00	0.00
Total	**238.2**	**0.00**	**0.00**	**0.00**	**0.00**
Total casual labour (formal)	15.0	−1.04	−1.53	1.36	8.06
Total casual labour (informal)	181.5	0.08	0.12	0.08	−0.41
AVERAGE CONSUMPTION WAGE RATE BY SKILL (REAL)					
CASUAL WAGE LABOUR	2632	2.56	6.76	−0.09	−2.26
REGULAR WAGE LABOUR	8657	−1.17	2.85	1.45	8.99

Table 3.6 Real household incomes (percentage change from baseline)

Variables	Base rupees	Flexible labour markets		Real wage rigidity in formal sector	
		Tariffs reduced by 60%	Tariffs and QRs reduced by 60%	Tariffs reduced by 60%	Tariffs and QRs reduced by 60%
PRIVATE GROSS INCOME		Simulation 1	Simulation 2	Simulation 3	Simulation 4
Rural					
Casual	3271	2.54	6.72	−0.09	−2.23
Regular	1875	−1.08	3.04	1.45	8.99
Self-employed	2299	2.28	7.18	0.00	−5.09
Employer	76	3.95	−26.75	3.69	−24.56
Urban					
Casual	2013	2.51	6.75	−0.05	−1.95
Regular	2028	−0.89	3.44	1.45	8.99
Self-employed	6797	1.42	6.23	2.08	11.16
Employer	1626	2.25	−48.92	2.68	−24.79
TOTAL BY HH groups					
TOTAL	19985	1.42	1.28	1.20	2.29
Rural	7522	1.57	5.60	0.36	−0.53
Urban	12463	1.33	−1.33	1.71	4.00
Casual	5284	2.53	6.74	−0.07	−2.13
Regular	3903	−0.98	3.25	1.45	8.99
Wage	9187	1.04	5.25	0.57	2.60
Capital	10798	1.74	−2.10	1.74	2.04

Though tentative, the model as currently constructed delivers a number of important insights. We find that trade reforms (taken to include the removal of QRs as well as a tariff reduction) generate real income gains when accompanied by revenue-neutral fiscal policies. Income gains emerge for regular wage-earners mainly when there is wage rigidity in the formal sector for the section of the workforce that is able to retain 'regular' status. On the other hand, casual workers suffer wage loss under such conditions. Our model findings convey that the way in which the labour market functions is highly significant in the casualization of the labour force, depressing their wages in the process. However, in consequence of reforms mostly all households enjoy improved real consumption wages (which themselves reflect the downward pressure on the relative price of imports and import substitutes). The gain is more favourable for regular workers when wage rigidity is introduced in the segmented labour market and for casual workers when there is no such rigidity.

As import prices fall as a result of liberalization, real import exchange rates of protected sectors decline in proportion to their protection. This results in higher imports of such items and, hence, domestic import substituting activities are squeezed. The transmission of this initial effect through the economy depends on two factors: (i) what happens to the structure of wages; and (ii) what happens to aggregate demand. It follows that factors that are used intensively in contracting (expanding) sectors would experience falling (increasing) relative remuneration. It is important here to discuss the degree of factor mobility. Factors that are fixed in contracting (expanding) sectors would experience falling (increasing) relative remuneration.[5]

As with all CGE models, certain features of the simulation results reflect the 'macroeconomic closure' adopted; that is, the assumptions imposed ensure that the model respects the macroeconomic balances of the economy. In this case, the choice of closure combined with the comparative-static nature of the model means that the model does not reflect the true nature of the investment process in India. Specifically, there is no capital accumulation in the model and while the capital stock is fixed by sector, labour is mobile across sectors. The model follows the 'neo-classical' closure rule in which aggregate investment is determined by total national savings. Hence, in a case where government savings fall due to tariff reduction, overall investment would fall in this model causing a decline in the *demand* for capital goods. This, however, has no effect on the capital stock itself.

Another important concern to examine is the role of capital in enhancing productivity in the informal sector. So far in this exercise, we have assumed that total capital available is fixed by sectors. The situation of the informal economy and informal workers can improve if there is flow of capital into this sector, as suggested by Marjit *et al.* (2003). However, the process of moving resources to the informal enterprises, where there is a lack of collateral, is a matter of serious deliberation. If these enterprises were able to raise their productivity while participating in the expanding market, they could bring forth further growth. Thereafter, such firms could contribute to public resources (by becoming 'formal' or 'registered'), and their workers could receive welfare benefits; these firms could be further supported to achieve viable growth. It was not possible to address these aspects in the current CGE model. Nevertheless, the analysis clearly shows the importance of the explicit inclusion of the informal sector and informal workers in future work on economic reforms, as this is relevant for developing countries. As a large section of the workers is being absorbed in informal activities during the process of economic reform, it is essential to understand how such workers would lose or benefit from the new policy changes. Such information could help in designing flanking policies that would help mitigate any negative influence of liberalization on the informal workers.

Appendix I

Sectoral classifications distinguished by informality

1. Agriculture (informal)
2. Agro-processing (formal)
3. Agro-processing (informal)
4. Other manufactured goods (formal)
5. Other manufactured goods (informal)
6. Capital goods (formal)
7. Construction (informal)
8. Other services (formal)
9. Other services (informal)
10. Government services (formal)

Household categories

(Label denotes principal source of factor income in each household type)

Rural

1. Casual wage-earners
2. Regular (formal sector) wage-earners
3. Self-employed workers (informal capitalists)
4. Employers (formal capitalists)

Urban
5 Casual wage-earners
6 Regular (formal sector) wage-earners
7 Self-employed workers (informal capitalists)
8 Employers (formal capitalists)

Appendix II

The model used for our simulations assumes households to consume a basket of goods containing both formal and informal types of all goods. Consumption choices in this set-up are governed by a common set of substitution elasticity that does not do full justice to the richness of consumer choices. An alternative, more nuanced approach that better reflects the reality of consumer choices would allow for a multi-stage consumption structure that recognizes consumer preferences over formal and informal varieties of goods. Specifically, we have initially defined consumption over broad groups of consumption (agricultural products, manufactured

Table 3A.1 Change in aggregate sectoral consumption by households

	Percentage change over baseline		
	EPSCZ = 0.25	**EPSCZ = 0.75**	**EPSCZ = 1.50**
Variables	**Scenario-1**	**Scenario-2**	**Scenario-3**
Aggregate sectoral consumption by households			
Rural			
Agriculture	0.3120	0.3237	0.3266
Manufactured goods (formal)	0.6819	0.8410	0.8808
Services (formal)	1.1081	1.1081	1.1081
TOTAL	0.4317	0.4657	0.4741
Urban			
Agriculture	0.3120	0.3237	0.3266
Manufactured goods (formal)	0.6819	0.8410	0.8809
Services (formal)	1.1081	1.1081	1.1081
TOTAL	0.6301	0.6760	0.6875
GRAND TOTAL	0.5303	0.5702	0.5801

Notes:
1 EPSCZ = consumption elasticity of substitution between formal and informal variants of goods.
2 Simulations assume fully flexible labour markets.
3 Base: the base line data are not based on actual statistics but are used for illustration only.

goods, services and so on) and then, within each group, allowed for preferences over imported versus domestic variants and further, within the domestic variant, between the formal and informal variants.

To investigate the qualitative relevance of this modification of the model, we developed a simple, stylized model that incorporates such a multi-stage consumer choice structure.

Simulations of the same trade liberalization experiment (Table 3A.1) suggest that the welfare effects of trade reforms are sensitive to consumers' preferences between formal and informal goods. Specifically, aggregate consumption, and hence welfare, is higher the greater the elasticity of substitution between formal and informal variants of the goods in response to relative price adjustments (which may be driven by trade policy reforms). This specific feature notwithstanding, however, the modification of consumer preferences in this fashion does not fundamentally alter the characteristics of the model reported in the main body of the chapter.

Notes

This chapter draws extensively on research funded by the UK Department for International Development (DfID) [The Impact of India's Trade Reforms on the Informal Sector, Grant No. R 7901]. We gratefully acknowledge the generous support of DfID. The views expressed in this chapter are, however, solely those of the authors.

1 For an overview of the Indian reform process, see Ahluwalia (1999); Srinivasan (2000); Kelkar (2001); Rangarajan (2001); Joshi and Little (2002) and Jha (2003).
2 We also provide for a richer characterization of consumer preferences across formal and informal variants of goods. This analysis is, however, rather sensitive to the baseline calibration and is therefore examined in the context of a stylized model, as reported in Appendix II.
3 Whether domestic goods prices rise or fall depends on the relative strength of demand side effects (caused by the substitution in consumption) and supply-side factors (caused by the substitution by producers away from domestic towards export markets).
4 We assume that world prices for imports and exports and the nominal exchange rate are fixed so that movements in the real exchange rate are brought about by movements in domestic prices.
5 It is also possible that the resulting change in the relative prices of primary factors (labour and capital) will affect sectors differentially according to their relative intensity in these primary factors.

References

Adam, C. and B. Harriss-White (2005) 'From Monet to Mondrian: Questioning Informal Economic Activity in Field Research and Simulation Models', Mimeo, Queen Elizabeth House, Oxford.

Ahluwalia, M.S. (1999) *Perspectives on India's Reforms* (New Delhi: Oxford University Press).

Chadha, R., S. Pohit, A.V. Deardorff and R.M. Stern (2001) *The Impact of Trade and Domestic Policy Reforms in India: A CGE Approach*, Ann Arbor: University of Michigan Press.

CSO (Central Statistical Organisation) (2000) 'Input–Output Transactions Table, 1993–94' (New Delhi: Government of India).

CSO (2002) National Accounts Statistics (New Delhi: Government of India).

De Soto, H. (1986) *El Otro Sendero* (Lima: Instituto de Libertad y Democracia).

Fortin, B., N. Marceau and L. Savard (1997) 'Taxation, Wage Controls and the Informal Sector', *Journal of Public Economics*, 66: 293–312.

Gibson, B. and B. Kelley (1994) 'A Classical Theory of the Informal Sector', *The Manchester School*, LXII, no. 1 (March): 81–96.

Government of India, *Statistics of the Customs and Excise Revenue Collections of the Indian Union, 1999–00*: DGCIS, various issues.

ILO (1972) 'Employment, Incomes and Equality. A Strategy for Increasing Productive Employment in Kenya' (Geneva: ILO).

Jha, R. (ed.) (2003) *Indian Economic Reforms* (New York: Palgrave Macmillan).

Joshi, V. and I. Little (2002) *India's Economic Reforms 1991–2001* (New Delhi: Oxford University Press).

Kelkar, V.L. (2001) 'India's Economic Reforms Agenda: Micro, Meso and Macro Economic Reforms, Fourth Annual Fellows Lecture', at Centre for the Advanced Study of India, University of Pennsylvania.

Kelkar, V.L. (2004) 'India: On the Growth Turnpike', a K.R. Narayanan Lecture at the Australian National University, Canberra.

Marjit, S., S. Kar and P. Sarkar (2003) *Trade Reform, Internal Capital Mobility and Informal Wage – Theory and Evidence* (Calcutta: Centre for Studies in Social Sciences).

Nagraj, N. (2004) 'Fall in Organised Manufacturing Employment: A Brief Note', *Economic and Political Weekly*, vol. XXXIX, no. 30, 24 July: 3387–90.

Pandey, M. (2004) 'Impact of Trade Liberalisation in Manufacturing Industry in India in the 1980s and 1990s', Working Paper, Indian Council for Research on International Economic Relations, New Delhi.

Portes, A., M. Castells and L. Benton, (eds) (1989) *The Informal Economy: Studies in Advanced and Less Developed Countries* (Baltimore: Johns Hopkins Press).

Rangarajan, C. (2001) 'Economic Reforms: An Assessment', Dr B.R. Ambedkar Lecture at University of Mumbai.

Sinha, A. and C.S. Adam (2004) 'Trade Reforms and Informal Economy in India: A CGE Analysis', Project Report Submitted to DFID in March, Mimeo, NCAER, New Delhi and Queen Elizabeth House, Oxford.

Sinha, A., K.A. Siddiqui and P. Munjal (2004) 'The Indian Informal Economy within a SAM Framework', Mimeo (New Delhi: NCAER).

Sinha, A., K.A. Siddiqui and N. Sangeeta (2003) 'The Impact of Alternative Economic Policies on the Informal Sector: A Multisectoral Study' (New Delhi: NCAER).

Srinivasan, T.N. (1998) 'India's Export Performance: A Comparative Analysis', in I.J. Ahluwalia and I.M.D. Little (eds) *India's Economic Reforms and Development Essay for Manmohan Singh* (Delhi: Oxford University Press).

Srinivasan, T.N. (2000) 'Eight Lectures on Indian Economic Reforms' (Delhi: Oxford University Press).

Wahba, J. and M. Moktar (2000) 'Informalization of Labor in Egypt', Report submitted to EPIC.

4

Evasive Reform: Informalization in a Liberalized Economy with Wage-setting Unions

Indraneel Dasgupta and Sugata Marjit

Introduction

Industrial labour markets in many developing countries exhibit a two-tiered structure. Unions, employers and the government negotiate an industry-wide pay agreement, which then acquires legal sanction. This 'formal', or 'official', wage rate is typically above the market-clearing rate, reflecting the institutionalized influence of the unions at the apex level. However, subsequent enforcement of this agreement is partial. Individual employers often employ workers on a lower, competitively-determined, 'informal' wage contract. This can be patently illegal, reflecting the failure of government monitoring and non-implementation of labour laws. This can also be legal, reflecting grey areas, loopholes and exceptions in labour laws governing coverage of formal contracts. In any case, the outcome is a dualistic labour market within the same industry, with some workers receiving relatively high remuneration, while others receive a lower, competitively-determined wage.[1]

Such dualism in labour markets has been criticized, on standard grounds, as generating low industrial employment and welfare losses.[2] A large wage differential also provides firms an incentive to evade formal agreements with unions and violate labour laws. This leads to deployment of resources in activities connected with directly unproductive profit-seeking, such as bureaucratic monitoring, litigation, political lobbying, bribery, industrial conflict and so on. Labour-market integration is therefore usually considered a key objective of strategies of economic liberalization.

Economic liberalization typically entails trade liberalization and deficit reduction. Import liberalization is expected to cause a contraction in import-substituting industries, at least in the short run. Deficit reduction, by reducing interest rates, is supposed to counteract this contraction.[3] These two elements carry a high profile in most, arguably all, deregulation packages, especially those put forward by the IMF. Yet, the nature of their joint impact on the wage differential within an industry, and on the extent of evasion of union-negotiated formal contracts, does not appear to have received much analytical attention.[4] The empirical literature, however, suggests that finance-compensated trade deregulation may be associated both with greater informalization of industrial labour contracts and deregulation of industrial labour markets.[5] Is there a direct causal connection, distinct from the impact of secondary factors such as greater capital mobility, technological change or exogenous ideological shifts in economic policymaking? The purpose of this chapter is to address this question.

We set up a static, partial equilibrium model of an industry characterized by price-taking firms facing a union. The union sets an official, or formal, wage rate, and employers hire workers on both this formal contract and a lower, competitively-set, 'informal' wage contract. Thus, employers partially evade the payment of the union-mandated wage rate, but have to pay a cost for such evasion due to subsequent government and union sanctions, litigation and so on. Unionized wage-setting combines with employer-evasion to generate a two-tiered labour market within the industry. Firms borrow to pay wages. However, an assumed time lag between evasion of formal contracts and the infliction of consequent costs implies that firms can pay their evasion costs out of their realized revenue.

Within this set-up, we model trade liberalization as a fall in the output price, and deficit reduction (or, more generally, financial deregulation) as a fall in the interest rate. We focus on a situation where the two balance one another, so that industrial employment is maintained at its pre-liberalization level. This benchmark is motivated by the observation that employment stability in import-competing industries is often enforced on liberalizing governments in developing countries as a political-economic constraint. Governments typically find themselves under short run pressure from both employers' and workers' lobbies to neutralize industrial contraction stemming from trade liberalization. Furthermore, employment stability would lead, given growth, to a fall in the share of import-competing industries in total output and employment over time. Such a strategy of gradual reorganization of the production structure is often politically easier to sustain than one involving a sharp employment contraction in the import-competing sector, and is therefore commonly observed in developing countries, especially those that are electoral democracies (see, for example, Edwards, 1989; and Ahluwalia, 2002 for discussions).

We show that, paradoxically, liberalization in this sense enables the union to raise the formal wage rate, thereby increasing the gap between formal and informal wage contracts. The proportion of the industrial labour force on informal contracts consequently rises, and so does directly unproductive firm expenditure necessitated by its evasion of formal contracts. These conclusions hold even with relatively small reductions in employment in the import-competing industry. Thus, liberalization increases the size of social losses due to employer–union conflicts over distribution. This happens, essentially, due to institutional weaknesses that generate delays in punishment of contract evasion.

Such a consequence, in turn, has important implications for regulatory policies in the labour market. It turns out that, if the state wishes to moderate this rise in social losses, then it must reduce the cost of contract evasion, yet raise the cost of loans. Weaker enforcement of existing labour laws, or creation of large grey areas, loopholes and exceptions in such laws, thus turn out to be deliberate strategies that may be forced upon a state that wishes simultaneously to (a) pursue a cheap import regime; (b) avoid a sharp contraction in import-competing industries; (c) avoid aggravating social losses stemming from union–employer conflicts; and (d) avoid a politically debilitating open confrontation with institutionalized unions. Import liberalization within existing political-economic constraints therefore appears to be causally connected to labour market deregulation.

Such evasion, if now engaged in by the state, must however reduce the total income accruing to workers in the import-competing industry. Ironically, employers' profits would fall as well. Lenders would be the only beneficiaries. Thus, labour-market deregulation, whether *de facto* or *de jure*, would enrich rentiers, at the cost of *both* workers and capitalists.

The next section sets up the model. We then go on to study the impact of credit-compensated import-liberalization on the extent of informalization of the labour force. Subsequently, we examine the implications for social losses stemming from union – employer conflict over employer evasion of formal contracts, and the state's responses to such losses. Possible extensions are addressed in the penultimate section and the chapter closes with our conclusions. Proofs are relegated to the Appendix.

The model

Consider a small open economy that both produces and imports a single industrial output, using capital and labour. The international price of the output is P, and a tariff rate t is imposed on imports.[6] The (exogenously given) domestic price of the industrial output is thus $p = P(1 + t)$. Labour supply to the industrial sector is perfectly elastic at the exogenously given wage rate w_I.[7]

Industrial production occurs in n price-taking firms. Firms are identical: they have identical capital stock and use identical technology, given by the production function $M(l)$, where l is the amount of labour employed. For notational convenience, we normalize the number of firms, n, to 1. A wage rate, w_F, is determined by a union on behalf of all industrial workers. Firms can choose to hire workers at this union-determined wage rate. We shall call payment of w_F a *formal sector* (F) contract. Firms can also choose to offer workers the competitive wage w_I. We term such offers *informal sector* (I) contracts.[8] Thus, output is given by $M(l_F + l_I)$, where l_F, l_I are the amounts of labour hired according to F and I contracts, respectively. Marginal product of labour is given by the decreasing function $m(l_F + l_I)$. Let $m^{-1} \equiv N$. Clearly, $N' < 0$; we shall assume that $N'' \leqslant 0$.

Labour payments are made at the beginning of the production cycle, whereas the firm's revenues are realized at the end of the cycle. The firm therefore has to borrow at a state determined interest rate $r > 0$ in order to pay wages: the nominal marginal labour cost for F contracts is thus $w_F R$, where $R = (1 + r)$. If the firm hires l_I amount of labour on I contracts, thereby evading the terms set by the union, then it has to pay an evasion cost, $al_I 2/2$ at the end of the production cycle; $a > 0$.[9] This evasion cost includes possible costs from hiring lawyers and professional union-busters, bribe payments to judges, government inspectors and union officials, loss of scale economies due to subcontracting and outsourcing, consumer boycotts, worker non-cooperation, sabotage and strike action. Nominal marginal labour cost for I contracts is thus, effectively, $[w_I R + al_I]$.

Evasion costs are costs associated with directly unproductive redistributive, or rent-seeking, activities by the firm. The union generates rents for workers by hiking the wage rate above its market-clearing level. The firm then attempts to redistribute these rents away from the workers, by evading the payment of the union determined wage rate. This, however, requires the use of resources, in the form of evasion costs, without directly generating any additional output. Note that since the firm has complete information and faces no uncertainty, court- or state-ordained monetary compensation to workers initially paid w_I, which can in principle be imposed with retrospective effect, is captured as F contracts. Such restitution payments are therefore not part of evasion costs.

The assumption that the evasion cost is paid at the end of the production cycle implies it can be paid out of realized revenue and is, therefore, independent of the interest rate. This is intended to capture a key institutional feature of industrial relations in developing countries such as India; namely, the pervasiveness of significant delays in the launching of punitive proceedings against evasion of labour laws and formal agreements. These delays reflect weaknesses in legal, administrative and union machinery, and high costs of hard information faced by both governments and unions. Courts and labour ministries are typically lethargic, employment records are commonly unavailable, workers are unaware of their legal rights, unions are often barred by law from taking strike action without prior recourse to a complex process of third party arbitration and attempted dispute-resolution, and large-scale strike action or consumer boycotts require time-consuming organizational efforts.[10]

We call a the *enforcement* parameter. A higher value of this parameter reflects one or more of the following: (a) more stringent laws against violation of agreements with unions; (b) better state machinery for detection and prosecution of such violations; (c) stronger union organization; (d) legal rights for unions to dictate more completely the hiring practices of firms; and (e) greater likelihood of courts and tribunals adjudicating in favour of the union in case of disputes with employers.

Labour demand

We now specify the labour demand function. Define:

$$\bar{l}_I(p, w_I, R, a) \equiv \underset{l_I}{\arg\max}\ pM(l_I) - w_I R l_I - \frac{a l_I^2}{2} \tag{4.1}$$

Thus, given a price vector (w_I, R, p), and an enforcement parameter a, $\bar{l}_I$ would yield the optimal employment level for the firm, if it did not offer any formal contract. Clearly, the firm would offer F contracts if, and only if, $m(\bar{l}_I) > w_F R/p$, m denoting the marginal product of labour. Now let:

$$\bar{w}_F(w_I, R, a, p) \equiv \frac{pm\left(\bar{l}_I(w_I, R, a, p)\right)}{R} \tag{4.2}$$

The firm will offer F contracts if, and only if, the formal wage is less than $\bar{w}_F$. Suppose now that this is indeed the case; that is, $w_F \in [w_I, \bar{w}_F)$. Then, noting that $N \equiv m^{-1}$, we must have:

$$\text{if } w_F \in [w_I, \bar{w}_F), \quad l_I + l_F = N\left(\frac{w_F R}{p}\right) \tag{4.3}$$

and

$$\text{if } w_F \in [w_I, \bar{w}_F), \qquad l_I = \frac{(w_F - w_I)R}{a} \tag{4.4}$$

Let total evasion cost be given by $K = al_I^2/2$. It follows from (4.4) that:

$$\text{if } w_F \in [w_I, \bar{w}_F), \qquad K = \frac{(w_F - w_I)^2 R^2}{2a} \tag{4.5}$$

Using (4.4)–(4.5), we find that the firm's profit is given by:

$$\text{if } w_F \in [w_I, \bar{w}_F), \qquad \pi = pM(l_I + l_F) - w_F R(l_I + l_F) + K \tag{4.6}$$

Note 1 By (4.4), some workers must be on I contracts if w_F is more than w_I.

Summarizing our discussion, we get the following specification for labour demand:

Note 2 *Let D^F (w_I, w_F, R, p, a), D^I (w_I, w_F, R, p, a), be the demand functions for F and I contracts, respectively. Then, given any* (w_I, R, p, a):

(i) if $w_F \geqslant \bar{w}_F$ (w_I, R, p, a), then $D^I = \bar{l}_I(w_I, R, p, a)$, $D^F = 0$; and

(ii) if $w_F \in [w_I, \bar{w}_F(w_I, R, p, a))$, then $D^I = \dfrac{(w_F - w_I)R}{a}$

$$D^F = N\left(\frac{w_F R}{p}\right) - D^I > 0$$

Unionized wage-setting

We now proceed to analyze the determination of the F wage rate. The union takes the labour demand functions, as specified in Note 2, along with the price vector (w_I, R, p) and the enforcement parameter a, as given, and chooses its optimal F contract. The union's problem is:

$$\underset{w_F}{Max}\ \hat{v} = \lambda w_F D^F + (1 - \lambda) w_I D^I \tag{4.7}$$

where $\lambda \in (\frac{1}{2}, 1]$. Thus, the union maximizes some weighted combination of total incomes received by workers with F and I contracts.[11] We assume that the union values additional income received by *F* workers more than that received by *I* workers, because its organizational base consists primarily of the former type of workers – a phenomenon commonly encountered in developing countries.

It follows from Note 2 and (4.7) that, for the union, setting $w_F = w_I$ must dominate setting $w_F \geqslant \bar{w}_F$. Hence, using Note 2 and (4.7), the union's problem can be rewritten as:

$$\underset{w_F}{Max}\; v = \left[\lambda w_F N\left(\frac{w_F R}{p}\right) - (\lambda w_F - (1-\lambda)w_I) \times \frac{(w_F - w_I)R}{a}\right] \text{ s.t. } w_F \in [w_I, \bar{w}_F) \quad (4.8)$$

Now,

$$\frac{\partial v}{\partial w_F} = \left[\lambda N + \lambda w_F\left(\frac{R}{p}\right)N' - \lambda\frac{(w_F - w_I)R}{a} - (\lambda w_F - (1-\lambda)w_I)\frac{R}{a}\right] \quad (4.9)$$

Noting that, since $N' < 0$, $\lambda > \frac{1}{2}$ and $N'' \leqslant 0$ by assumption, we then have from (4.9):

$$\text{for all } w_F \in [w_I, \bar{w}_F),\; \frac{\partial^2 v}{\partial w_F^2} = \left[\frac{2\lambda R N'}{p} + \frac{\lambda w_F R^2 N''}{p^2} - \frac{2\lambda R}{a}\right] < 0 \quad (4.10)$$

To make the problem in (4.8) both non-trivial and well defined, we need to assume the following:

A1. $\frac{\partial v}{\partial w_F}\Big|_{w_F = w_I} > 0, \frac{\partial v}{\partial w_F}\Big|_{w_F = \bar{w}_F} < 0.$

Note 2, (4.8)–(4.10) and A1 together yield the following:

> **Note 3** *There exists a unique* w_F^* *which solves (4.7); furthermore,* $w_F^* \in (w_I, \bar{w}^F)$.

Thus, by Note 3, the union sets the *F* wage at some level above the competitive rate w_I, and firms employ workers on both types of contracts. Union power and management evasion combine to generate a two-tiered labour market. The situation is depicted in Figure 4.1.

We now note two properties of the model, which are easy to check. First, the higher the weight put by the union on *F* workers, the lower the

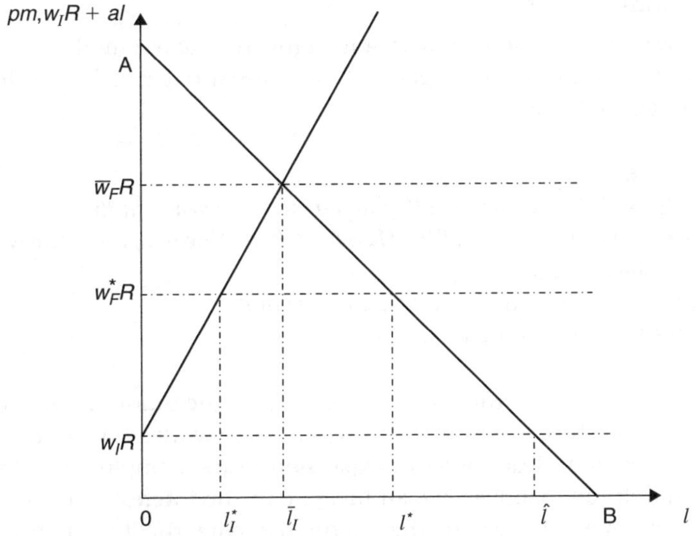

Figure 4.1 The two-tiered labour market
The schedule AB represents the value of the marginal product. At the union-chosen F wage rate w_F^*, the firm employs l^* workers, of whom l_I^* receive I contracts, while the remaining number, $l^* - l_I^*$, receive F contracts. The competitive employment level is $\hat{l}$.

formal–informal wage gap. Second, total income accruing to workers is higher under unionization, regardless of the relative weight that the union puts on F workers. Unionized wage-setting makes workers as a group better off, even if unions only care about workers on F contracts; that is, even if $\lambda = 1$. We specify these properties formally below.

Note 4 (i) $\partial w_F^*/\partial\lambda < 0$, *and* (ii) *total income accruing to workers is higher under* $w_F = w_F^*$, *than under* $w_F = w_I$.
Note 5 It is often simultaneously claimed that unions (a) ignore the interests of workers in the informal sector; and (b) generate and maintain a large formal–informal wage gap. Note 4(i) casts doubt on the internal consistency of such a two-part claim. Intuitively, higher formal wage implies greater 'leakage' of labour income to the lower paid segment of the workforce. This is costlier to a union leadership reflecting the interests of the 'labour aristocracy' compared to one that can balance such losses with gains for its membership among the poorer section of the workforce.[12]

Comparative statics

We now specify the comparative static properties of our model. We shall combine these properties to generate our substantive conclusions in the subsequent sections.

Note 6

(i) *w_F^* is increasing in both p and a, and decreasing in R;*

(ii) *Let $\theta^*(p,a,R) \equiv w_F^* R/p$. Then θ^* is decreasing in p, and increasing in both a and R;*

(iii) *l_I^* is increasing in p and decreasing in R.*

Proof: See the Appendix.

By Note 6, a rise in the output price leads to the union hiking up the formal wage. The real cost to the firm of hiring a worker on an F contract nevertheless falls, leading to an expansion in total employment in the new equilibrium. Conversely, an increase in the interest rate contracts total employment, despite the union reducing the formal wage in response. The union also raises the formal wage in response to more stringent enforcement of labour laws; that is, a rise in a. This increases the real cost of an F contract, contracting total employment. A rise in the output price, by increasing the F wage rate, induces firms to hire more workers on I contracts. A rise in the interest rate generates a fall in the F wage, which is sharp enough to induce firms to replace some I contracts with F contracts.

Note 7 The impact of a rise in the enforcement parameter on informal employment is ambiguous: the direct effect reduces it, but the associated rise in the formal wage increases it. Notice further that a fall in the output price has an ambiguous effect on the share of I contracts in total employment: thus, greater import competition, by itself, does not necessarily imply greater informalization, interpreted as a rise in the proportion of I contracts in total employment.

Liberalization and informalization

We now proceed to analyze the impact of liberalization on the extent of informalization of the labour market. To fix ideas, we think of a state that has two objectives: (a) implementing a given reduction in tariff protection (exogenously determined, say, by WTO norms); and (b) maintaining employment in the import-competing industry at its pre-liberalization level. The state's problem is to choose an interest rate that permits both objectives to be attained simultaneously.

Consider first trade liberalization via a tariff cut. This would lower the price of the industrial output.[13] By Note 6, industrial employment would consequently contract, despite the union lowering the formal wage. Now, suppose the state also reduced the fiscal deficit, thereby lowering the firm's cost of borrowing. By Note 6, this fall in the interest rate, by itself, would generate an industrial expansion, despite the union hiking up the formal wage. Suppose the interest rate exactly counteracted the tariff reduction, so that industrial employment remained at its pre-liberalization level. What would be the net impact of these two conflicting moves on the extent of informalization?

It turns out that, if the state counteracts the trade-liberalization-induced contraction through a cheap credit policy, then the union will find it optimal to hike up the formal wage. Consequently, the formal–informal wage gap will rise. This hike will be large enough to induce firms to replace formal contracts with informal contracts, despite a fall in the nominal cost, w_F^*R, of offering F contracts. The liberalization process, if successful in maintaining the level of industrial employment, must also have the unintended consequence of expanding both the extent of wage dualism and the size of the low-paid segment in the industrial labour force. Total income accruing to workers will however increase, despite greater informalization.[14] We summarize these results in Proposition 1.

Proposition 1 *Suppose the government compensates a fall in the output price through a reduction in the interest rate, so as to keep total industrial employment invariant. Then:*

(i) *the formal wage rate must increase;*
(ii) *the proportion of the industrial workforce employed on informal contracts must increase; and*
(iii) *total income of workers must increase.*

Proof: See the Appendix.

Note 8 Proposition 1 is essentially generated by the time lag between wage payments and the payment of evasion costs. Due to this time lag, while the present discounted value of the gain from the marginal evasion is $[w_F^* - w_I]$, that of the marginal cost of evasion in equilibrium is $[al_I^*/R]$. A credit-compensated tariff reduction increases the former more than the latter, generating greater informalization. Now, suppose instead that both wage payments and evasion payments had to be made simultaneously. Then the present discounted value of the gain from the marginal evasion would remain at $[w_F^* - w_I]$, but that of the marginal cost of evasion in equilibrium would simply become al_I^*. It can be checked that, in this case, a credit-compensated tariff-reduction, which keeps total employment invariant, must also keep the formal wage rate, and thus the marginal gain from evasion, invariant. Consequently, the distribution of the labour force between formal and informal contracts will remain unchanged as well. Total labour income will likewise remain invariant. Thus, it is the delay in punitive response to evasions in developing countries, reflective of weaknesses in legal, administrative and union machinery, and of high information costs, that generates greater informalization and wage dualism as an unintended consequence of the liberalization process.

Note 9 Since all the relevant functions are continuous in R, it can be seen that Note 6 and Proposition 1 together imply that the consequences of import liberalization noted in Proposition 1 will all continue to hold even if total employment falls, provided such a fall is not too drastic. Thus, the employment stability constraint facing the government can be relaxed to permit a relatively small magnitude of job losses without altering any of our conclusions.

Informalization and labour-market deregulation

Suppose now that the government has largely offset a trade-liberalization-induced contraction through financial liberalization. As discussed, this would be associated with greater informalization, and hence (noting (4.4)) greater unproductive firm expenditure on evasion.[15] The state may therefore wish to implement further changes in order to reduce the extent of this waste, while maintaining both the magnitude of tariff reduction and the level of employment in the industry.

To fix ideas, we now think of the state's problem, post-liberalization, as that of reducing total evasion expenditure by firms to its pre-liberalization level, subject to (a) the employment stability constraint; and (b) an exogenously-given tariff rate. Clearly, this would require the simultaneous use of credit and enforcement policies. What would be the nature and consequences of such policies?

Given an output price, if employment is to remain invariant despite changes in the interest rate and the enforcement parameter, then unit nominal cost of a formal contract, $w_F^* R$, must remain invariant as well. Recall now that this effective nominal cost rises both with the interest rate, R, and the enforcement parameter, a (Note 6(ii)). It follows that credit policy and enforcement policy must now move in opposite directions. But should the enforcement parameter rise or fall?

Since the marginal cost of evasion, al_I, rises with the enforcement parameter, it might appear, at first glance, that the enforcement parameter should rise. However, once the impact, on the marginal gain, of the union's response is taken into account, the opposite turns out to be true.

Proposition 2 *Given the output price, suppose the government compensates a change in the enforcement parameter through a change in the interest rate in the opposite direction, so as to keep total industrial employment constant, while reducing total evasion cost incurred by firms. Then:*

(i) *the enforcement parameter, the formal wage rate and the proportion of the industrial workforce employed on informal contracts must all fall, while the interest rate must rise;*

(ii) *total income of workers must fall; and*

(iii) *firms' profits must fall.*

Proof: See the Appendix.

Proposition 2 implies that, if the government wishes to reduce total resource wastage due to evasion activities, while keeping employment constant, then it must reduce the marginal cost to firms of evading formal contracts, yet increase the cost of credit. The reduction in the enforcement parameter, by making it cheaper for firms to substitute informal contracts for formal contracts, will force the union to reduce the formal wage. This will expand total employment. The interest rate will have to rise in order to counteract this expansion. The net consequence will be an expansion in the proportion of the industrial workforce employed on *F* contracts, as well as a fall in the formal wage rate. Thus, there will be a rise in the proportion of the workforce on relatively higher pay. However, this will be more than negated by the fall in the absolute level of such higher pay, in that total income accruing to workers as a group will go down. Paradoxically enough, despite the reduction in total labour income and evasion costs, and despite their revenue staying constant, firms will be worse off. This will happen simply because their interest costs will go up more than commensurately.

Note 10 A fall in the enforcement parameter alone need not reduce evasion expenditure, since *I* employment may go up in response (recall Note 7). A rise in the interest rate alone would reduce evasion expenditure (Note 6(iii)), but at the cost of a contraction in employment.

Propositions 1 and 2 can be directly combined into the following conclusion:

Corollary 1 *Suppose the government compensates a fall in the output price through changes in both credit and enforcement policies, so as to keep total industrial employment invariant without increasing total evasion expenditure by firms. Then the enforcement parameter must fall.*

Note that the implications, for the interest rate, the formal wage rate, total labour and profit incomes and the distribution of the industrial labour force between formal and informal contracts, of the scenario considered in Corollary 1, are all ambiguous.

In light of Corollary 1, one expects a process of import liberalization to give rise to endogenous generation of incentives for regimes to reduce the enforcement parameter; that is, opt for labour market deregulation. Notice that these incentives, operating through the intensification of industrial conflict, would impact even regimes that find the standard economic case for labour-market deregulation unpersuasive, once they sign up for import liberalization. What would be the likely forms such deregulation would assume in democratic developing countries with strong industrial unions?

Major changes in labour laws are difficult to implement, at least in the short run. Direct attempts to strip workers of rights granted by the law would involve open confrontations with unions that could be politically debilitating for governments. One would instead expect a hollowing away, gradual deactivation and weakening of the state machinery for detection and prosecution of employer evasion. Such weakening is often ascribed to administrative inefficiency. Our analysis suggests, in contrast, that it may be viewed as a deliberate, effective response to a liberalization-generated rise in distributive conflicts, within existing political constraints.[16] One would also expect an increasing tendency for courts, labour tribunals and government arbitrators to adjudicate in favour of employers in case of industrial disputes involving grey areas of contract interpretation, and to define the scope of existing loopholes and discretionary exceptions in pro-union legislation more expansively.[17]

While non-discretionary governance is often considered a critical component of economic liberalization, our analysis therefore suggests that the liberalization process may itself generate outcomes that create governmental incentives to expand the scope of discretionary decision-making. One cannot hollow away the substantive content of legal rights conferred upon organized labour, while maintaining their formal shell, without utilizing the power of selective application.[18] Somewhat ironically, employers might have an incentive to resist such creeping labour-market deregulation, which would, in employment-invariant equilibrium, benefit only lenders.

Extensions

While we have focused on the import-competing sector, trade liberalization may also involve removal of export restrictions on globally competitive sectors. We then have a fall in the interest rate and a rise in the output price. By Note 6, total employment, the formal wage rate, informal employment and evasion expenditure must all go up. Thus, social losses from industrial conflict over employer evasion must rise in this case as well. Proposition 2 and the subsequent discussion (except, clearly, Corollary 1) would continue to be applicable. However, in developing countries, these sectors are often in agriculture or services, with negligible union presence to begin with.

We have assumed that the informal wage rate, w_I, is invariant with respect to industrial employment. Intuitively, this abstraction amounts to assuming that short run variations in employment in the import-competing sector impinge on a relatively small proportion of the total workforce in the economy, or that other factors counteract these variations. This appears to be a reasonable approximation for many developing countries. However, one may extend our analysis, by assuming that the informal wage is determined according to, for example, the function $[w_I = \underline{w}_I + \eta N(w_F\, R/p)]$, where $\underline{w}_I > 0$, $\eta \geqslant 0$, and that the union takes into account its impact on the informal wage when choosing the formal wage. Evidently, the analysis in this chapter would then constitute the special case where $\eta = 0$. It can be shown that, if (i) the union completely ignores informal workers (that is, $\lambda = 1$); and (ii) a rise in the interest rate contracts the industry, then our conclusions, as presented in Propositions 1 and 2, would hold even under this extended scenario.[19]

We have modelled the objective of the government simply as the simultaneous satisfaction of three constraints: (a) implementation of an exogenously given tariff reduction; (b) employment stability in the import-competing industry; and (c) maintenance of social losses due to employer–employee conflicts at the pre-liberalization level. We have already noted that (b) and (c) are to be interpreted broadly, in that they can be partially relaxed without altering our conclusions. One can derive these intuitively and empirically plausible objectives endogenously from a prior specification of the state's utility function, where the income distribution figures explicitly. This, however, comes at the cost of a major increase in notational complexity, and provides little or no additional insight.

Conclusion

This chapter has examined the impact of trade liberalization on the extent of wage dualism and evasion of formal, union-mandated, wage-contracts by employers in an import-competing industry. We have shown that, if the government largely maintains the employment level in the industry despite greater import competition, by reducing the cost of credit to firms, then the extent of employer evasion of formal contracts will increase, in response to a rise in the formal–informal wage gap. Thus, liberalization may causally exacerbate existing labour market distortions. These effects are generated essentially by institutional delays in punitive response to employer evasion. Greater employer evasion will entail greater diversion of resources to socially wasteful employer–union distributive conflicts. This, in turn, may generate incentives for the state to moderate such social waste. To do so, however, the state will be forced to (a) evade or attenuate its own responsibilities as the enforcer of contracts between unions and employers; and (b) thereby reduce the total income of workers, as well as profits of firms, while benefiting rentiers. Identical conclusions will follow if the initial price reduction is instead caused by, say, a cut in industrial subsidy. Our results provide theoretical comprehension of observed trends in industrial labour markets in developing countries such as India.

The political-economic and distributive implications of finance-compensated import-liberalization (or subsidy-reduction) that we have highlighted need to be subjected to greater empirical scrutiny. In particular, our theoretical analysis points to the need for quantitative assessment of social losses due to wage dualism and industrial conflicts in liberalizing economies in the developing world. Furthermore, our theoretical investigation has been carried out within a static, partial equilibrium context. Extension of this investigation to dynamic and general equilibrium contexts, with investment and capital mobility, can constitute a fruitful avenue of future research.

Our objective has been to highlight some logical implications of liberalizing policies, not to generate policy prescriptions from deregulatory first principles. This exercise may contribute towards a better understanding of distributive tensions and conflicts emerging in developing countries as consequences of the liberalization process. It does not, by itself, directly translate into technocratic policy advice in any straightforward way. Yet, it also appears to raise concerns that neither students nor practitioners of the political art of economic policy-making can quite afford to ignore.

Appendix

Proof of Note 6

(i) Using (4.9), since $w_F^* > w_I$, noting that by assumption, $N'' \leqslant 0$, $\lambda > \frac{1}{2}$, we get:

$$\frac{\partial^2 v}{\partial w_F \partial p}\Big|_{w_F = w_F^*} = -\lambda\left[2\left(\frac{w_F R}{p^2}\right)N' + \left(\frac{1}{p}\right)\left(\frac{w_F R}{p}\right)^2 N''\right] > 0 \tag{N1}$$

$$\frac{\partial^2 v}{\partial w_F \partial a}\Big|_{w_F = w_F^*} = \left[\lambda\frac{(w_F - w_I)R}{a^2} + (\lambda w_F - (1-\lambda)w_I)\frac{R}{a^2}\right] > 0 \tag{N2}$$

and

$$\frac{\partial^2 v}{\partial w_F \partial R}\Big|_{w_F = w_F^*} = \left[2\lambda\left(\frac{w_F}{p}\right)N' + \lambda R\left(\frac{w_F}{p}\right)^2 N'' - \lambda\frac{(w_F - w_I)}{a} - \frac{(\lambda w_F - (1-\lambda)w_I)}{a}\right] < 0 \tag{N3}$$

Together, (4.10) and (N1)–(N3) yield Note 6(i).

(ii) Since a rise in a must raise w_F^* (Note 6(i)), it follows trivially that θ^* must rise. Note now that, from (4.9), the union's first-order condition implies:

$$\lambda\left(N\left(\theta^*\right) + \theta^* N'\left(\theta^*\right)\right) = \frac{(w_F^* - w_I)R}{a} + (2\lambda - 1)\frac{w_F^* R}{a} \tag{N4}$$

Since $\lambda > \frac{1}{2}$, Note 6(i) implies that the right hand side of (N4) must rise with an increase in p. Since the left hand side is decreasing in θ^*, it follows that θ^* must be decreasing in p. Now rewrite (N4) as:

$$\lambda\left(N\left(\theta^*\right) + \theta^* N'\left(\theta^*\right)\right) - 2\lambda\frac{\theta^* p}{a} = -\frac{w_I R}{a} \tag{N5}$$

Since the left hand side is decreasing in θ^*, it follows from (N5) that θ^* must be increasing in R.

(iii) That l_I^* must increase with a rise in p follows from (4.4) and Note 6(i). Note 6(ii) implies that the left hand side of (N4) must fall with an increase in R, and that $w_F^* R$ must rise. Noting $\lambda > \frac{1}{2}$, it follows from (N4) that l_I^* must fall with a rise in R. □

Proof of Proposition 1

From (4.4) and (N4) we get:

$$\lambda N\left(\theta^*\right) + \lambda\theta^* N'\left(\theta^*\right) = l_I^* + (2\lambda - 1)\frac{w_F^* R}{a} \tag{N6}$$

Noting that $\lambda > \frac{1}{2}$, and that, given θ^*, a fall in p must be matched by a fall in $w_F^* R$, we get parts (i) and (ii) of Proposition 1 from (N4) and (N6). Now consider equilibrium total income of workers:

$$V^* = \left[w_F^* N\left(\theta^*\right) - (w_F^* - w_I)^2\left(\frac{R}{a}\right)\right] \tag{N7}$$

Let the F wage rates in the post and pre-liberalization equilibria be w_{F1}^*, w_{F2}^* respectively. Let R_1,R_2 be the corresponding interest rates. Consider the post-liberalization equilibrium. From (4.9):

$$\frac{\partial v}{\partial w_F}\bigg|_{w_F = w_{F1}^*} = \left[\lambda\left(N + \theta^* N' - \frac{2(w_F - w_I)R_1}{a}\right) + (1 - 2\lambda)w_I\frac{R_1}{a}\right] = 0.$$

Then, since $\lambda > \frac{1}{2}$, noting that N is held constant by assumption, and using (N7), we get:

$$\frac{\partial V^*}{\partial w_F^*}\bigg|_{w_F^* = w_{F1}^*} = \left(N - \frac{2(w_F^* - w_I)R_1}{a}\right) > 0.$$

Since, given N, $\partial^2 V^*/\partial w_F^{*2} < 0$ for any $w_F^* > 0$, and by Proposition 1(i), $w_{F1}^* > w_{F2}$, we thus get:

$$\left[w_{F1}^* N(\theta^*) - (w_{F1}^* - w_I)^2\left(\frac{R_1}{a}\right)\right] > \left[w_{F2}^* N(\theta^*) - (w_{F2}^* - w_I)^2\left(\frac{R_1}{a}\right)\right].$$

Noting that $R_1 < R_2$, and using (N7), part (iii) of Proposition 1 follows. □

We shall prove Proposition 2 via the following lemma, which follows directly from (N6).

> **Lemma N1** *Given the output price, suppose the government compensates a change in the enforcement parameter through a change in the interest rate in the opposite direction, so as to keep total industrial employment constant. Then, the proportion of the industrial workforce employed on informal contracts will increase if, and only if, the enforcement parameter rises.*

Proof of Proposition 2

Part (i) of Proposition 2 follows directly from Lemma N1 and (4.4). The proof of part (ii) of Proposition 2 is analogous to that of part (iii) of Proposition 1 and is therefore omitted. Note now that, using (4.4) and (N7), the firm's total profit is: $[pM(N(\theta^*)) - p\theta^*N(\theta^*) + al_f^2/2]$. Noting that p and θ^* remain constant by assumption, part (iii) of Proposition 2 is immediate. □

Notes

We thank Daniel Seidmann and seminar participants at the Indian Statistical Institute, Kolkata and UNU-WIDER, Helsinki, for helpful comments. Dasgupta thanks the Calcutta Centre for Studies in Social Sciences, and Marjit, Nottingham, for hosting visits, which facilitated this research.

1 For example, by law Indian firms with over ten workers are subject to labour regulations, but in practice most firms with labour forces above this threshold have a substantial casual labour force that is undeclared under the Factories Act and hence not state-regulated. Estimates of unregulated labour in various Indian corporations range from 40 per cent to 85 per cent (Davala, 1992; Bhowmik, 1998). A recent study of the garment industry in Ahmedabad found that 50 per cent of workers in all registered firms did not have written contracts and about 10 per cent did not receive any benefits (Jhabvala and Kanbur, 2004). See Agenor (1996) for other developing countries.
2 See, for example, Besley and Burgess (2004) for an analysis of related Indian evidence. However, Aidt and Tzannatos (2002) cast doubt on the claim that economies perform better with non-unionized labour markets.
3 For example, trade liberalization in India in the 1990s was associated with monetary and financial sector deregulation, which led to a fall in the prime lending rate of banks from about 19 per cent in 1991–92 to 10.5–11 per cent in 2001–02. The actual lending rates for top-rated borrowers could be even lower (see Reddy, 2004). Brazil and Colombia also experienced a phase of declining interest rates in the 1990s (Marjit and Maiti, 2004).
4 There is a small but growing theoretical literature on economic reform and informal labour. A common concern is the impact of deregulation of trade and labour laws on the informal wage. Building on Carruth and Oswald (1981) and Agenor and Montiel (1995), this issue is addressed by Marjit (2003), Marjit *et al.* (2003) and Marjit and Maiti (2004). Our focus is quite different.
5 See, for example, Jenkins (1999) and Dev (2000) for India; Galli and Kucera (2003) for Latin America; Amin (2002) for Asia; and Xaba *et al.* (2002) for sub-Saharan Africa.
6 Note that t can alternatively be interpreted as the rate at which a subsidy is provided to domestic producers.
7 Thus, returns to labour in non-industrial occupations (that is, agriculture and services) are assumed constant, as in the classical two-sector labour surplus economy of Lewis (1954). See the section on extensions, p. 63.
8 This can be *transparently* illegal, or involve exploitation of incompleteness, loopholes, interpretative ambiguities and grey areas in labour laws and/or

agreements with unions – actions that are open to subsequent contestation by the union or the government. Common examples of such friction-generating grey areas are clauses allowing limited outsourcing, hiring of apprentices and part-time/temporary workers on lower pay, relocation of part of the production base to a region with lower wage rates, and so on. The phenomenon of firms subcontracting out to smaller firms legally free to offer *I* contracts is also captured through our formulation.

9 At the cost of expositional inconvenience, we can specify the evasion cost function more generally as a strictly convex function without affecting our substantive conclusions.

10 Despite delays, evasion costs should depend on *r* if fines with retrospective effect, accruing to the state, constitute the major component of such costs. This does not appear to be the case in developing countries.

11 It is likely that the union itself would incur significant costs from imposing evasion penalties on the firm. Our formulation involves, in effect (a) modelling these as a fixed cost (for example, costs of employing permanent union staff, running union offices and so on); and (b) normalizing this fixed cost to 0. More complicated cost schedules for the union, while compatible with our analysis, make the exposition cumbersome without adding any insights.

12 In a general equilibrium setting, one can show, following Marjit *et al.* (2003), that whether a higher unionized wage will increase the informal wage depends on the degree of capital mobility across sectors.

13 Alternatively, such a fall could reflect a cut in industrial subsidy. See note 6.

14 Note, from (4.6), that the firm's profit measured in *output* units, $[M - \theta^* N + a l_I^{*2}/2p]$ must rise as well. However, the direction of change in the firm's *monetary* profit is indeterminate. The firm's total cost, $[w_F^* RN - a l_I^{*2}/2]$, must fall, but the price reduction will reduce the firm's revenue as well.

15 Greater employer evasion of formal contracts, and the consequent increase in conflict between the union and firms, may also force the government to extend its adjudicating and enforcing activities through the courts, labour bureaus, industrial tribunals, police and so on, thereby imposing additional pressure on the public exchequer.

16 One reads an echo of this interpretation in the official position of the largest Left political formation in India, the Communist Party of India (Marxist). 'This phenomenon of non-enforcement of labour laws is not just administrative default, but is being deliberately promoted by those in governant through dismantling of labour-inspectorates, drastic weakening of the enforcement machineries including tribunals etc. and curbing trade union rights' (Communist Party of India (Marxist), 2005).

17 See Jenkins (1999: 188–94) for a number of telling examples from India in the 1990s. Recently, the Supreme Court of India, overturning the concurrent decision of three lower courts, upheld an employer's right to fire a worker for abusing his supervisor. A legal commentator interpreted the ruling thus: 'Pro-globalisation proponents should welcome this trend of judicial interpretation of labour laws ... Their view – labour laws have to be made flexible to make Indian industry more competitive. The Supreme Court's recognition of the employer's right of termination confirms this workplace reality' (Sen, 2005). In another interesting judgement, a five-judge bench of the Supreme Court decided to refer the definition of 'industry', in the context of the Industrial

Disputes Act of 1947, to a larger bench for reconsideration. The bench argued that the current, broad, definition was excessively 'worker-oriented' and 'unmindful of the interests of the employer and the public'. 'Has the Supreme Court taken it upon itself to direct India on the path of free market and globalisation?', a Left Parliamentarian queried. See Joshi (2005).

18 In his study of economic liberalization in India in the 1990s, Jenkins (1999) uses the phrase 'reforms by stealth' to characterize this process of hollowing out. 'State governments have been waging a guerrilla war ... taking action in isolated incidents and sapping the power of unions to resist encroachments upon their rights. This has taken place without alterations to official policy ... Indeed, India still has some of the most pro-worker labour laws in the world. *Implementation is another matter*' (Jenkins, 1999: 192, emphasis added).

19 With $\eta > 0$, and given (ii), $\lambda = 1$ is sufficient, but not necessary, to maintain our conclusions. One can do so even with $\lambda < 1$, but at the cost of imposing additional, intuitively opaque restrictions.

References

Agenor, P.R. (1996) 'The Labour Market and Economic Adjustment', *IMF Staff Papers*, 43: 261–335.

Agenor, P.R. and P. Montiel (1995) *Development Macroeconomics* (Princeton, NJ: Princeton University Press).

Ahluwalia, M.S. (2002) 'Economic Reforms in India since 1991: Has Gradualism Worked?', *Journal of Economic Perspectives*, 16: 67–88.

Aidt, T. and Z. Tzannatos (2002) *Unions and Collective Bargaining: Economic Effects in a Global Environment* (Washington, DC: World Bank).

Amin, T.M.N. (2002) *The Informal Sector in Asia from the Decent Work Perspective*, Working Paper on the Informal Economy no. 4 (Geneva: ILO).

Besley, T. and R. Burgess (2004) 'Can Labour Regulation Hinder Economic Performance? Evidence from India', *Quarterly Journal of Economics*, 119: 91–134.

Bhowmik, S. (1998) 'The Labour Movement in India: Present Problems and Future Perspectives', *Indian Journal of Social Work*, 59: 147–66.

Carruth, A. and A. Oswald (1981) 'The Determination of Union and Non-union Wage Rates', *European Economic Review*, 16: 285–302.

Communist Party of India (Marxist) (2005) '18th Congress Resolution on Working Class Struggles', *People's Democracy*, XXIX (16), 17 April.

Davala, S. (ed.) (1992) *Employment and Unionization in Indian Industry* (Delhi: Friedrich Ebert Stiftung).

Dev, M. (2000) 'Economic Liberalization and Employment in South Asia', *Economic and Political Weekly* (January): 40–51.

Edwards, S. (1989) 'On the Sequencing of Structural Reforms', Working Paper no. 3138 (Cambridge, MA: NBER).

Galli, R. and D. Kucera (2003) 'Informal Employment in Latin America: Movements over Business Cycles and the Effects of Worker Rights', Discussion Paper no. 145 (Geneva: ILO).

Jenkins, R. (1999) *Democratic Politics and Economic Reform in India* (Cambridge: Cambridge University Press).

Jhabvala, R. and R. Kanbur (2004) 'Globalization and Economic Reform as seen from the Ground', in K. Basu (ed.) *India's Emerging Economy: Performance and Prospects in the 1990s and Beyond* (Cambridge, MA: MIT Press).
Joshi, P. (2005) 'All's Not Quiet on Industry Front', *Telegraph*, 29 August.
Lewis, W.A. (1954) 'Economic Development with Unlimited Supplies of Labour', *The Manchester School*, 22: 139–91.
Marjit, S. (2003) 'Economic Reform and Informal Wage – A General Equilibrium Analysis', *Journal of Development Economics*, 72: 371–8.
Marjit, S., S. Kar and K. Sarkar (2003) 'Trade Reform, Internal Capital Mobility and Informal Wage', Mimeo (Kolkata: CSSS).
Marjit, S. and D.S. Maiti (2004) 'Globalization, Economic Reform and the Informal Sector', presented at the EGDI-WIDER Conference on the Informal Sector, Helsinki, September. (See also Chapter 2, this volume.)
Reddy, Y.V. (2004) 'Monetary and Financial Sector Reforms in India: A Practitioner's Perspective', in K. Basu (ed.) *India's Emerging Economy: Performance and Prospects in the 1990s and Beyond* (Cambridge, MA: MIT Press).
Sen, K. (2005) 'Labour Laws: Change in Judicial Thinking', *Financial Express*, 8 March.
Xaba, J., P. Horn and S. Motala (2002) 'The Informal Sector in sub-Saharan Africa', Working Paper on the Informal Economy no. 10 (Geneva: ILO).

5
Township and Village Enterprises and Employment Generation in China

Guanghua Wan and Yuchun Zhu

Introduction

Having emerged in the 1960s, town and village enterprises (TVEs) form a unique sector in China. Not only do they have no formal institutional arrangement, but also their property rights are difficult to define. As implied by the name, TVEs are located in non-urban areas and they are more related to the local economy than other enterprises. Despite lack of government support, TVEs have evolved into an integral part of the Chinese economy. They have been playing a crucial role in China's industrialization and development processes. Today, neither the formal sector nor the agricultural sector can survive without the TVEs. In 2002, they constituted 31 per cent of China's GDP, totalling 3180 billion RMB, and 65 per cent of the entire rural economy, where some 70 per cent of China's population lives. In the same year, their exports amounted to 1050 million RMB, accounting for 40 per cent of China's total exports. In reality, many local governments derive much of their operating budget from TVEs.

While an extensive literature exists that focuses on the evolution, growth path and institutional framework of TVEs (Putterman, 1997; Jin and Qian, 1998; Bowles and Dong, 1999), much less is written on their labour absorbing role. This is rather disappointing, particularly given that China faces some 200 million surplus labourers from the farming sector and a major perceived role of TVEs lies in job creation (Zhou *et al.*, 1992). Further, there existed some 80–100 million internal migrants in China (Wan, 1995). This number may have doubled in recent years. A significant proportion of migrants seek employment opportunities in TVEs. Meanwhile, under a massive industrial reform programme implemented in state-owned enterprises (SOEs), tens of millions of urban labourers are being laid off. Thus, the formal sector has been releasing rather than absorbing labour, despite the miraculous growth of the Chinese economy in the last 25 years. One simply cannot imagine the state of the employment situation in the absence of TVEs in China. With the development of the tertiary sector lagging behind, TVEs represent the major avenue for alleviating the serious unemployment and underemployment problems in China. To a large extent, development of TVEs has also helped significantly to ease the pressure of migration on major cities. Clearly, an examination of TVEs labour-absorbing role is both timely and important.

On the other hand, TVEs are not evenly developed across regions in China, partly because they were germinated in those regions of the country where residents were traditionally business-minded. In the early stages, and long after their emergence, society was rather closed and fragmented; markets of any kind were treated as anti-revolutionary. More importantly, the Chinese government did not appreciate the value of TVEs and they were often subject to unfair criticism and various discriminations. These contributed to the regional imbalance in TVE development. As TVEs in a few regions (for example, Jiangsu, Zhejiang and Shandong) struggled to survive and grow in the 1960s, 1970s and early 1980s, the entry costs, requirement of expertise and competition pressure had also risen. These formed obstacles to late-comers wishing to set up TVEs, let alone maintain profitable operation. Recognizing their unbalanced development, TVEs have been identified as one of the most significant contributors to the worsening regional inequality in China (Rozelle, 1994; Wan, 2001). However, economists seem to have overlooked the fact that TVEs must have also led to reductions in regional inequality, since they have helped to close up the urban–rural income gap, which constitutes more than 70 per cent of the overall regional inequality (Kanbur and Zhang, 2005). To say the least, past studies do not provide a complete and fair picture, as the two offsetting forces of TVEs (disequalizing on the spatial dimension and equalizing on the rural–urban dimension) render the overall impact on inequality indeterminate. A proper evaluation appeals for consideration of both the disequalizing and the equalizing impacts. Nevertheless, this chapter will focus on the role of TVEs in absorbing surplus labour. Their relevance to the urban–rural income gap will be addressed in a separate paper. These two issues, though not intrinsically linked, are broadly related as development of TVEs is rightly expected to help generate employment but is wrongly accused of having caused high regional inequality in China.

In the following section, an effort is made to classify TVEs as an informal sector. This has not been attempted before. Following this, an econometric framework is developed for exploring the capacity of TVEs to absorb surplus labour; labour absorption elasticities are also obtained and discussed in this section. The chapter concludes with policy recommendations.

TVEs as an informal sector

Do TVEs constitute an informal sector? To answer this question requires a clear definition of 'informality'. Despite its wide use, no consensus has been reached on the exact meaning and interpretation of this term. Some even go so far as to question the validity of the very concept of informality (Sindzingre, 2006).

Hart is the first proponent of this concept, and highlights uncertainty of production activities in terms of income and employment as the distinctive feature of informality (Hart, 2006). In other words, as long as an economic activity is associated with a highly unstable income stream and highly vulnerable employment conditions (particularly job insecurity for employees), it can be regarded as part of the informal sector. Chen (2006) refers this group of scholars as dualists. On the other hand, the legalist school, according to Chen (2006), emphasizes the illegality of institutions as a major characteristic of informality where illegality means non-registration or avoidance of taxes and other costs (such as employee pensions or insurance (OECD, 2002)). Following this definition, the informal sector will continue to survive as long as government procedures are cumbersome and costly. Finally, structuralists propose that the informal sector should be viewed as micro firms and employees that strive to reduce costs and, thereby, increase the competitiveness of larger firms. From this perspective, formal and informal sectors are complementary to each other and they may co-exist in the long run.

It should be pointed out that the TVE sector has evolved over many years. Nowadays, a few of them are possibly as formal as large corporations. Nevertheless, one must treat TVEs in their entirety, and it seems inappropriate to ignore the historic origin of TVEs completely when attempting to characterize this sector. With these caveats in mind, one can classify TVEs as an informal sector if informality is taken as a negative connotation (Sindzingre, 2006), at least relative to the large-scale SOEs. The same can be said when TVEs are examined in terms of size, contractual arrangements, level of organization, possession of human capital and so on (Sindzingre, 2006), as discussed below.

To the extent that many TVEs are processing or outsourcing plants for large corporations, China's TVEs match the informality definition of the structuralists. Indeed, the growth and development of TVEs in China have helped to intensify pressure on SOEs to reform and to improve efficiency.

The potential threat to SOEs from TVEs is real and considerable, as evidenced by an increasing number of acquisitions of SOEs made by peasant entrepreneurs or owners of TVEs.

Typically, TVE employees do not enjoy job security; many are seasonal or casual workers. There is little contractual arrangement between TVEs and their employees. Very few, if any, employees are entitled to pensions or insurance of any kind. In some cases, employees are required to contribute capital as part of employment conditions. On the other hand, there are no strict accounting, reporting or monitoring standards on TVEs. It is common that a sizable portion of TVE profits goes to the local government. Tax evasion was and still is prevalent among TVEs. These features clearly indicate that China's TVEs are operating informally.

At present, 89 per cent of TVEs are located in villages, 9 per cent in rural townships and the remaining 2 per cent in county-level townships or cities. Most TVEs are small scale, achieving low-productivity and low income. They do not have advanced machines or highly skilled workers. These are perceived to be significant characteristics of an informal sector (Hart, 2006).

For a long time, TVEs have been discriminated against by non-local governments and financial institutions. In a BBC radio programme, Wan (1997) referred to the TVE sector as an orphan because of the lack of official support or attention. Even today in China, there is no line ministry to administer this important sector. The only relevant government organ is the so-called TVE Bureau under the Ministry of Agriculture. This bureau has little executive power and it is a semi-public or semi-official organization. Since the inception of TVEs, central government has either supported SOEs at the expense of TVEs, or simply ignored the latter. It seems appropriate to say that TVEs are perceived to be an informal sector by policy-makers in China.

Except the legalist school, both structuralist and dualist schools recognize the relevance of the employment issue in defining informality. While the dualists attribute absorption of surplus labour as the driving force of informal activities, structuralists emphasize reduction of labour cost as the basis of informality. TVEs in China were created to take advantage of surplus and cheap labour in rural China, and are still playing a prominent role in alleviating employment problems in China.

Modelling the TVE sector

Since their emergence, TVEs have absorbed a remarkable proportion of the labour force. In 2002, some 135 million labourers were employed by TVEs in China, including, surprisingly, 1.47 million urban labourers. This represents 18 (28.6) per cent of the total (rural) labour force. Most of this employment (105 million) was created after the commencement of economic reform in 1978, when only 2.7 per cent of the rural labour force was in TVEs. This increase in TVE employment helped to put 55 per cent of the increased labour force into employment during this period. Some researchers believe that approximately half of the 80–100 million migrants are working in TVEs. These data confirm the informal nature of TVEs in China.

The amount of labour absorbed by TVEs differs considerably across regions, so does the proportion of TVE employees in the regional rural labour force (Table 5.1). It seems that a positive correlation exists between the formal sectors and the TVEs, as evidenced by the high percentages of labour force working in TVEs in more industrialized regions such as Beijing, Shanghai, Tianjin, Fujian, Guangdong and Zhejiang. The positive correlation is even better reflected by the reasonably high percentages of TVE employment in less-developed regions of Shaanxi, Liaoning, Jilin and Heilongjiang. These regions were major industrial bases in pre-reform China, where many large scale SOEs still operate. As expected, the labour absorption-capacity of TVEs is strong in east China followed by central China, with west China lagging far behind.

However, it is observed that increases in TVE job creation have slowed down, and appear to have come to a halt. From Table 5.1, there was a drop, though negligible, in the absolute number of TVE employees from 1995 to 2000. Worse still, the percentage of TVE employees in China's rural labour force actually declined from 29.5 per cent to 27.1 per cent during this period. These observations have worried development experts, the rural mass and policy-makers. While there is no doubt that this has been caused by the slow down in the output growth of TVEs (now averaging 10–15 per cent annually rather than over 20 per cent in the 1980s and early 1990s), a concerted push into capital and technology-intensive operations is also responsible. The push is largely driven by competition from reforming SOEs, the WTO accession (thus, competition from other countries) and inflows of FDI, which have mostly been directed into technology and capital-intensive production entities.

Nevertheless, TVEs may regain their trend for growth as the domestic economy picks up. Efforts to develop TVEs in less developed inland areas are expected to generate more employment; the inland areas are where the unemployment problem is most acute and income levels are low. In any case, how much employment would be created requires careful analysis, for China as a whole and for inland areas in particular.

Table 5.1 Regional number of employees in TVEs and proportion in rural labour force (%)

Region	Number of employees (10 000 persons)				Percentage in rural labour force			
	1990	1995	2000	2002	1990	1995	2000	2002
Beijing	108.82	98.72	101.41	113.58	56.67	54.04	61.17	68.59
Tianjin	88.69	104.67	120.43	130.60	50.77	61.64	71.68	77.42
Hebei	641.22	852.02	849.58	886.15	26.93	33.11	31.38	32.44
Shanxi	240.42	207.29	287.44	319.10	26.86	21.89	29.07	31.90
Neimenggu	97.62	223.97	205.05	188.82	17.00	37.99	32.47	29.03
Liaoning	305.09	434.23	464.49	487.45	34.91	50.14	48.09	49.06
Jilin	155.26	213.78	250.95	202.72	24.35	33.87	39.15	30.90
Heilongjiang	162.21	209.47	154.32	153.00	25.69	35.90	16.90	16.46
Shanghai	151.58	139.94	144.12	173.19	57.29	60.74	56.39	68.32
Jiangsu	896.17	924.71	855.76	972.28	31.75	33.35	31.84	36.70
Zhejiang	495.49	795.71	880.39	993.64	24.19	37.95	41.76	45.46
Anhui	462.29	595.03	479.75	502.03	19.92	22.95	17.15	17.67
Fujian	279.16	471.00	555.56	575.23	27.17	41.01	44.66	45.13
Jiangxi	232.69	440.13	307.17	330.84	16.23	28.28	19.85	20.97
Shandong	943.90	1439.77	1311.57	1447.29	28.07	40.30	36.04	39.17
Henan	881.88	716.05	889.18	938.94	25.64	40.01	18.87	20.02

Hubei	388.98	663.65	629.69	647.90	21.01	36.66	35.34	36.04
Hunan	418.36	722.55	938.85	779.62	15.85	26.22	32.87	26.90
Guangdong	658.33	1072.11	928.29	1178.60	27.38	42.56	33.33	42.39
Guangxi	199.11	182.84	353.15	374.00	11.11	9.31	16.46	17.09
Hainan	24.45	37.89	28.17	29.67	10.15	18.69	12.58	12.70
Sichuan	705.74	1150.72	761.09	828.08	14.38	22.22	20.09	22.01
Guizhou	106.95	85.66	140.59	172.11	7.59	5.40	7.80	9.34
Yunnan	148.44	273.38	270.79	301.13	8.88	14.90	13.89	15.13
Shaanxi	253.53	328.97	400.99	400.83	20.93	24.83	29.85	29.42
Gansu	129.36	204.26	156.95	176.98	15.55	23.32	16.80	17.55
Qinghai	14.68	9.31	23.41	24.78	10.49	6.10	13.61	13.97
Ningxia	23.53	14.27	49.81	53.70	15.95	8.78	25.16	26.43
Xinjiang	46.40	49.98	80.64	86.67	11.99	15.99	22.77	23.21
East China	4792.01	6553.60	6592.92	7361.68	27.25	35.81	34.52	38.10
Central China	3039.71	3991.90	4142.39	4062.97	21.08	30.11	24.56	23.84
West China	1428.64	2116.56	1884.27	2044.26	13.35	18.52	17.87	19.07
China	9260.36	12662.06	12619.57	13468.92	21.68	29.46	27.13	28.61

To analyze the capacity of TVEs for labour absorption, we first specify and estimate a production function for TVEs, using panel data from 29 regions (with Chongqing merged with Sichuan, and Tibet excluded due to data incompleteness). To minimize the specification errors, an extended Box–Cox model is adopted:

$$Y^{(\lambda)} = \alpha + \beta_1 X_1{}^{(\theta)}\,(2) + \beta_2 X_2{}^{(\theta)} + \cdots \beta_K X_K{}^{(\theta)} \\ + \textit{dummy variable terms} + U \qquad (5.1)$$

where Y = regional total TVE output deflated by regional CPIs, Xs = various inputs, and dummy variables are used to control for possible heterogeneity. Further, λ and θ are transformation parameters. In (5.1), $Y^{(\lambda)} = (Y^{\lambda} - 1)/\lambda$ and $X_k^{(\theta)} = (X_k^{(\theta)} - 1)/\theta$. As λ approaches 0, the limit of $(Y^{\lambda} - 1)/\lambda$ is *Log Y* by L'Hopital's rule. Hence, $Y^{(\lambda)}$ = *Log Y* when $\lambda = 0$ (Judge *et al.*, 1988). The same arguments apply to $X_k^{(\theta)}$. Model (5.1) encompasses many functional forms, including the semilog function if $\lambda = 0$ and $\theta = 1$, and the standard linear function if $\lambda = \theta = 1$. In the case that $\lambda = \theta = 0$, a double-log or Cobb–Douglas equation is obtained. When $\lambda = -1$ or $\theta = -1$, the relevant variable becomes its reciprocal. Clearly, one can restrict each of the two transformation parameters to be 0, 1, −1 or unrestricted. The 4 by 4 combinations produce 16 different functional forms. Moreover, one can impose $\lambda = \theta$ although they are not restricted to a particular numerical value. Thus, at least 17 different models can be derived based on Equation (5.1). The standard χ^2 test will be used to select the preferred model (see Wan, 2004).

Data are taken exclusively from the TVE Statistical Yearbook of China (NBS, various years). The selection of input variables depends on the dependent variable to be used. When gross output is considered, energy and material inputs should be included (the so-called KLEM model). Since data on these inputs are not available, a net output production process can be modelled instead, which typically requires inclusion of the capital and labour variables (see Fu and Balasubramanyam, 2003). Unfortunately, net output or value added data are only available to us for limited years and we are thus forced to restrict the time horizon to the period 1995–2002.

There are two reasons why this restriction is not as serious as it may initially seem. First, the sample size is 232 (8 years by 29 regions), which is quite reasonable. Second, the long run relationship can be identified despite the short time-span of the panel data, since the level of TVE development differs considerably from region to region. As a matter of fact, using more recent data is necessary, as TVE data are notorious for their low quality. However, the quality of data is believed to have been improving as auditing and taxation rules are being gradually enforced. One major drawback of earlier data lies in the exaggeration of output values, primarily driven by the desire of local officials to overreport their performance. This must have been gradually corrected as, in addition to the enforcement of various rules, privately run TVEs gain larger shares and collectively TVEs are privatized in one way or another (Ho *et al.*, 2003).

Before proceeding to econometric estimation, it is useful to plot the observations as a form of preliminary data analysis. Two figures are obtained to this end; Figure 5.1 shows the correlation between labour and output, and Figure 5.2 displays the relationship between capital stock and output. Interestingly, Figure 5.2 exhibits little heterogeneity; it looks quite similar to a plot of time series data. However, Figure 5.1 demonstrates possible differences in the labour–output relationship from region to region. These findings point to the need for separate treatment of the labour absorption issue for eastern, central and western China, not necessarily for each individual region.

Given the unbalanced nature of TVE development across locations and visual detection of potential heterogeneity in the labour–output relationship, it is necessary to interact the labour variable with location dummy variables. Since the time span of the panel data is short, it is not sensible to

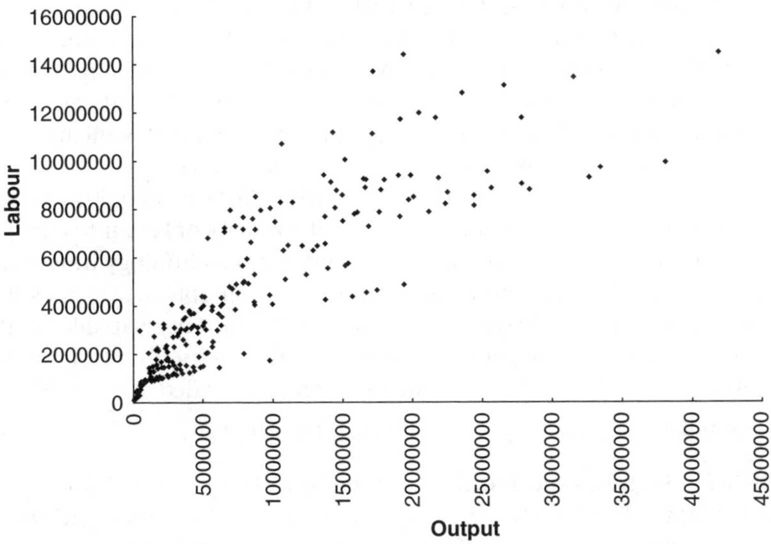

Figure 5.1 Output–labour plot

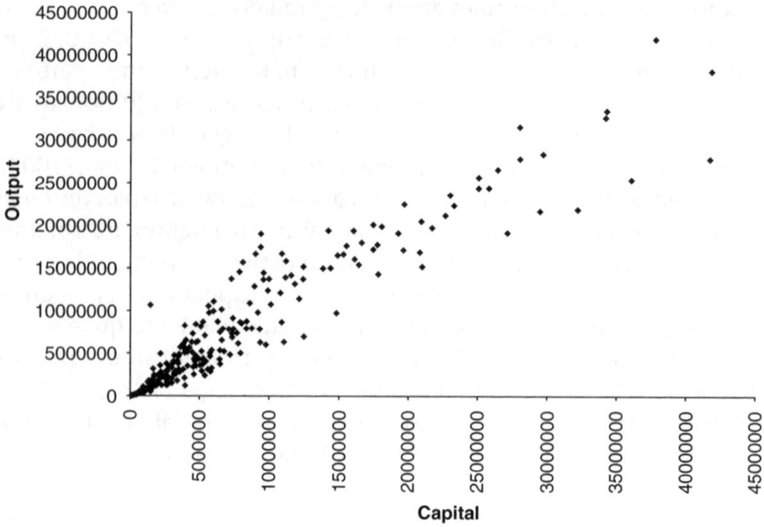

Figure 5.2 Output–capital plot

treat every region as a distinct location. In fact, this is unnecessary, as indicated by the broadly homogeneous plots of Figures 5.1 and 5.2. Consequently, we divide China into eastern, central and western areas, and define two area dummies accordingly. As in most of the earlier studies, central provinces refer to Shanxi, Inner Mongolia, Jilin, Heilongjiang, Anhui, Jiangxi, Henan, Hubei and Hunan. Western provinces include Sichuan, Guizhou, Yunnan, Shaanxi, Gansu, Qinghai, Ningxia, and Xinjiang. The remaining provinces constitute the east or coastal China.

Adding the location dummies to Equation (5.1) is straightforward. However, it is important to allow the output elasticity of labour to change over time, as TVEs are becoming more capital and technology intensive. This can be achieved by allowing the time trend variable to interact with labour input. Also, it is sensible to interact the dummy variables with labour input so that output elasticity is allowed to vary from location to location. Thus, the production function can be specified as

$$Y^{(\lambda)} = f(K, L, K \times L, T \times L, T, D1, D2, D1 \times L, D2 \times L) \quad (5.2)$$

where f = Box–Cox specification as given by (5.1), K = capital stock, L = labour input, T = time trend, D1 = dummy for central China and D2 = dummy for west China. It is important to mention that the Box–Cox transformation cannot be applied to variables with non-positive observations.

Table 5.2 Model selection

Model		Log-likelihood	χ^2	p-value
$\lambda = \theta$	$\lambda = \theta$	−3530.76	17.1	0.000
λ	0	−3522.39	0.36	0.549
λ	1	−3573.19	101.96	0.000
λ	−1	−7096.55	7148.68	0.000
0	θ	−3529.52	14.62	0.000
0	0	−3540.42	36.42	0.000
0	1	−3684.57	324.72	0.000
0	−1	−9999.00	12953.58	0.000
1	θ	−3679.13	313.84	0.000
1	0	−3856.41	668.4	0.000
1	1	−3682.42	320.42	0.000
1	−1	−9999.00	12953.58	0.000
−1	θ	−4328.42	1612.42	0.000
−1	0	−4328.42	1612.42	0.000
−1	1	−4353.68	1662.94	0.000
−1	−1	−9999.00	12953.58	0.000
λ	θ	−3522.21		

Further, in the actual estimation stage, it is not possible to transform the time trend variable. Thus, the last five variables in (5.2) will enter the function linearly.

Estimation results of the production functions are not presented but are available from the senior author upon request. Instead, we use Table 5.2 to tabulate the log-likelihood values for the 17 empirical models. In Table 5.2, the symbol or value in the first (second) column represents Box–Cox transformations applicable to the dependent (independent) variables. For example, the eighth row '0 –1' means that $\lambda = 0$ and $\theta = 1$ are imposed on model (5.1) during estimation. As another example, the last row '$\lambda - \theta$' means both transformation parameters are not restricted and are determined by data. This is the most flexible specification in the Box–Cox setting, where both the dependent and independent variables are transformed differently. Except the '$\lambda = \theta$' specification, where both transformation parameters are assumed to be identical but not restricted to any specific value, all other models are nested with the most flexible specification of '$\lambda - \theta$'. A large sample test – χ^2 test – is often employed for model selection among the nested specifications, although a standard F-test can be used. The former statistic can be easily obtained as twice the difference between the log-likelihood values of the restricted specification and the non-restricted counterpart. Test results are tabulated in Table 5.2.

According to Table 5.2, the '$\lambda - \theta$' model is the most preferred choice as it has a log-likelihood value almost identical to that of the most flexible model. Although the selected model is not nested with the specification of '$\lambda = \theta$', it is preferred when the model selection procedure of Pollak and Wales (1991) is applied, as recommended by Granger *et al.* (1995). Thus, the finally chosen model is similar to the classical Box–Cox specification where the dependent variable is subject to the Box–Cox transformation and the independent variables are in logarithms unless they contain non-positive observations. When subject to logarithmic transformations, some of the right hand side variables can be expanded and common terms can be collected. Performing these algebraic manipulations, Equation (5.2) becomes:

$$Y^{(\lambda)} = \beta_0 + \beta_1 \text{ Ln K} + \beta_2 \text{ Ln L} + \beta_3 \text{ Ln T} + \beta_4 \text{ T} + \beta_5 \text{ D1} + \beta_6 \text{ D2} + \beta_7 (\text{D1} \times \text{L}) + \beta_8 (\text{D2} \times \text{L}) \quad (5.3)$$

Estimation results of model (5.3) are presented in Table 5.3. The overall quality of the model is indicated by its reasonable *t*-ratios for the parameters. Most signs of the parameter estimates are consistent with normal expectations. In particular, the area dummy for west China and its interaction with labour are significantly negative. The location dummy for central China and its interaction with labour are both insignificant, although suspiciously positive. The time trend does not affect the net output of TVEs at any conventional level of significance. This may imply little technical progress over the sample period. It may also be attributable to the short span of the time horizon. Time trend is typically used as a proxy of technical progress, which is unlikely to occur in such a short time.

Table 5.3 Model estimation results

Variable	**Coefficient**	***t*-ratio**
D1	0.079	1.559
D2	−0.270	−5.302
T	0.020	1.161
K	0.363	11.61
L	0.390	12.81
Log T	−0.015	−0.2438
D1*L	0.000	1.139
D2*L	0.000	1.925
CONSTANT	0.926	3.983

Note: D1 = dummy for central China; D2 = dummy for west China.

Labour-absorption by TVEs

Once the empirical production models are obtained, there are two approaches through which to explore the impact of TVE development on labour-absorption. Labour demand functions can be derived from the production functions, and various simulations can be performed to examine the response of labour demand to prices (see Wan, 1996) or output growth. This approach usually presumes competition, at least in the factor markets, and requires price data that are not available. There is little or no competition in formal capital markets in rural China; however, the labour market conforms more closely to the supposition. An alternative approach is to compute output elasticity with respect to labour and use its inverse to indicate percentage changes in labour input induced by output growth. This inverse may be termed as labour absorption elasticity. This method, while not perfect, is simple and sufficient to serve our purpose.

Based on Equation (5.3), it can be easily shown that the output elasticity of labour, denoted by E, is a function of output:

$$E = \beta_2 / Y^{\lambda} \tag{5.4}$$

In obtaining (5.4), we omitted terms associated with the relevant dummy variables as coefficient estimates of these dummies are very close to 0 (see the second and third rows from the bottom of Table 5.3).

When an elasticity expression involves variables, the usual practice is to evaluate the elasticity at the mean values of these variables. Rather than using the global mean, we undertake two sets of calculations based on (5.4). The first calculation uses mean outputs for east, central and west China, producing elasticity estimates for the three locations (see the top panel of Table 5.4); the second uses mean output for each year, giving elasticity estimates over time (see the bottom panel of Table 5.4). A quick glance over Table 5.4 reveals that the labour elasticities are all around 0.6, which is in line with the typical estimate provided in the literature (Wan, 1996). This finding, once again, demonstrates the quality of our modelling work. Under perfect competition, the elasticity is equivalent to labour's share in the total output. Since TVEs have long been operating under competition, one can state that labour's share in the total output is increasing over time. This increase is attributable to both wage rises and increased labour input.

As expected, the labour elasticity in coastal areas is higher than that in central China, which, in turn, is higher than that in western China. The higher elasticity not only implies higher efficiency of labour input, but is also necessary for firm survival as labour is much more expensive in developed areas. These arguments can also be used to explain the increasing trend in the elasticity over time.

Table 5.4 Output elasticity of labour and labour-absorption elasticity

	Output elasticity	**Absorption elasticity**
East China	0.63	1.60
Central China	0.62	1.62
West China	0.60	1.67
For China as a whole		
1995	0.61	1.64
1996	0.61	1.63
1997	0.61	1.64
1998	0.62	1.62
1999	0.62	1.61
2000	0.62	1.61
2001	0.62	1.60
2002	0.63	1.60

Attention is now turned to the labour-absorption elasticities. For China as a whole, absorption elasticity was almost 1.7 in the mid-1990s. It decreased to 1.6 in 2002, implying that for every 1 per cent increase in the value added of TVE output, employment could grow by 1.6 per cent. This elasticity is quite high in comparison with empirical evidence from industrialized countries. Such a high elasticity must be related to the informal nature of the TVE sector as a major job-creator. The lack of modern technologies and capital forces TVEs to rely on the cheap labour in rural China as the major input when expanding output.

It is clear that the labour-absorption capacity is declining over time, though at a moderate rate. The decrease in the job-generation capacity of TVEs is almost uniform from year-to-year. Such an empirical regularity matches the reality well and offers an analytical basis for examining the prospect of job creation by TVEs in China. Although beyond the scope of this chapter, one can infer that reasons for this declining capacity may include rising wages, which promote substitution of labour by other production factors, and technical changes, which are typically biased towards capital. It is important to note that the effects associated with the substitution and technology bias are somewhat small at present.

The output induced effect is close to 1.7 per cent in the west, while it is less than 1.6 per cent in the coastal areas. Given that TVEs are growing at an annual rate of 10 per cent or so, such a difference in labour-absorption capacity is not negligible. Therefore, it is more effective to promote TVE development in the inland areas, not only for raising rural income but for generating jobs too. Generally speaking, internal migration in China mainly involves flows of the labour force from inland rural to coastal urban areas. Temporary migration incurs significant economic costs to migrants. It is also perceived to be a cause of a rising crime rate in major cities, implying significant social costs of migration. From this perspective, enhancing job-creation by supporting TVE development in non-coastal areas is justifiable on social, economic and political grounds.

It is crucial to mention that, by their very definition, these estimates and their interpretations are conditional on the assumption of 'holding everything else constant'. This explains why recent growth in TVE output did not bring about a large demand for labour, as suggested by the absorption elasticities previously discussed. The major contributor to output growth has been capital rather than labour, and the importance of capital has been on the rise. An immediate policy implication is that government should promote labour-intensive rather than capital- or technology intensive TVE development. This policy will better help inland regions as capital is lacking in these regions and TVEs there are not as capital-intensive as in the other parts of China.

Conclusion

This chapter focuses on the capacity of TVEs in China to absorb labour. By employing a Box–Cox modelling technique, it is expected that misspecification errors are minimized and goodness of fit improved. The finally-chosen model appears to provide a good description of the production process of TVEs in China, as is indicated by the statistical properties of the model and its implied labour elasticities.

The analysis reveals that the labour-absorption potential of TVEs is considerable. Every 1 per cent increase in output is capable of inducing a 1.6 per cent increase in employment. Using this estimate, the growth rate of over 10 per cent in recent years could have produced a 16 per cent increase in TVE employment every year. That means the labour force in TVEs doubling every five years. This, of course, has not happened in reality because TVEs in China are becoming more and more capital-intensive. In other words, capital has been displacing labour in China. This point should be borne in mind by policy-makers when making decisions about TVE-related government policies.

Further research can be directed towards the projection of labour demand by TVEs in China, making allowance for changing capital input. It is certainly recommended that data be extended back to the early 1980s, when TVEs were primarily labour-intensive. This kind of analysis will help shed light on the likely trend in labour-absorption capacity of TVEs. The limited time span of data represents a major limitation of this chapter.

Note

We wish to thank Yin Zhang for computing assistance and Jin Yao for help with data-collection.

References

Bowles, P. and Xiao Yuan Dong (1999) 'Enterprise Ownership, Enterprise Organisation, and Worker Attitudes in Chinese Rural Industry: Some New Evidence', *Cambridge Journal of Economics*, 23(1): 1–20.

Chen, M. (2006) 'Rethinking the Informal Economy: Linkages with the Formal Economy and the Formal Regulatory Environment', in B. Guha-Khasnobis, R. Kanbur and E. Ostrom (eds) *Linking the Formal and Informal Economy: Concepts and Policies*, UNU-WIDER Studies in Development Economics (Oxford: Oxford University Press).

Fu Xiaolan and V.N. Balasubramanyam (2003) 'Township and Village Enterprises in China', *Journal of Development Studies*, 39(4): 27–46.

Granger, C.W.J., M.L. King and H. White (1995) 'Comments on Testing Economic Theories and the Use of Model Selection Criteria, *Journal of Econometrics*, 67: 173–87.

Hart, K. (2006) 'Bureaucratic Form and the Informal Economy', in B. Guha-Khasnobis, R. Kanbur and E. Ostrom (eds) *Linking the Formal and Informal Economy: Concepts and Policies*, UNU-WIDER Studies in Development Economics (Oxford: Oxford University Press).

Ho, S.P.S., P. Bowles and Xiao Yuan Dong (2003) ' "Letting go of the Small": An Analysis of the Privatisation of Rural Enterprises in Jiangshu and Shandong', *Journal of Development Studies*, 39(4): 1–26.

Jin, Hehui and Yingyi Qian (1998) 'Public versus Private Ownership of Firms: Evidence from Rural China', *Quarterly Journal of Economics*, 113(3): 773–808.

Judge, G.G., C.R. Hill, W.E. Griffiths, H. Lutkepohl and Tsoung-Chao Lee (1988) *Introduction to the Theory and Practice of Econometrics* (New York: Wiley).

Kanbur, R. and Xiaobo Zhang (2005) 'Fifty Years of Regional Inequality in China: A Journey through Central Planning, Reform and Openness', *Review of Development Economics*, 9(1): 87–106.

NBS (National Bureau of Statistics) (various years) *Town and Village Enterprises Statistical Yearbook* (Beijing: China Statistical Publishing House).

OECD (2002) *Measuring the Non-observed Economy: A Handbook* (Paris: OECD).

Pollak, R.A. and T.J. Wales (1991) 'The Likelihood Dominance Criterion: A New Approach to Model Selection', *Journal of Econometrics*, 47: 227–42.

Putterman, L. (1997) 'On the Past and Future of China's Township and Village-Owned Enterprises', *World Development*, 25(10): 1639–55.

Rozelle, S. (1994) 'Rural Industrialization and Increasing Inequality: Emerging Patterns in China's Reforming Economy', *Journal of Comparative Economics*, 19: 362–91.

Sindzingre, A. (2006) 'The Relevance of the Concepts of Formality and Informality: A Theoretical Appraisal', in B. Guha-Khasnobis, R. Kanbur and E. Ostrom (eds) *Linking the Formal and Informal Economy: Concepts and Policies*, UNU-WIDER Studies in Development Economics (Oxford: Oxford University Press).

Wan, Guanghua (1995) 'Peasant Flood in China: Internal Migration and Its Policy Determinants', *Third World Quarterly*, 16(2): 105–28.

Wan, Guanghua (1996) 'Measuring Input Substitution and Output Expansion Effects: A Nonparametric Approach with Application', *Empirical Economics*, 21(3): 361–80.

Wan, Guanghua (1997) 'TVEs as an Orphan', BBC Radio Talk.

Wan, Guanghua (2001) 'Changes in Regional Inequality in Rural China: Decomposing the Gini Index by Income Sources', *Australian Journal of Agricultural and Resource Economics*, 43: 361–81.

Wan, Guanghua (2004) 'Accounting for Regional Inequality in Rural China', *Journal of Comparative Economics*, 32(2): 348–63.

Zhou, Z.Y., J.L. Dillon and G.H. Wan (1992) 'Development of Township Enterprises and Alleviation of Employment Problem in Rural China', *Agricultural Economics, Journal of the International Association of Agricultural Economists*, 6(3): 201–15.

6 The Informal Sector During Crisis and Transition

Ralitza Dimova, Ira N. Gang and John S. Landon-Lane

Introduction

During economic transition, the public sector shrinks and the unemployed population expands, as do both the formal and informal private sectors. The formal private sector is usually portrayed as the more 'productive' sector and often policy is oriented to expanding the size of that sector. On the other hand, we do find stylized stories of the transition and development process giving an important role to the informal private sector, usually characterized by relatively free entry by labour, competition, low wages and low overheads. These characteristics are viewed as a potential source of great expansion.

We examine the labour market links of the informal private sector to other parts of an East European economy in transition: the 'before and after' of the Bulgarian 1996–97 crisis and market-oriented policy reforms. We adopt a broad definition of informal sector work that goes beyond non-contractual work for an employer and encompasses any substantial effort undertaken to enhance one's standard of living beyond reported income. Conventional thinking about job mobility during crises in economic transition places its emphasis on the shutting down of the public sector and the expansion of the formal private sector, as well as on large scale movement into unemployment. Indeed, the conventional transition literature has proliferated, almost without exception, along two lines of analysis.

Firm level studies have scrutinized the job-creation and job-destruction aspects of post-communist structural adjustment. They established that while both public and privatized (or *de novo*) firms destroyed a significant number of jobs, private firms were better at simultaneously creating new job opportunities than their state-owned counterparts (Bilsen and Konings,

1998; Acquisti and Lehmann, 2000; Faggio and Konings, 2003). However, these studies, based on balance sheet and aggregate employment information from manufacturing sector firms, do not shed light on human capital reallocation.

Household level research established that while the labour flow out of employment into unemployment was significant, the simultaneous unemployment to employment flow was far from being negligible (Bellmann *et al.*, 1995; Sorm and Terrell, 2000; Hunt, 2002). The risk of permanent job loss was lowest among highly-skilled and young individuals; it was most significant among women with low education levels (Jones and Kato, 1997; Hunt, 2002; Ham *et al.*, 1998; Sorm and Terrell, 2000). This literature explores the determinants of unemployment and labour mobility between working and unemployed, but does not address the fate of people falling in between.

We use a Markov chain to model labour mobility among public and private employment, the informal sector and the unemployed. We explore the subtleties in choices facing a potential employee, including the possibility of a preference for public sector employment and the distinction between public and formal/informal private sector labour-absorption from the pool of those not in employment. We also study the effect of various characteristics on labour mobility.

We use a panel constructed by merging the 1995 and 1997 Bulgarian Integrated Household Surveys (BIHS). The Bulgarian experience during this period was unique due to the drastic financial crisis, the ensuing rapid structural reform and massive public sector labour-shedding. The panel allows us to track the labour market history of people from before until after the 1996 crisis.

Economic transition, crisis, labour market and poverty in Bulgaria

During the first half of the 1990s, Bulgaria experienced significant output loss and rising inflation, considerably more than in most other Central and East European (CEE) countries. Whereas the CEE economies joining the European Union (EU) in 2004 reached the trough of their output loss in 1991–92 and had contained inflation by 1993, Bulgaria's GDP continued to fall during 1993, while hyperinflation was witnessed as late as 1997.

Reforms were initiated in earnest only after the financial crisis of 1996–97. They included rapid privatization, reform of the pension and social welfare structure, and the establishment of a currency board. One of the immediate outcomes of this programme was the transfer of most of Bulgaria's productive resources from public into private hands, such that by the end of the 1990s, the private sector accounted for nearly 70 per cent of GDP (Bulgarian Privatization Agency, 2000; National Statistical Institute, 2003). In the process, official employment declined at the rate of about 2 per cent per annum and, as late as 2001, the unemployment rate was as high as 17.3 per cent, with 62 per cent of the unemployed people remaining unemployed for more than a year. The unemployment benefit system in Bulgaria remained one of the least generous in Europe (Garibaldi *et al.*, 2001).

The crisis of 1996–97 contributed not only to rapid restructuring and labour-shedding, but also to a significant real wage decline, such that by 1997 the average real wage in Bulgaria was 61.1 per cent lower than its 1990 level (Rutkowski, 2003). Besides earnings, hyperinflation also eroded savings; indeed, much more than in other transition economies in Central and Eastern Europe (Rutkowski, 1999; IMF, 2002). All of these contributed to a 77 per cent increase in poverty during the period 1995–97 (Sahn *et al.*, 2002).

Despite the low level of unemployment benefits, one of the highest unemployment rates in CEE, and high correlation between unemployment and poverty, reservation wages in Bulgaria apparently remained high throughout the transition period (Rutkowski, 1999). This observation, together with the extraordinarily high level of discouragement among unemployed males indicates that a high proportion of the Bulgarian population may have found its way to the informal economy (Garibaldi *et al.*, 2001). The plausibility of this proposition is further augmented by the extraordinary payroll tax burden in transition Bulgaria, leading to a 41 per cent tax wedge between labour costs to employer and take-home earnings, as well as by an excessively restrictive business environment leading to a lower number of officially registered small and medium enterprises (SMEs) than elsewhere in Central and Eastern Europe. According to existing macroeconomic estimates, the informal economy in Bulgaria accounts for at least a quarter of the country's GDP (Nenovski and Hristov, 2000).

Data

Gallup International conducted the BIHS under the auspices of the Bulgarian Ministry of Labour, the Ministry of Social Affairs and the National Institute of Statistics. These surveys provide detailed information about employment, income, education, and demographic characteristics for all members of about 2500 households in 1995, 1997 and 2001.[1] We create a panel from the 1995 and 1997 BIHS, spanning the crisis and watershed period during which large-scale industrial restructuring and privatization occurred. Sample attrition prevented creating a panel data set across all three years; the 2001 sample is unrelated to that of the earlier two. After accounting for discrepancies in the data, we are left with a total of 2873 individuals, of whom we use the subsample of 1639 individuals (from 781 households) who are 15–65 years of age and, if working, report positive income.[2]

We use a Markov chain in the first step and a multinomial logit in the second step of our analysis. We allocate individuals to one of four labour market sectors based on the sector in which they are employed in their main job (public sector, formal private sector, informal private sector, and unemployed).[3] We categorize both government employees and employees of state-owned enterprises as belonging to the public sector.[4]

Key to our analysis is how we assign individuals to the informal sector. First, we look at the self-employed and their specific jobs. Those who are in jobs that are likely to be in the informal sector, such as taxi drivers, hairdressers and salespeople, we assign to the informal sector. Otherwise, they are placed in the formal private sector. Second, we carefully examine those people claiming to be not working, and determine whether they are truly not working or whether they are in the informal sector. We implement this by first establishing the expenditure to income ratio of households for which we feel comfortable in asserting that no one is in the informal sector. We consider two-worker households in 1995 where both spouses state they do not have a second job, and find that their median expenditures exceeded median income by 18 per cent. With this information we then assign to the informal sector anyone who is not working and is in a household in which household expenditures exceed household income by 100 per cent. Our rationale is quite obvious; to fund this lifestyle income must be coming from somewhere. Borrowing was fairly primitive in Bulgaria at this time, and our income measure already includes transfers and incomes from real estate and financial assets.

In Table 6.1, we report sample statistics. We separate individuals by their labour market status in both 1995 and 1997. For example, the average age of individuals who worked in the public sector in 1995 and in 1997 is 41.27 years of age, while the average age of people who moved from the public sector in 1995 to the private sector in 1997 is 40.59 years.

These descriptive statistics highlight some interesting patterns. The average number of years of education did not vary significantly for labourers who were employed in either the public or private sectors in both 1995 and 1997. However, the educational attainment of people who were employed in either of these sectors for both years was noticeably higher than that of people who were in the informal sector or not working during at least one of the surveys. This observation is consistent with both the existing literature that finds a significant skill-based gap between employed and unemployed people across the CEE economies, and the presumption that the informal sector in Bulgaria might have developed along the low-skilled outskirts of the economy.

Next, the average number of years of education of people in the informal sector who found employment in the public sector exceeded that of informal sector people who found employment in the private sector. At the same time, the difference between years of education of non-working people who found employment in either the public or the private sector is not statistically significant. Taken together, our observations on the skill-based labour reallocation of individuals across sectors does not suggest that the formal private sector in Bulgaria developed as a sector employing low-skill labourers who lost their jobs in the public sector. Arguments to the contrary arise when the informal sector is not treated as a separate labour market state distinct from either formal employment or unemployment (see, for example, Falaris, 2004).

Third, the average age of individuals who left either public or private sector employment for the informal sector exceeds the average age of individuals who remained in either the public or private formal sector. At the same time, the average age of people who entered the private sector is significantly lower than the age of individuals who faced alternative labour-market states. These observations are consistent with the presumption that employers in the formal private sector are more willing to hire labourers whose work habits are not influenced by the socialist era work culture. They also indicate that the informal sector in Bulgaria might have developed as a cushion for older labourers who lost their employment in the formal economy.

Another observation we can make from Table 6.1 is that, in all cases, the proportion of people working who come from an urban area is between 60 per cent and 80 per cent, while the proportion of people not working who come from an urban area is 17 per cent to 44 per cent. This suggests that jobs, both formal and informal, are hard to come by in rural areas.

Finally, there appears to be easily distinguishable gender differences in the patterns of formal employment, unemployment and informal sector employment. The proportion of women who retained public sector employment or moved from unemployment or private sector employment into the public sector exceeds the proportion of women who retained private employment or exited the public sector or unemployment to embrace private employment. However, the proportion of women who left the

Table 6.1 Summary statistics in 1997 (by 1995 sector)

	Public sector in 1995				**Private sector in 1995**			
	Pub97	**Pvte97**	**Inf97**	**NW97**	**Pub97**	**Pvte97**	**Inf97**	**NW97**
Age (years)	41.27	40.59	42.50	40.15	38.80	32.71	39.30	42.67
	(8.73)	(10.37)	(11.05)	(12.16)	(9.48)	(9.40)	(11.79)	(10.50)
Education	11.68	11.70	10.71	9.92	11.52	11.57	10.78	7.50
(years)	(3.02)	(2.73)	(2.70)	(3.25)	(3.48)	(2.83)	(2.47)	(2.81)
Female	0.53	0.35	0.52	0.41	0.36	0.38	0.44	0.50
	(0.50)	(0.48)	(0.50)	(0.50)	(0.49)	(0.49)	(0.50)	(0.55)
Married	0.88	0.83	0.87	0.63	0.88	0.67	0.75	1.00
	(0.32)	(0.38)	(0.34)	(0.49)	(0.33)	(0.48)	(0.44)	(0.00)
Children	0.26	0.41	0.33	0.11	0.28	0.63	0.42	0.33
<6	(0.53)	(0.60)	(0.59)	(0.32)	(0.61)	(0.87)	(0.55)	(0.82)
Ethnic	0.08	0.06	0.11	0.19	0.08	0.21	0.17	0.50
minority	(0.28)	(0.23)	(0.32)	(0.40)	(0.28)	(0.41)	(0.38)	(0.55)
Urban	0.83	0.80	0.78	0.44	0.68	0.79	0.73	0.17
	(0.38)	(0.41)	(0.42)	(0.51)	(0.48)	(0.41)	(0.45)	(0.41)
HH income	14.36	15.49	19.43	13.98	14.02	14.28	17.92	13.17
(000's)	(7.72)	(8.50)	(45.34)	(5.90)	(6.45)	(8.87)	(12.98)	(8.20)
Obs	464	54	141	27	25	48	64	6

	Informal sector 1995				**Not working 1995**			
	Pub97	**Pvte97**	**Inf97**	**NW97**	**Pub97**	**Pvte97**	**Inf97**	**NW97**
Age (years)	49.31	30.89	41.81	40.78	34.83	32.14	41.2	41.4
	(8.38)	(11.57)	(15.92)	(14.66)	(12.87)	(12.26)	(18.10)	(18.07)
Education	11.96	11.07	10.08	8.00	10.71	10.77	9.15	7.93
(years)	(3.51)	(2.34)	(3.58)	(2.56)	(3.92)	(3.02)	(3.33)	(3.09)
Female	0.48	0.61	0.43	0.44	0.50	0.49	0.59	0.56
	(0.51)	(0.50)	(0.50)	(0.51)	(0.51)	(0.51)	(0.49)	(0.50)
Married	0.83	0.67	0.65	0.83	0.64	0.62	0.60	0.66
	(0.38)	(0.49)	(0.48)	(0.38)	(0.48)	(0.49)	(0.49)	(0.48)
Children	0.31	0.22	0.34	0.06	0.38	0.43	0.21	0.22
<6	(0.67)	(0.55)	(0.62)	(0.24)	(0.62)	(0.69)	(0.52)	(0.52)
Ethnic	0.07	0.22	0.22	0.50	0.19	0.43	0.20	0.35
minority	(0.26)	(0.55)	(0.62)	(0.51)	(0.38)	(0.50)	(0.40)	(0.48)
Urban	0.90	0.78	0.76	0.22	0.57	0.65	0.62	0.28
	(0.31)	(0.43)	(0.43)	(0.42)	(0.50)	(0.48)	(0.49)	(0.45)
HH income	6.46	7.70	7.14	8.33	12.16	14.57	12.59	14.29
(000's)	(6.74)	(8.43)	(7.09)	(11.25)	(8.98)	(13.17)	(10.53)	(9.27)
Obs	29	18	140	18	42	37	422	104

informal sector for private employment significantly exceeded that of women who transited from the informal sector into public sector employment, and the proportion of women who exited from unemployment to enter the informal sector exceeded the proportion of women who remained in the pool of unemployed people. The above patterns are difficult to interpret. While there is an apparent preference among women who work in the formal sector to retain public-sector employment, perhaps due to child related or other benefits, the preference for private over public employment after exiting the informal sector might be an indication of either bad signals sent to potential public-sector employers, or self-selection of more entrepreneurial women into the ranks of either the formal or the informal private sector. These hypotheses will be explored further in our formal analysis.

Overall, the data do not indicate that the formal private sector in the Bulgarian economy has developed along the low-skilled outskirts of the economy. We find a clear pattern whereby both younger (and perhaps more entrepreneurial) and higher skilled individuals tend to reallocate towards the formal private sector. In addition, we find a weak indication that the informal sector might have developed as a cushion to both older and lower-skilled individuals against the adversities of the crisis period.

A Markov chain model of Bulgarian transition

Here, we characterize the transition in Bulgaria from 1995 to 1997, with particular attention paid to movements into and out of the informal sector. We have data from 1995 and 1997, and a natural way to think about how the cross-sectional distribution evolves over this period is via the first order Markov chain model (FOMC).[5] This approach to modelling the dynamics of the cross-sectional distribution of individuals has a long history in economics. Early work by Champernowne (1953) and Prais (1955) looked at the cross-sectional dynamics of individual incomes and social status, respectively.

We are interested in the labour-market outcomes of individuals in Bulgaria, where we place an individual in one of four labour market categories: public, private, informal and unemployed. The first three categories are working categories while the last category is the out-of-labour force category. Individuals in this category include those who have retired, those who are studying and those who have left the labour force and have stopped searching for a new job.[6] We characterize the evolution of the cross-section distribution of individuals via the FOMC model introduced in Champernowne (1953).

The FOMC model is defined as follows. In each period we allocate each individual one of the four categories defined above. Let $s_{it} \in \{1,2,3,4\}$ represent the category of which individual i is a member in period t. Here, an individual is in category 1 if they work in the public sector, category 2 if they work in the private sector, category 3 if they are assigned to the informal sector, and category 4 if they report themselves to be out of the labour force. Let $\pi_{jt} = P[x = j]$ be the probability that an individual is in category j in period t. Then, the vector $\pi_t = (\pi_{1t}, \pi_{2t}, \pi_{3t}, \pi_{4t})'$ represents the cross-sectional probability distribution of individuals in period t. The FOMC model aims to describe the dynamics of this probability distribution over time. In particular, the FOMC model states that the conditional distribution for period t is a function of the information available from period $t-1$ only. That is, the FOMC model is

$$\pi_t' = \pi_{t-1}P \tag{6.1}$$

where P is the probability transition matrix.

The probability transition matrix $P = [p_{ij}]$ has individual elements, p_{ij}, representing the probability that an individual moves from category i in period $t - 1$ to category j in period t. As the categories that an individual can move to encompass all possibilities, the sum of each row of P must be 1.

The FOMC model described in (6.1) has a unique limiting (ergodic) distribution if there is only 1 eigenvalue of P that has modulus equal to 1.[7] Given some initial state, π_0, it follows that

$$\pi_t' = \pi_0' P^t \tag{6.2}$$

so that the limiting distribution implied by the FOMC is

$$\bar{\pi}' = Lim_{t\to\infty}\pi_0' P^t \tag{6.3}$$

We are interested in a number of parameters, including the initial probability distribution, π_{95}, the final probability distribution, π_{97}, the probability transition matrix P and the limiting state, $\bar{\pi}$, of the Markov chain. The first three parameters can be estimated using likelihood methods. However, the limiting state is a highly complicated non-linear function of P. It is the left eigenvector of P associated with the eigenvalue 1. The maximum likelihood estimates of the limiting state are difficult to obtain and require asymptotic approximations. As Bayesian methods allow for exact finite distributions of all parameters, we use them for parameter estimates with the priors chosen to be as diffuse as possible within a specific distributional family.

The Bayesian methods used to estimate the FOMC model are described in Geweke *et al.* (1986) and Geweke (2003). Summarizing, let $S_{MT} = \{s_{it}\}_{i=1}^{M}{}_{t=1}^{T}$ be the observed categories for each individual for each time period in our sample. Define the indicator variable δ_{ijk} to be 1 if individual i, is in category k, in period j and 0 otherwise. That is, $\delta_{ijk} = 1$ only if $s_{ij} = k$. Then the information contained in S_{MT} can be summarized by the following two summary statistics: n_1, the number of individuals each category initially, and N, the data transition matrix. Here

$$n_{1k} = \sum_{i=1}^{M} \delta_{i1k}$$

is the number of individuals in category k in period one. The data transition matrix, $N = [n_{kl}]$ where

$$n_{kl} = \sum_{i=1}^{M} \sum_{t=2}^{T} \delta_{it-1k}\delta_{itl}$$

is the number of observed transitions from category k to category l across all individuals and all time periods.[8]

Given these sufficient statistics, the likelihood function for the FOMC model is

$$p(S_{MT}|\pi_1, P) = \prod_{k=1}^{4} \pi_{1k}{}^{n_{1k}} \prod_{k=1}^{4} \prod_{l=1}^{4} p_{kl}{}^{n_{kl}} \tag{6.4}$$

The likelihood function is the product of independent Dirichlet (multivariate Beta) densities. This suggests that the appropriate form of conjugate prior for π_1 and for each row of P is also Dirichlet.[9]

Therefore, the prior for P will be made up of independent Dirichlet distributions, one for each row, and the prior for π_1 will also be independent Dirichlet. Thus

$$p(\pi_1|a_1) \propto \prod_{j=1}^{4} \pi_{1j}{}^{a_{1j}-1}, \quad \text{and } p(P|A) \propto \prod_{i=1}^{4} \prod_{j=1}^{4} p_{ij}{}^{a_{ij}-1} \tag{6.5}$$

where the priors are parameterized by a_1 and $A = [a_{ij}]$ respectively.

The prior densities given in (6.5) together with the likelihood function given in (6.4) yields a posterior density of

$$p(\pi_1, P|S_{MT}) \propto \prod_{i=1}^{4} \pi_{1i}{}^{a_{1i}+n_{1i}-1} \prod_{j=1}^{4} \prod_{k=1}^{4} p_{jk}{}^{a_{jk}+n_{jk}-1} \tag{6.6}$$

Thus, the posterior distribution is a product of independent Dirichlet distributions parameterized by vectors of the form $a_{ij} + n_{ij}$ in the case of the rows of P and $a_{1i} + n_{1i}$ in the case of the initial distribution, π_1. From the posterior distribution given in (6.6) it is simple to draw independent and identically distributed pseudo-random draws. The results presented below are calculated using these i.i.d. draws from (6.6).

Summary of transition results

The following results are for the FOMC model described above. Table 6.2 reports the posterior means and standard deviations for the full sample (males plus females) and for the male and female subsamples respectively. In all cases, the prior distribution for the initial distribution (π_{95}) and each row of P is

$$p(\pi) \sim Dirichlet((0.1,0.1,0.1,0.1)) \tag{6.7}$$

With $a = (0.1,0.1,0.1,0.1)$ we have a prior mean of 0.25 for each parameter of the distribution π_{95} or row of P, and a prior standard deviation of 0.366. Thus, the prior used, while proper, is chosen to be very diffuse. In this way, the results presented below reflect information coming from the observed sample and not from our prior. It is clear that the posterior standard deviations are significantly smaller than the prior standard deviations, which implies that the prior is having minimal impact on the results.

The FOMC model's parameters are the initial distribution and the probability transition matrix. We are also interested in the final distribution and the limiting distribution, which is what the cross-sectional distribution of job categories would look like if the transitions continued on forever without change. Bayesian methods allow us to construct finite sample distributions for all parameters of the model and, most importantly, any well-defined function of these parameters, including the limiting distribution of the Markov chain. Given the prior, the results presented are very similar to estimates we would have obtained had we used maximum likelihood as our estimation method.

These results show the effect of the economic crisis that hit Bulgaria in 1996. Before the crisis, the informal sector was relatively small and accounted for about 12.5 per cent of the population. After the crisis, the informal sector grew to about 47 per cent of the population. If this process continued without change, the informal sector would grow to about 51 per cent, as we can see from the limiting distribution. This change appears to be facilitated by a reduction in the size of the public sector and movement out of unemployment into the informal sector. The private sector has grown slightly after the crisis but it appears that most people could not find jobs in the formal private sector, leaving them to find work in the informal private sector. The fact that the proportion of people not working shrank suggests that households had lost income during the crisis and individuals belonging to these households were forced to exit unemployment in order to survive.

Table 6.2 also reports the results for males and females. While the pattern of movement is similar for males and females, there are some differences. In 1995, males were slightly more likely to work in the public sector than females, with 42.6 per cent of all males working in the public sector compared to 41.2 per cent of all females. Subsequent to the crisis, the percentages of males and females in the public sector are about the same at 34.1 per cent and 34.2 per cent, respectively. Thus, the proportion of males working in the public sector fell by more than the proportion of females working in the public sector.

Conditional on moving from the public sector, it appears that males are more likely to move to the private sector than are females. The probability of a male moving from the public sector in 1995 to the private sector in 1997 is 0.104, while the probability for a female making the same move

Table 6.2 Estimation results for Markov chain

	Public	Private	Informal	Not working
Full Sample				
Initial distribution (1995)	0.42	0.09	0.13	0.37
	(0.01)	(0.01)	(0.01)	(0.01)
Final distribution (1997)	0.34	0.10	0.47	0.10
	(0.01)	(0.01)	(0.01)	(0.01)
Limiting distribution	0.30	0.11	0.52	0.08
	(0.03)	(0.02)	(0.03)	(0.01)
Males				
Initial distribution (1995)	0.43	0.11	0.14	0.33
	(0.02)	(0.01)	(0.01)	(0.02)
Final distribution (1997)	0.34	0.12	0.45	0.09
	(0.02)	(0.01)	(0.02)	(0.01)
Limiting distribution	0.28	0.11	0.54	0.08
	(0.04)	(0.02)	(0.04)	(0.02)
Females				
Initial distribution (1995)	0.41	0.07	0.11	0.41
	(0.02)	(0.01)	(0.01)	(0.02)
Final distribution (1997)	0.34	0.08	0.49	0.10
	(0.02)	(0.01)	(0.02)	(0.01)
Limiting distribution	0.32	0.12	0.49	0.07
	(0.05)	(0.02)	(0.04)	(0.02)

is 0.055. Conditional on moving, these probabilities are 0.29 and 0.185, respectively. The unconditional probability of moving from the public sector to the informal sector is identical for males and females but, given that females are less likely to move out of the public sector, this yields a conditional probability of moving from the public sector to the informal sector for males and females of 0.564 and 0.707, respectively. Females, however, if they move from the public sector, are more likely to move to the informal sector.[10]

When looking at individuals who worked in the private sector in 1995, we again see different male and female patterns. Females have a 5 per cent lower probability of staying in the private sector compared to males. Of people who do move, males are again less likely to move to the informal sector. Males have a conditional probability of moving to the informal sector of 0.65 compared to 0.695 for females. The conditional probability of a male moving to the public sector is 0.29 compared to 0.22 for females. Again, we see that if an individual moves from their 1995 job, females are more likely to move to the informal sector compared to males, although it is always the case that most people move to the informal sector rather than to a formal job. Taken together, the gender-based mobility patterns confirm our observations from the descriptive statistics.

When comparing the initial distribution to the final and/or limiting distributions, we see that the increase in the informal sector comes from two main sources: movements out of the public sector, and movements out of unemployment. We saw above that for people who separated from the public sector, females were more likely to move to the informal sector. The same is true for those who moved out of unemployment. The probability of remaining unemployed is roughly the same for males and females but the probability of moving from unemployment to the informal sector is significantly higher for females than for males. Most of the movement out of unemployment is to the informal sector. However, it seems that males are more likely to find formal employment, while females are more likely to work in the informal sector.

Regression results

Above, we examined the Bulgarian transition's overall properties from before to after the 1996 crisis. In this section, our aim is to further analyze the transition and control for individuals' observed characteristics. We use a multinomial logit model to capture the labour choice of individuals.[11] While individuals may not have a great deal of choice over their separation from their employment in 1995, they do have choices as to where they

Table 6.3 Public sector employment in 1995 (marginal effects from multinomial logit)

	Pub97	Pvte97	Inf97	NW97
Age	0.050***	−4.00e−4	−0.045***	−0.005*
	(0.013)	(0.007)	(0.012)	(0.003)
Age-squared	−0.001***	1.31e−06	0.001***	6.00e−04*
	(1.00e−04)	(9.00e−04)	(1.00e−04)	(3.00e−04)
Education	0.017***	0.001	−0.016***	−0.003*
	(0.006)	(0.004)	(0.006)	(0.001)
Female	0.022	−0.054**	0.037	−0.005
	(0.037)	(0.022)	(0.032)	(0.008)
Married	0.102*	−0.037	−0.022	−0.044
	(0.064)	(0.040)	(0.055)	(0.028)
Children <6	−0.041	0.032*	0.030	−0.021*
	(0.034)	(0.017)	(0.029)	(0.011)
Ethnic minority	0.037	−0.033	−0.019	0.015
	(0.063)	(0.031)	(0.055)	(0.018)
Urban	0.081*	−0.005	−0.015	−0.062***
	(0.049)	(0.027)	(0.041)	(0.023)
HH income	−1.57e−06	3.04e−07	1.50e−06	−2.29e−07
	(0.049)	(0.000)	(0.000)	(0.000)
Pseudo R^2	0.076			
Obs	676			
LR χ^2	94.68			

Note: *, **, *** significant at 10, 5 and 1 per cent respectively.

move. Hence, we believe that the logit specification is the appropriate means for looking at the mobility of workers during the transition.

The marginal effects from our multinomial logit regressions are reported in Tables 6.3 and 6.4.[12] Our dependent variable includes the four choices facing a potential labourer; namely, public sector employment, private (formal) sector employment, work in the (private) informal sector and unemployed. The labour force state held by a respondent in 1997 is regressed on a set of 1995 characteristics of that respondent. The multinomial logit is performed over four different samples. We start with those who were in the public sector in 1995 and ask what the determinants of where they worked in 1997 are. We ask the same question of those who were in the formal private sector in 1995.[13] We are able to identify the effect of the 1995 demographic and other characteristics on

Table 6.4 Private sector employment in 1995 (marginal effects from multinomial logit)

	Pub97	**Pvte97**	**Inf97**	**NW97**
Age	0.026	−0.013	−0.013	3.00e−05
	(0.023)	(0.029)	(0.031)	(7.00e−05)
Age-squared	−3.00e−04	5.00e−05	3.00e−04	−3.11e−07
	(3.00e−04)	(4.00e−04)	(4.00e−04)	(0.000)
Education	0.114	0.013	−0.025	−1.00e−05
	(0.119)	(0.018)	(0.019)	(3.00e−05)
Female	−0.015	−0.078	0.093	−4.11e−06
	(0.064)	(0.089)	(0.096)	(4.00e−05)
Married	0.146**	−0.065	−0.087	0.006
	(0.061)	(0.123)	(0.128)	(0.008)
Children <6	−0.101*	0.092	0.009	−5.00e−05
	(0.059)	(0.069)	(0.077)	(1.00e−04)
Ethnic minority	−0.144**	0.134	0.010	1.00e−05
	(0.059)	(0.146)	(0.148)	(7.00e−05)
Urban	−0.245**	0.139	0.105	−3.00e−05
	(0.119)	(0.105)	(0.124)	(6.00e−04)
HH income	−4.50e−06	−5.34e−06	9.85e−06**	−1.37e−09
	(0.000)	(0.000)	(0.000)	(0.000)
Pseudo R^2	0.169			
Obs	140			
LR χ^2	55.25			

Note: *, **, *** significant at 10, 5 and 1 per cent respectively.

the probability of a person starting from the public or formal private sector remaining in their origin sector or moving into one of the three remaining labour market categories.

Public employment as the sector of origin

The marginal effects from the multinomial logit using public employment in 1995 as the sector of origin are reported in Table 6.3. These results confirm our prior of a skill gap between public-sector employees and individuals who exited public-sector employment for unemployment. Education has a significant and positive marginal effect on the probability of staying in the public sector, while education has a significant and negative marginal effect on moving from the public sector to either the informal sector or unemployment.

The urban variable has a significant and positive effect on the probability of staying in the public sector, suggesting that a disproportionate number of lost public jobs occurred in the rural area. If an individual leaves public employment, then those in the urban areas are significantly less likely to move into the unemployed category, suggesting that it is easier to find an informal sector job in urban areas than in rural areas.

We see that age has a non-linear, inverted U shape, effect on the probability of staying in the public sector. Thus, it appears that both the young and the old are more likely to move from the public sector. The inverse of this relationship is found in the marginal effects of age on movements from the public sector into either the informal sector or not working. Age does not have any significant marginal effect on the probability of moving into the private sector. The only characteristics that had a significant marginal effect on moving into the private sector from the public sector were gender and whether you had a child under the age of six. We found that there was a significantly negative marginal effect for a female of moving into the private sector from the public sector. This accords with our earlier finding that females are less likely to move to the private sector from the public sector. We also find that individuals who have children have a higher marginal probability of working in the private sector. This could be because these people are willing to take any job that is offered. We cannot test this hypothesis, as we do not know the type of jobs at which these people work. However, we do see that individuals with children under the age of six are less likely to move into unemployment, which is consistent with this theory.

Private employment as the sector of origin

The marginal effects of the individual characteristics for those individuals who were working in the private (formal) sector in 1995 are reported in Table 6.4. As we have seen, the size of this sector is very small (around 10 per cent) and does not change much after the transition (around 11 per cent). We do see some characteristics having a significant marginal effect on the probability of moving from the private sector to the public sector. In particular, married people are more likely to move to the public sector, while ethnic minorities, people who live in urban areas, and people with children under the age of six are less likely to move. Given the small number of individuals in this category it is difficult to draw any strong conclusions from these results, though there appears movement to the public sector in rural areas.

Conclusion

As transition to a market-based economy proceeds, the private sector grows. The private sector discussed above is composed of two very different groups of labourers: those who obtain formal private sector jobs and those who obtain informal private sector jobs. The cause of the coexistence of the formal and informal sectors appears to be the side effects of deliberate government policy. Government policy *vis-à-vis* extra taxes, protective labour legislation, support for unions, payoffs, and a variety of other measures ensures, 'artificially', that the formal private sector will be a high-cost sector.

The informal sector is largely unobserved, and it is of interest to consider its relationship to other sectors of the economy. Even our simple presentation, however, points out how complicated this relationship is, and how intertwined the informal sector is with the rest of the economy. In Bulgaria, the political economy of transition led to policy inertia during the first half of the 1990s. A banking crisis struck in December 1996–January 1997. Rapid privatization of SOEs followed. Between 1995 and 1997, the informal sector grew both absolutely and relative to the private sector, while the public sector shrank in absolute and relative terms.

Overall, the pattern of the transition is one of movement out of formal employment into informal employment. The crisis caused a large reduction in the size of the public sector, and displaced workers could not find jobs in the formal private sector. Hence, they were forced to find work in the informal private sector. Also, the economic crisis forced people who were initially out of the labour force to rejoin the labour force, mostly in the informal sector. In our sample, we did observe some retired individuals who left retirement and found a job in the public or formal private sectors between 1995 and 1997. While most of the movement was into the informal sector for both males and females, there were some gender differences. Females were more likely to join the informal sector than males but also less likely to leave the public sector.

When we studied the movement of workers, controlling for a number of individual characteristics, we saw several interesting results. First, more education meant increased likelihood of obtaining a job in the formal sector (either public or private). We also saw that it was more likely for someone to move into the informal sector if they lived in an urban area, suggesting that the informal sector was mainly an urban phenomenon. The regression results also reinforced the aggregate results that females were less likely to move to formal private jobs and more likely to move to the informal sector. We also saw that individuals who had children under the age of six were also more likely to have a job, either formal or informal.

The results reported above (pp. 94–102) indicate that there was a significant increase in the size of the informal sector after the crisis in 1996. The increase in the informal sector came from two sources: a downsizing of the public sector and a movement out of unemployment. The crisis in Bulgaria caused a great deal of hardship and many people found informal work in order to get by.

Notes

This is a shortened version of Dimova, Gang and Landon-Lane (2005).

1 The surveys included information about 2466 households with a total of 7199 members in 1995, 2323 households with 6947 members in 1997, and 2633 households with 7844 members in 2001.
2 In restricting the sample to age group 15–65, we use the ILO standards applied by the National Statistics Institute in Bulgaria in its labour force surveys and by World Bank reports based on these surveys. We use the sample including 1639 individuals for our descriptive statistics and transition analysis. However, missing observations, primarily with respect to years of education, reduce this sample further and we use 1470 observations in our regression analysis.
3 An average of 30 individuals reported having a second job for each of the survey years, so the categorization of labourers in accordance with their main job should not affect our analysis.
4 Since in our sample only 60 individuals in 1995 and 59 individuals in 1997 worked for the government, it is impractical to analyze them as a separate category.
5 As a practical consideration, we are restricted to looking at only the FOMC model as we only have data for two years.
6 We include retirees and students, as there is an element of choice in their decision to be a student or a retiree. Indeed, many came out of retirement between 1995 and 1997 and went back into the labour force.
7 Note that P is a row stochastic matrix, which implies that the rows of P sum to 1. In this case, the maximum eigenvalue of P has modulus equal to 1. If there are no repeated eigenvalues with modulus equal to 1, then the limiting distribution is unique.
8 It is implicitly assumed that there is no structural break in the transition probability matrix, P, in this formulation.
9 See Bernado and Smith (1994: 134–5) for a complete description of the Dirichlet distribution.
10 The probabilities noted in the previous paragraph refer to the transition probabilities found in the transition probability matrices. For brevity, these are not reported in Table 6.2. However, the full results (including the estimates of the transition probability matrices) can be found in Dimova *et al.* (2005).
11 We could have used a multinomial probit model instead of a multinomial logit model but we found that because of small sample size in some of the regressions,

the logit model was more stable than the probit model. In any case, the test of independence of irrelevant alternatives (IIA) was never rejected so the use of the logit specification is not rejected on IIA grounds.

12 The numbers of observations in the regressions differ from the transition matrices above, as we have lost cases because of missing observations.

13 For the same analysis on those who were in the informal private sector in 1995 and those not in employment in 1995, see Dimova *et al.* (2005).

References

Acquisti, A. and H. Lehmann (2000) 'Job Creation and Job Destruction in the Russian Federation', Economic Paper 2000/1 (Dublin: Department of Economics, Trinity College).

Bellmann, L., S. Estrin, H. Lehmann and J. Wadsworth (1995) 'The East German Labor Market in Transition: Gross Flow Estimates from Panel Data', *Journal of Comparative Economics*, 20: 139–70.

Bernado, J.M. and A.F.M. Smith (1994) *Bayesian Theory* (Chichester: John Wiley).

Bilsen, V. and J. Konings (1998) 'Job Creation, Job Destruction and Growth of Newly Established, Privatized and State-Owned Enterprises in Transition Economies: Survey Evidence from Bulgaria, Hungary and Romania', *Journal of Comparative Economics*, 26: 429–45.

Bulgarian Privatization Agency, http://www.priv.government.bg/ap/bg/

Champernowne, D.G. (1953) 'A Model of Income Distribution', *Economic Journal*, 63: 318–51.

Dimova, R., I.N. Gang and J.S. Landon-Lane (2005) 'The Informal Sector During Crisis and Transition', WIDER Research Paper 2005/18 (Helsinki: UNU-WIDER).

Faggio, G. and J. Konings (2003) 'Gross Job Flows and Firm Growth in Transition Countries: Evidence Using Firm Level Data on Five Countries', *Economic Systems*, 27: 129–54.

Falaris, E. (2004) 'Private and Public Sector Wages in Bulgaria', *Journal of Comparative Economics*, 32: 56–72.

Garibaldi, P., M. Makovec and M. Stoyanova (2001) 'From Transition to Accession: The Bulgarian Labour Market over the 1990s', World Bank Technical Paper 494 (Washington, DC: World Bank).

Geweke, J.F. (2003) *Contemporary Bayesian Econometrics and Statistics*, unpublished manuscript, http://www2.cirano.qc.ca/~bacc/outgoing2003/july2003.pdf

Geweke, J.F., C. Marshall and G.A. Zarkin (1986) 'Exact Inference for Continuous Time Markov Chain Models', *Review of Economics and Statistics*, 53: 653–69.

Ham, J., J. Svejnar and K. Terrell (1998) 'Unemployment, the Social Safety Net and Efficiency During Transition: Evidence from Micro Data on Czech and Slovak Men', *American Economic Review*, 88: 1117–42.

Hunt, J. (2002) 'The Transition in East Germany: When is a Ten Point Fall in the Gender Wage Gap Bad News?', *Journal of Labor Economics*, 20: 148–69.

International Monetary Fund (2002) 'Bulgaria: Selected Issues and Statistical Appendix', IMF Country Report 02/173 (Washington, DC: IMF).

Jones, D. and T. Kato (1997) 'The Nature and the Determinants of Labor Market Transition in Emerging Market Economies: Evidence from Bulgaria', *Industrial Relations*, 36: 229–54.

National Statistical Institute of Bulgaria: http://www.nsi.bg/Index-e.html

Nenovski, N. and K. Hristov (2000) 'Currency Circulation after Currency Board Introduction in Bulgaria', Bulgarian National Bank DP\13\2000.

Prais, S.J. (1955) 'Measuring Social Mobility', *Journal of the Royal Statistical Society, Series A*, Part I: 56–66.

Rutkowski, J. (1999) 'Labor Markets and Poverty in Bulgaria', SP Discussion Paper 9918 (Washington, DC: World Bank).

Rutkowski, J. (2003) 'Why is Unemployment so High in Bulgaria', World Bank Policy Research Working Paper 3017 (Washington, DC: World Bank).

Sahn, D., S. Younger and C. Meyerhoefer (2002) 'Rural Poverty in Bulgaria: Characteristics and Trends', http://people.cornell.edu/pages/des16/sahn/wp132.pdf

Sorm, V. and K. Terrell (2000) 'Sectoral Restructuring and Labor Mobility: A Comparative Look at the Czech Republic', *Journal of Comparative Economics*, 28: 431–55.

Part II
Survival Strategies of the Urban Poor

7

An Investigation of the Labour Market Earnings in Deprived Areas: Evaluating the Sources of Earning Differentials in the Slums

João Pedro W. de Azevedo

This chapter presents empirical evidence on the determinants of labour market earnings for males and females in the slums of Rio de Janeiro. The data used are from a survey of 21,704 households at 51 slums from the city of Rio de Janeiro, augmented with contextual information from the 2000 census as well as GIS information on the location of these communities. Several tests of the labour-market segmentation hypothesis were implemented. This work suggests that the informal sector can be a rational choice from the workers' point of view, particularly at a younger age. In addition, it also supports the existence of selection effects, which suggests that occupational choices are non-random, and must be taken into consideration through a two-step estimation of the earnings equation. The chapter also provides evidence of the importance of entrepreneurial activities, in particular those that are not home-based.

Introduction

In some areas of the world, such as Latin America, the urbanization of poverty is already a fact. Although poverty rates are higher in rural areas than in urban areas in the region (55 per cent and 39 per cent respectively), in absolute terms there are more than twice as many urban poor than rural poor – 68 million rural poor compared with 138 million urban poor (Cira, 2002).

Most of the time, the urban poor are only able to afford housing in areas characterized by precarious public health, a lack of basic infrastructure (including water delivery), inadequate public services, substandard sanitation, and widespread violence and insecurity; such areas are also referred to as slums. According to a report from the United Nations

Human Settlements Programme, *The Challenge of Slums: Global Report on Human Settlements 2003*, at least one billion people worldwide currently live in urban slums (UN-HABITAT, 2003). Within 30 years, if current trends continue, one out of every three people on the planet will live in such conditions. It is clear, then, that urban poverty and the dynamics of the slums have a substantial importance in the development debate.

For a long time, studies on economic development have emphasized the agriculture and industry sector, following the prevailing paradigms of Lewis (1954) and Fei and Ranis (1964), thus underestimating the importance of the entrepreneurial sector. However, the work by Harris and Todaro (1970) illustrated that migrants from agriculture to industry may face a period of unemployment or, if unemployment is unaffordable, may be forced to provide for themselves through a low-productivity household enterprise. The latter idea took further shape when an ILO (1972) report defined the so-called informal sector, which has proved to be one of the most influential concepts in development economics.

More often than not, in the most deprived areas of developing countries entrepreneurship and informal sector activities are, in spite of the numerous hurdles, an important port of entry to the labour market (De Soto, 1989; Gill *et al.*, 1999; De Soto, 2000). In this context, it is extremely relevant to understand the labour market in these areas, and identify ways to support the entrepreneurial initiatives of this segment, both as employment- and income-generation strategies.

This chapter intends to contribute to a virtually non-existent literature on the labour market in extremely deprived urban areas in developing countries, with a particular interest in understanding the wage differential of the residents in these communities and how it is related to the entrepreneurial activity within these communities.

Most of the previous works comparing wages in developing countries analyze occupation as a binary choice, either formal or informal, or wage-earners and self-employed (see Van Der Sluis *et al.* (2004) for a recent survey of this literature). One of the problems in these studies is the assumption that some categories can be pooled together; another is the exclusion of some important categories, such as the self-employed or the wage-earner. This work follows a smaller literature that models the multinomial nature of these choices (Cohen and House, 1996; Saavedra and Chong, 1999). Moreover, this chapter shows through an often neglected specification test of the multinomial logit model that these categories cannot be pooled together, and applies a relatively recent polynomial selection bias correction model (Bourguignon *et al.*, 2002) which, to the best of the author's knowledge, has never been applied in this literature.

Another problem in the existing literature is its frequent narrow focus on the gender dimension, either by pooling males and females together, or by analyzing only one gender. This work tries to provide a more complete picture of the labour market under scrutiny, analyzing the labour-market conditions of both males and females separately.

Many of the contributions of this chapter have only been made possible given the unique character of the data set used, which comprises interviews of 21,704 households from 51 different slums in the city of Rio de Janeiro. This data set has been augmented with contextual information from the 2000 census data at the neighbourhood level in which each community is located, as well as geographical information on the position of each of these communities in the city of Rio de Janeiro.

The next section of this chapter presents a review on the literature on earnings and occupational choice, and how these models are often estimated. The subsequent section describes the data set used in this study. The empirical results of the study are then presented, with several tests for the labour-market segmentation for the residents of the slums of Rio de Janeiro. The final section highlights the major findings of this chapter.

Models of labour earnings and occupational choice and their estimation

Various models of labour-market earnings and occupational choice have been advanced in the economic literature. Mincer (1958; 1974) and Becker (1964) human capital models represent one of the most prominent representatives of this literature.

The simple schooling model of Mincer (1958) is given by:

$$\ln(y_i) = \beta_0 + \beta_1 s_i + \mu_i \tag{7.1}$$

where y_i is earnings, s_i is schooling, and μ_i is an error term for the model representing unobserved determinants of earnings. β_1 can be interpreted as the average return to schooling with β_0 as the logarithm of the base earnings on an individual with no schooling.

In latter works, such as Mincer (1974) and Becker and Chiswick (1966), Equation (7.1) is augmented to include the effect of investment after formal schooling. In this specification the log of earnings is written as

$$\ln(y_i) = \beta_0 + \beta_1 s_i + \beta_2 t_i + \beta_3 t_i^2 + \mu_i^* \tag{7.2}$$

where t_i and t_i^2 are, respectively, post-schooling labour-market experience and experience squared, and μ_i^* is an unobserved disturbance term. Often this basic equation is enlarged, including hours of work, regional dummy variables, and other covariates (see Mincer, 1974). Model (7.2) is the basic specification of the earnings equations adopted in this study.

Another important extension of (7.2) is when the sample is divided in J subsamples, and separate earning equations are estimated for each segment. Models such as this are often used when separate earnings equations are estimated for different gender, occupational and geographical groups. This model can be formally presented as follows:

$$\ln(y_{ij}) = \beta_0 + \beta_1 s_{ij} + \beta_2 t_{ij} + \beta_3 t_{ij}^2 + \mu_{ij}^* \tag{7.3}$$

where the subscript j indicates the subsample to which this earnings equation refers.

Model (7.3) will provide unbiased estimates of (β_k)s as long as the population is randomly distributed across the j segments. In other words, this model will no longer hold if individuals are heterogeneous with respect to their preferences, their observed and unobserved productivity-enhancing characteristics, and the strength of their contacts in the labour market. Nevertheless, when the sample separation is known, combining a set of observable characteristics for each individual and the knowledge of the j segment in which individuals are located provides both an insight into the nature of the covariance and a means by which to construct unbiased estimates of the parameter vectors β_k. Hence, to achieve this goal, it is necessary also to model the occupational choice process.

In order to combine the equation of earnings-determination with occupational choice – omitting the individual-specific subscript i and j is a categorical variable that describes the choice of an economic agent among J occupational alternatives – this work follows Bourguignon *et al.*'s (2002) notation:

$$y_j = x_j\beta_j + \mu_j^* \tag{7.4}$$

$$y_j^* = z_j\gamma_j + \eta_j, \quad j = 1 \ldots J \tag{7.5}$$

where all the variables x_j and z_j are exogenous, and the disturbance $E(\mu_j^* \mid x, z) = 0$ and $V(\mu_j^* \mid x, z) = \sigma_j^2$. The outcome variable y_j is observed if, and only if, the category j is chosen, which happens when

$$y_j^* > \max_{s \neq j}(y_s^*) \tag{7.6}$$

Condition (7.6) can also be written as:

$$z_j\gamma_j > \varepsilon_j \tag{7.7}$$

where

$$\varepsilon_j = \max_{s \neq j}(y_s^* - \eta_j) \tag{7.8}$$

Now it is possible to assume that the (η_j)s are independent and follow, identically, a Gumble distribution, with cumulative and density functions as, respectively: $G(\eta) = \exp(e^{-\eta})$ and $g(\eta) = \exp(-\eta - e^{\eta^0})$. This specification leads to the familiar multinomial logit model, presented as:

$$P(z_j\gamma_j > \varepsilon_j) = \frac{\exp(z_j\gamma_j)}{\sum_s \exp(z_s\gamma_s)} \tag{7.9}$$

where maximum likelihood estimates of the (γ_s)s can be easily obtained. Note that Equation (7.9) represents the probability that an individual with characteristics z_j chooses the segment j. Therefore, this can be taken as the empirical estimation of the occupational choice process.[1] Often, vector z_j contains variables such as education,[2] age,[3] and marital status.[4]

In order to estimate unbiased β_js, Heckman (1979), in a seminal article, proposes a two-stage technique to correct for selection bias in the case of a dichotomous choice model ($J = 2$).

A few authors have extended this work and proposed similar two-stage correction procedures for polychotomous choice models; for instance, Lee (1983), Dubin and McFadden (1984) and Bourguignon *et al.* (2002).

A paper by Schmertmann (1994) demonstrates that when the number of potential outcomes exceeds two ($J>2$), the Lee technique imposes implicit and unnecessary restrictions on the structure of the error terms that generally render this method inappropriate for a study of this sort. Thus, a few authors, such as Cohen and House (1996), have argued that the Dubin and McFadden (1984) procedure was the most adequate. In this alternative procedure, each segment-earnings equation also includes a separate selection term for each pairwise utility comparison, which sets for a J sector model $J - 1$ selection terms.

However, Bourguignon *et al.* (2002) propose an alternative selective correction method that involves all correlation coefficients between the disturbance term of the outcome equation of interest (Equation (7.5)) and the disturbance term of all categorical latent expression (Equation (7.4)). Thus, in a J sector model there are J selection terms.

This chapter applies this recent contribution, and uses the following equation to estimate unbiased β_js:

$$y_1 = x_1\beta_1 - \sigma_1\left[\tilde{\rho}_1 m(P_1) + \sum_{j>1} \tilde{\rho}_j \frac{P_j}{(P_j - 1)} m(P_j)\right] + \nu_j \tag{7.10}$$

where ν_j is orthogonal to all other terms in the right hand side and has zero expectation. Because of this property, least squares may now be used to estimate the β_1s. It is important to notice that $(\sigma_1 \tilde{\rho}_1), \ldots, (\sigma_1 \tilde{\rho}_j)$ are the coefficients for the correction terms that adjust for selection bias, and $(m(\hat{P}_j))$s are the fitted probabilities of Model (7.9). Henceforth, this model is referred to as BFG (after Bourguignon *et al.*, 2002).

Overall, the estimation procedures in this chapter will consist of the following: first, according to the tradition of a well-established empirical literature, this work estimates embellished variations of equation (7.2) by ordinary least squares (OLS). Second, Model (7.10) is estimated through a two-step procedure: (i) estimate the multinomial logit (Model (7.9)), and derive from it the fitted probabilities $(\hat{P}_j)$ using the $(\hat{\gamma}_j)$s;[5] and (ii) estimate Equation (7.10) by least squares.

Data and summary statistics

Data definitions

The data for this study was obtained from a survey carried out by the municipality of Rio de Janeiro, between January 1998 and March 2000. The survey covered households and enterprises in 51 out of the 462 slums in the city of Rio de Janeiro at the time of the survey.[6] The survey had two modules that were carried out independently: household (PCBR-Dom) and enterprises (PCBR-Est). The data from both modules were collected through face-to-face interviews conducted by the Brazilian National School of Statistics (ENCE), which is part of the Brazilian National Office of Statistics (IBGE).

In addition, this study also uses two complementary data sets; namely, the 2000 census (IBGE, 2000) and the 1996 geographical boundaries of the slums and neighbourhoods of the city of Rio de Janeiro (LabGeo, 1996).

The 2000 census data was used to generate average incomes for each neighbourhood in which the analyzed slums are located. The goal of this variable is to capture geographical effects that might arise from slums near more, or less, affluent neighbourhoods.

The data from the 1996 geographical boundaries of the slums and the city of Rio de Janeiro were used to generate distance measures from the centroids of each slum to downtown Rio, in order to control for transportation effects that might affect the labour market of each of these communities.

The household survey followed a questionnaire similar to the World Bank LSMS, and covered a sample of 21,704 households in the 51 slums selected. The enterprise module is a census of all the 4,553 business establishments located in these slums. This was one of the most extensive efforts to map these communities. A full description of the survey is contained in Silva *et al.* (1998). The current study only uses the data of the household module (PCBR-Dom).

From the 21,704 households covered by the survey, it was possible to access information on 82,948 individuals. From these 82,948 individuals, the final sample was obtained by restricting the analysis according to five criteria:

(a) All men and women between the ages 15 to 65, inclusive. This choice reduced the sample to 52,514 individuals;
(b) Individuals who were working on the week of the survey. This restricted the analysis to 29,320 individuals – from the sample 4,169 students, 2,965 early retirement, 3,986 unemployed, 9,551 unpaid/domestic workers and approximately 2,500 classified as others were removed (see Table 7.1);
(c) Individuals with only one occupation on the week of reference. This restricted the sample to 28,930 out of the 29,320 workers;
(d) In the household survey, there were six occupational segments: wage earners, domestic workers, cooperative members, employers, self-employed and unpaid (see Table 7.2). The segments of domestic workers,[7] unpaid workers, unemployed and cooperatives members were also excluded;
(e) The sample was further reduced by the absence of data on other covariates, including earnings, used in the empirical analysis.

The final sample therefore comprises 19,332 individuals, of whom 13,608 (70.4 per cent) are male.

Table 7.1 Activity during the reference week (age 15–65)

Item	Number	Percentage
Worked	29,320	56
Had work but did not work	327	1
Looked for job	3,986	8
Early retired	2,965	6
Student	4,169	8
Domestic	9,551	18
Other	2,196	4
Total	52,514	100

Table 7.2 Occupational distribution (age 15–65 and only one occupation)

Item	Number	Percentage
Wage earner	19,579	68
Domestic worker	3,799	13
Cooperative members	161	1
Employer	353	1
Self-employed	4,804	17
Unpaid	234	1
Total	28,930	100

Due to the timing differences of the data collection, the consumer price index of the metropolitan region of Rio de Janeiro's city was used to deflate all the monetary values in the survey to the prices of March 2000.

The description of the variables used can be found in the Appendix. Most of the variables were computed directly from the replies to the survey questionnaire. One notable exception is OCCUPFOR, which was generated by crossing the information from occupational choice with the data on social security enrolment and enterprise location. Formal and informal wage-earners were classified according to their social security status: workers with no social security were classified as informal, while workers with social security were classified as formal.

This chapter follows the standard literature, and takes self-employment and employer categories as a working definition of entrepreneurs (see Parker, 2004 and Le, 1999). The ideal variable to define entrepreneurs as formal or informal is business registration; however, the survey used did not contain this question. In order to overcome this limitation, the definition of formality and informality based on the business infrastructure proposed by Magnac (1991) was adopted. Entrepreneurs who operated their enterprise from home were classified as informal, while entrepreneurs who operated their business from a separate address were classified as formal.

Table 7.3 shows the sample distribution of OCCUPFOR by gender. A couple of interesting features of this table are worth highlighting. First, most of the final sample comprises formal wage-earners (11,419). Second, although gender distribution is very similar in the formal sector (with around 70 per cent of males as both wage-earners and entrepreneurs), females tend to dominate, in the informal sector, the entrepreneur category, forming approximately 57 per cent of this occupation.

A few aspects of the data need to be borne in mind when the present results are analyzed and compared with results from other studies. It is

Table 7.3 Occupation and formality by gender

OCCUPFOR	Male	Female	Total
Formal wage-earner	7,993	3,426	11,419
	70	30	100
Informal wage-earner	3,276	977	4,253
	77	23	100
Formal entrepreneurs	2,019	900	2,919
	69	31	100
Informal entrepreneurs	320	421	741
	43	57	100
Total	13,608	5,724	19,332
	70	30	100

important to recognize that the data are not statistically representative of the entire population residing in slums in the city of Rio. The selection criterion used to include each community in the survey sample was its involvement in a housing and infrastructure programme from the municipality of Rio (for more details, see Acioly, 2001 and Riley *et al.*, 2001). The 1998/2000 phase of this programme prioritized small and medium-size slums that already had some infrastructure, leaving the most challenging and destitute communities out. If anything, the existing anecdotal evidence seems to suggest that these communities are among the least problematic, and should be interpreted as an upper boundary of the reality of slums in Rio de Janeiro.

Empirical analysis

This section analyses the wage differential among male and female workers employed in both the formal and informal sectors, either as wage-earners or entrepreneurs.

Labour-market segmentation

In order to investigate the possibility of labour-market segmentation in the slums of Rio de Janeiro, this study presents a simple stylized model of a dualistic labour market. It then moves to the empirical estimation of a few models that gradually shed light on this issue.

Dualistic or segmented models of the labour market have pervaded the economic development literature since the seminal work of Lewis (1954) (for a survey of dual market theory, see Cain, 1976). According to this hypothesis, the existence of dual labour markets will be reflected in dualism in earnings as long as workers with similar characteristics are paid different wages, given the sector in which they work (Saavedra and Chong, 1999).

The wage segmentation hypothesis can be formally simplified. To do this, consider an economy populated by agents who differ in terms of a finite list X of personal characteristics. They are employed either in the formal (F) sector or the informal (I) sector. Both sectors offer a menu of jobs described by a vector Y of characteristics that include industry and establishment size.

Let $\omega^F(X, Y, \varepsilon)$ and $\omega^I(X, Y, \varepsilon)$ denote integrable random variables that give the agent's log earnings in, respectively, the formal and the informal sector, as a function of their personal and job characteristics, and an exogenous source of uncertainties denoted by ε. The wage segmentation hypothesis can be stated as:

$$S : E(\omega^F(X, Y, \varepsilon) - \omega^I(X, Y, \varepsilon) \,|\, X, Y \in A) > A$$

for a non-negligible subset A or characteristics. This section asks whether such a subset of personal and job characteristics can be found in the set of workers sampled in the slums of Rio de Janeiro.

One way of assessing whether or not there are differences in income determination is to compare income differentials of individuals that are observationally equivalent. If they persist, it may be because such differentials cannot be explained by the differences of the observable characteristics of the individuals, but rather by the characteristics of the job.

It is now possible to estimate a variant of the model in which monthly earnings, y, is assumed to be log-linear, and the controls used are: dummy variables created from OCCUPFOR (D_{wi}, D_{of} and D_{ow}) that indicate whether or not the individual is a wage-earner from the informal sector, an entrepreneur who belongs to the formal sector, or an entrepreneur from the informal sector;[8] years of schooling; experience; gender; marital status; migrant status; occupational sector; number of hours per week; job location; neighbourhood average income; and average distance from the community to downtown Rio.

Earning differentials in the distinct occupational categories are obtained from the parameters γ_1, γ_2 and γ_3, which respectively measure the effects of variables D_{wi}, D_{of} and D_{ow}. The results of the regressions are shown in Table 7.4.

At first glance, the coefficients of Table 7.4 show that earnings across the different occupational categories are systematically different. Even after controlling for the above-mentioned covariates, the parameters for formal entrepreneurs, informal entrepreneurs and informal wage-earners remained positive and statistically significant. This suggests that these occupations

Table 7.4 Earnings differential between formal and informal workers

	Lnwage
educ	0.048
	(0.001)***
exp	0.019
	(0.001)***
expsq	−0.00009
	(0.00002)***
female	−0.166
	(0.007)***
marital	0.058
	(0.007)***
mig	0.049
	(0.006)***
hhouse	0.056
	(0.008)***
renda	0.0001
	(9.11e−06)***
dist	9.97e−07
	(3.35e−07)**
inside	−0.122
	(0.014)***
γ_1	0.056
	(0.008)***
γ_2	0.215
	(0.011)***
γ_3	0.149
	(0.025)***
Obs	19,309
R^2	0.27
F-statistic	299.457

have a higher return than the reference category; namely, formal wage-earners. Moreover, the gender coefficients suggest that the controls do explain part of the earning differential between men and women. Given that this differential has now dropped from 30 per cent to 16 per cent, it is, nevertheless, still present and significant.

A more general comment on the findings of Table 7.4 is the already noted much lower return to education of the residents of these communities, when compared with the existing empirical evidence for developing countries. Another point is the average 12 per cent wage increase for occupations outside the slums.

It is important to note that the rejection of the single market hypothesis, as with the rejection of the hypothesis of no geographical segmentation, may simply result, as previously noted, from sample selection bias (Heckman and Hotz, 1986). According to Cain (1976), creating a sample of the basis of the dependent variable of a regression analysis and running separate regressions within each subsample can produce sharply biased estimated coefficients if, in fact, a common regression function characterizes all populations. Figure 7.1 illustrates the point.

The solid line in this figure shows hypothetical population earnings equations based on the simple schooling model of Equation (7.1). The line assumes a positive relationship between income and schooling. The dots around that line represent the residual variability in the earnings equation caused by unmeasured variables such as ability and motivation; that is, the μ_i[9] of Equation (7.1).

Suppose that there is no segmentation of the market, in the sense that the solid line represents the mean earnings function for everyone at all levels of schooling. Creating a sample of low-earners (people whose earnings are below *C*), and running regression on the sample, produced

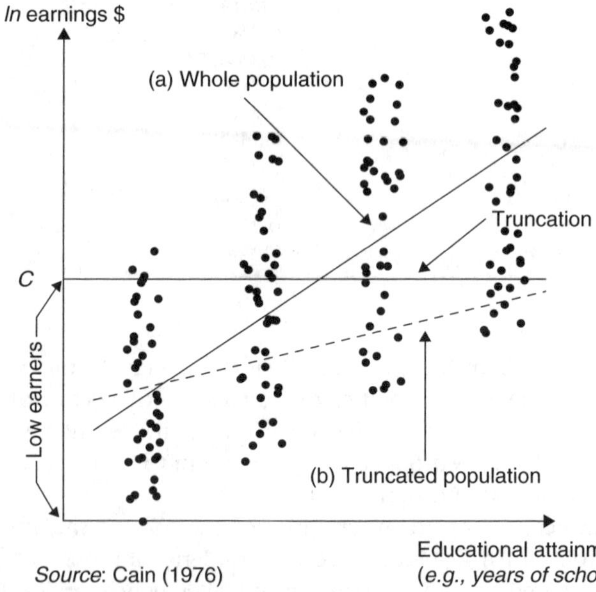

Source: Cain (1976)

Figure 7.1 Hypothetical scatter diagram and regression of earnings on educational attainment, with and without truncated earnings

biased estimates of the true regression function. As the level of education increases, the proportion of people in the low-income category declines. Those who are in that category tend to have low values of μ_i (the error terms representing unobserved determinants of earnings) as in Equation (7.1). As Heckman and Hotz (1986) explain, the measured relationship between income and schooling from samples of low-income workers is biased towards zero because the level of μ_i in the sample of low-income workers is negatively correlated with s_i (years of schooling), even though μ_i is uncorrelated with s_i in the population. The dashed line in Figure 7.1 indicates the impact of this bias on fitted regression equations. Low-income workers and high-income workers whose behaviour is generated by a common regression function (the solid line) appear to be different (the dashed line) only because of the statistical methods used.

Nevertheless, it is possible to correct for this bias using sample selection techniques, which account for the effect of income-truncation (or other selection rules) on the mean of μ in the low-income sample. This is the aim of the next section.

Earnings equation adjusted for occupational choice

So far, wage premium has been calculated on the basis of the estimated coefficient of the sectoral earning functions. However, if workers freely choose between the occupation segments, the wage and the sector are simultaneously determined, and the same individual peculiarities that drive one result may also drive the other. In other words, the same unobservable personal characteristics that make an individual more likely to choose the informal sector may also be raising his or her wage in the informal sector above that of a person with the same observed characteristics drawn randomly from the population.

Following Equation (7.10) (p. 113), this chapter now estimates the two-step procedure suggested by Bourguignon *et al.* (2002).

The segment allocation equation and identification

The first step in testing the model of wage determination is to consider a reduced form selection equation that summarizes what it is known about the recruitment procedures and participation decision (as described in Model (7.9)). In reduced form, the choice of a particular segment is a function of segment-specific prices, exogenous income, hours worked, job characteristics, and other individual-specific exogenous variables. The main proxy variables available to capture these effects are: education, age, marital status, partner's occupation, a dummy variable indicating whether

Table 7.5 Marginal effect: multinomial logit

	Formal wage-earner	**Informal wage-earner**	**Formal entrepreneur**	**Informal entrepreneur**
	(1)	(2)	(3)	(4)
educ	0.009	−0.00002	−0.008	−0.0003
	(0.001)***	(0.001)	(0.0009)***	(0.0004)
age	0.011	−0.025	0.012	0.002
	(0.002)***	(0.002)***	(0.002)***	(0.0006)**
agesq	−0.00009	0.0003	0	0
	(0.00003)***	(0.00002)***	(0.00002)***	(7.71e−06)
female	0.009	−0.088	0.034	0.047
	(0.009)	(0.007)***	(0.007)***	(0.005)***
marital	−0.0009	−0.025	0.017	0.01
	(0.009)	(0.008)**	(0.006)**	(0.002)***
hhouse	0.025	−0.042	0.018	0.0002
	(0.01)	(0.009)***	(0.007)**	(0.003)
spouse	−0.103	0.03	0.053	0.021
	(0.016)***	(0.014)	(0.011)***	(0.005)***
own	−0.022	−0.0004	0.017	0.007
	(0.012)	(0.01)	(0.008)	(0.003)
mig	0.031	−0.041	0.0009	0.01
	(0.008)***	(0.007)***	(0.006)	(0.003)***
kids	−0.004	0.0005	0.005	−0.00009
	(0.002)	(0.002)	(0.002)**	(0.0007)
m11	0.0003	−0.00009	−0.0002	0.0002
	(0.0003)	(0.0003)	(0.0002)	(0.00008)
asset2	0.017	−0.012	−0.006	0.003
	(0.003)***	(0.002)***	(0.002)***	(0.0008)***
asset2sq	−0.004	0.004	0.002	−0.0004
	(0.0007)***	(0.0005)***	(0.0003)***	(0.0002)

Note: Significance levels, **: 5%, ***: 1%.

the person is the head of the household, and a dummy variable indicating whether the respondent owns a house.

Table 7.5 provides the marginal effects of the MNL estimates for the occupation equation. The model proved reasonably successful, converging rapidly with the majority of coefficients significant at the 1 per cent level.

Figures 7.2 and 7.3 plot the predicted values of Equation (7.9). In this particular exercise, all continuous variables were set at mean values while the categorical variables were set at the most representative figure (married males who own their own house, and whose wives work as entrepreneurs). It is important to note that, in these figures, age is being used as a proxy for financial and human capital factors.

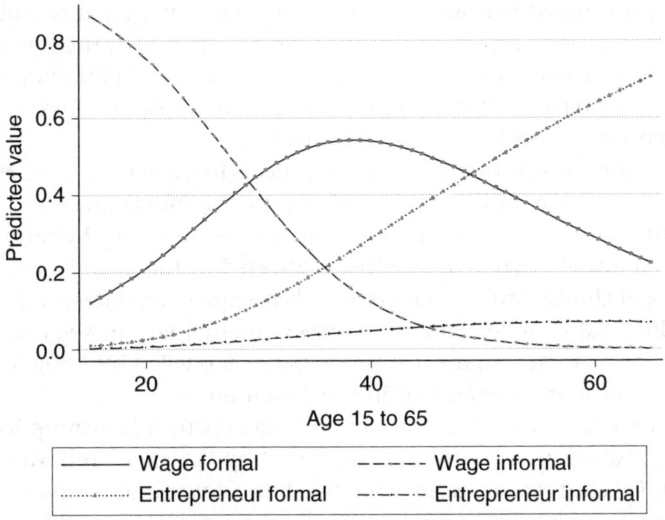

Figure 7.2 Occupational choice and experience

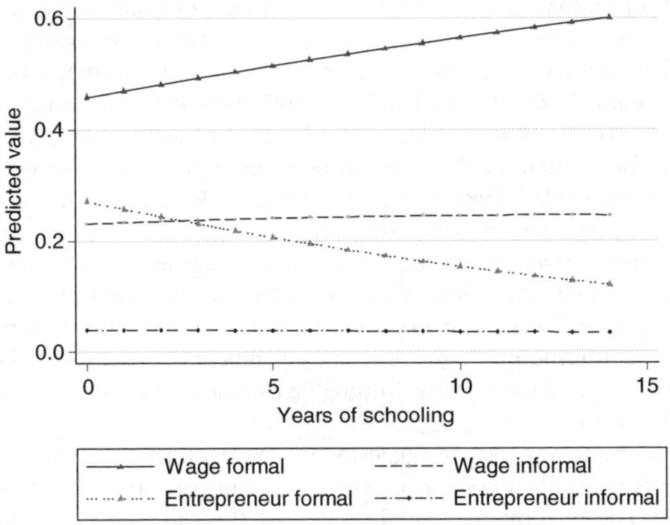

Figure 7.3 Occupational choice and education

The main message from these figures is that entrepreneurs (both formal and informal) represent the only category in which the probability of entering increases over time, suggesting the degree of importance these occupations have in these communities, and that formal education only has a positive effect for formal wage-earners.

Given the key role of the allocation process in the model, there is need to ensure that it conforms to the assumption of 'independence of irrelevant alternatives' (IIA). This condition is violated when the ratio probability of one alternative to another is affected by the introduction of an additional choice. This amounts to workers expressing differential substitutability and complementarity between alternatives. In such case, the process of sectoral assignment can be better modelled by using a multinomial probit or a nested multinomial logit model.

Testing whether a particular data set adheres to this assumption can be established by using the test suggested by Hausman and McFadden (1984). This test systematically compared the four-segment model against all possible three-segment models, all of which rejected the null hypothesis at the 1 per cent level. The IIA property holds (for the full results, see the Appendix).

More often than not, the empirical literature on labour market segmentation in developing countries pools together self-employed workers with informal sector wage-earners in order to create the informal sector category (Telles, 1993; Marcouiller *et al.*, 1997; Saavedra and Chong, 1999). In other cases they ignore formal and informal sector differences, and simply focus their analysis on differences among wage-earners and entrepreneurs (Blau, 1985; Cohen and House, 1996). The combination of such categories can be dangerous, and is only valid if no fundamental underlying differences among the distinct groups are found. The literature mentioned above has failed to notice an important contribution made by Hill (1983) who noticed that the condition for pooling two states of a multinomial logit lies in the equality of the multinomial coefficient vectors, and can be tested through a likelihood ratio test.[10] This chapter tests for this.

Following the procedure suggested by Cramer and Ridder (1991), this study sequentially tests for all possible combinations of all four categories. The possibility of pooling any of the categories together was rejected at the 1 per cent level for all cases (for the full results, see the Appendix).

One extremely important factor when estimating any two-stage model is the identification of exclusion restrictions; in other words, variables that affect the occupation decision, but do not affect the earnings equation.

The specification used relies on the existing literature on entrepreneurship and self-employment in order to choose a set of regressors that fit this quality; in particular, house-ownership and partner-occupation. The first variable is a proxy of the physical assets of the household, often an important factor when deciding to become an entrepreneur. The second variable, partner occupation, is also often discussed in the literature as being a relevant factor when making the decision as to occupation.[11]

Estimating the earnings equation

The second stage of this economic procedure involves estimating earnings equations for each segment, including the additional synthetic regressors (Model 7.10). The chosen earning equation is a variant of Mincer's standard human capital equations, and includes controls for education, experience and experience squared, marital status, migration, work journey, sector, household position (head of the household), neighbourhood average income, and distance to downtown Rio.

As usual, the dependent variable in this analysis is the natural logarithm of monthly earnings. Each segment's earnings equation also includes a separate selection term for each categorical latent expression. Hence, in a four-sector model there are four selection terms, derived from the predicted values of Equation (7.9), $(\sigma_s \widetilde{\rho}_1)$, $(\sigma_s \widetilde{\rho}_2)$, $(\sigma_s \widetilde{\rho}_3)$, and $(\sigma_s \widetilde{\rho}_4)$, where s represents the chosen occupation.

The estimated coefficients are reported in Table 7.6 for males, and Table 7.7 for females.

Under this elaborate method, an F-test was conducted to test the hypothesis that all the $(\sigma_s \widetilde{\rho}_j)$s are 0. In each segment, the rejection of the null hypothesis[12] indicates the presence of unobservables in the occupational choice process. Overall, the test results seem to suggest that the effects of unobservables seem to be stronger for the wage-earners than for entrepreneurs.

Comparison of Tables 7.6 and 7.7 shows that females still present a higher return to education than males. Nevertheless, returns to education, for both males and females, are slightly smaller once adjustments for occupation selectivity are made (see Table 7A.2 in the Appendix for the OLS coefficients). Having said that, it is important to note that in the case of female wage-earners, returns to previously experienced employment became much higher as the correction for the selection bias was made. These results suggest the existence of selection effects, which implies that occupational choices are non-random and must be taken into consideration through a two-step estimation of the earnings equation.

Table 7.6 Selected coefficients sector wage equations, male workers: BFG

	Formal wage earner	**Informal wage earner**	**Formal entrepreneur**	**Informal entrepreneur**
	(1)	(2)	(3)	(4)
educ	0.032	0.031	0.017	−0.025
	(0.005)***	(0.006)***	(0.007)	(0.02)
exp	−0.003	−0.008	−0.043	−0.031
	(0.008)	(0.009)	(0.017)**	(0.023)
expsq	0.00003	0.0001	0.0006	0.0003
	(0.0001)	(0.0001)	(0.0002)	(0.0004)
marital	0.043	0.091	0.017	0.165
	(0.051)	(0.063)	(0.085)	(0.169)
mig	−0.05	−0.021	−0.084	0.035
	(0.03)	(0.034)	(0.053)	(0.108)
hhouse	−0.036	−0.088	−0.039	0.132
	(0.046)	(0.059)	(0.092)	(0.155)
renda	0.00007	0.0001	0.0001	0.0001
	(1.00e−05)***	(0.00002)***	(0.00003)***	(0.00009)
dist	9.16e−07	2.47e−06	5.91e−07	−3.44e−06
	(4.87e−07)	(8.25e−07)**	(1.08e−06)	(2.64e−06)
$(\sigma_s \tilde{\rho}_1)$	1.392	−0.322	0.998	−2.123
	(0.512)**	(0.74)	(1.245)	(4.098)
$(\sigma_s \tilde{\rho}_2)$	3.434	0.471	2.938	−1.771
	(1.07)**	(0.367)	(1.364)	(3.79)
$(\sigma_s \tilde{\rho}_3)$	1.46	−0.555	−0.028	0.293
	(0.859)	(0.858)	(0.385)	(2.828)
$(\sigma_s \tilde{\rho}_4)$	−0.92	−1.801	−1.936	−0.946
	(1.462)	(1.448)	(1.675)	(0.54)
Obs	7,850	3,177	1,967	314
R^2	0.213	0.31	0.229	0.309
F-statistic	111.227	74.668	30.485	6.908
F-test:[a]				
$\lambda_{ij} = 0$	94.03***	48.87***	40.05***	8.16***

Notes:
Bootstrapped standard errors in parentheses; significance levels: *: 10%, **: 5%,***: 1%.
[a] A test statistic is approximately F(4,N − 17) distributed.

Conclusion

This chapter provides evidence on the labour market from extremely deprived areas in a developing country – the slums of Rio de Janeiro – and examines how the labour market relates to the entrepreneurial activities of the residents of these communities. Some main features are highlighted.

Table 7.7 Selected coefficients sector wage equations, female workers: BFG

	Formal wage earner	**Informal wage earner**	**Formal entrepreneur**	**Informal entrepreneur**
	(1)	(2)	(3)	(4)
educ	0.034	0.044	−0.007	0.006
	(0.009)***	(0.011)***	(0.017)	(0.026)
exp	0.037	0.043	0.032	0.044
	(0.01)***	(0.009)***	(0.017)	(0.023)
expsq	−0.0004	−0.0005	−0.0003	−0.0006
	(0.0001)**	(0.0001)***	(0.0002)	(0.0003)
marital	0.153	0.165	0.177	0.036
	(0.09)	(0.089)	(0.117)	(0.229)
mig	0.049	0.059	0.046	0.196
	(0.033)	(0.04)	(0.053)	(0.099)
hhouse	0.127	0.146	0.132	0.123
	(0.056)	(0.061)	(0.09)	(0.153)
renda	0.00008	0.00004	0.00007	0.0001
	(0.00002)***	(0.00004)	(0.00005)	(0.00009)
dist	−9.88e−08	1.42e−06	1.63e−06	8.09e−06
	(7.66e−07)	(1.58e−06)	(2.19e−06)	(3.46e−06)
$(\sigma_s\tilde{\rho}_1)$	1.299	2.251	0.626	1.209
	(0.535)	(0.942)	(0.649)	(1.44)
$(\sigma_s\tilde{\rho}_2)$	0.558	0.283	0.05	−0.684
	(0.636)	(0.246)	(0.658)	(1.222)
$(\sigma_s\tilde{\rho}_3)$	2.855	2.333	0.72	2.118
	(1.084)**	(1.011)	(0.323)	(1.683)
$(\sigma_s\tilde{\rho}_4)$	1.383	1.205	0.149	0.072
	(1.021)	(0.842)	(0.712)	(0.442)
Obs	3,376	958	877	415
R^2	0.19	0.317	0.281	0.41
F-statistic	41.492	22.884	18.585	16.197
F-test:[a]				
$\lambda_{ij} = 0$	27.79***	9.41***	10.26***	3.93***

Notes:
Bootstrapped standard errors in parentheses; significance levels: *: 10%, **: 5%, ***: 1%.
[a] A test statistic is approximately F(4,N − 17) distributed.

One important finding is the substantially lower returns to education for the residents of the slums of Rio de Janeiro, when compared with the existing empirical literature for developing countries. While the latest survey on the return to education of wage-earners and entrepreneurs in developing countries showed average returns of approximately 10 per cent and 5 per cent (Van Der Sluis *et al.*, 2004), this study found returns of approximately 6 per cent and 3 per cent for wage-earners and entrepreneurs, respectively. This result was robust in several model specifications and estimation procedures, including a selection-adjusted earnings equation designed to correct for occupational choice bias.

This chapter also provides empirical evidence of significant neighbourhood effects in the city of Rio de Janeiro, through which it can be seen that the slums closer to the more affluent areas of the city had greater earnings, particularly in the case of males.

Following a well established empirical literature on labour market segmentation in developing countries, this chapter shows a substantial earning differential between formal entrepreneurs and formal wage-earners, as well as informal entrepreneurs and informal wage-earners, with formal sector entrepreneurs earning 15 per cent more and informal entrepreneurs earning 8 per cent less than formal wage-earners.

Another important analysis was the scrutiny of the process of occupational choice of the population from the various communities. Two important features, in agreement with the existing literature, emerged from this analysis. Entrepreneurs (both formal and informal) form the only occupational category in which the probability of entering increases with age, suggesting that this is an extremely important segment for the older population (over 40 years of age). Furthermore, it is clear that formal education only has a positive effect on the probability of becoming a formal wage-earner, playing a minor role on entrepreneurial choice, and informal wage earnings.

The information from the occupational choice model implemented is included in the earnings equation to adjust for unobservable factors that might influence both the occupational choice and the earnings equation simultaneously. The procedure implemented in this study has never been used in this literature, and has the advantage of including a correction term for all occupational possibilities. The coefficients of the selection correction terms were statistically significant, suggesting both the effect of unobservables and the necessity of taking them into account on the estimation.

In a nutshell, the present work corroborates other studies of developing countries, showing that returns to education for entrepreneurs are much fewer than for wage-earners. However, returns to education found in residents from the slums of Rio de Janeiro are fewer than those in the developing countries literature. The chapter also provides evidence that the residents of the slums of Rio who do not manage to find work outside their communities will, in general, receive substantially lower remuneration for their work. This work also shows that, once selection is accounted for, the returns to education for formal and informal entrepreneurs are much fewer than for wage-earners. Such findings can potentially legitimize targeted interventions to help the labour markets of these communities to operate better, in particular, the entrepreneurial initiatives within these communities.

Appendix

Testing the Independence of Irrelevant Alternative assumption (IIA)

A crucial assumption of the multinomial logit model is the IIA property. Testing whether a particular data set adheres to this assumption can be established by using the test suggested by Hausman and McFadden (1984).

Table 7A.1 Variables description

Variable	Description	Type
Logwage	Log monthly wages	Continuous
educ	Education (Years of Schooling)	Continuous
exp	Experience (Age – Years of Schooling – 6)	Continuous
Expsq	Experience squared	Continuous
female	Female	Dummy
marital	Marital status	Dummy
hhouse	Head of household	Dummy
mig	Migrant	Dummy
age	Age (15–65)	Continuous
Agesq	Age squared	Continuous
spouse	Spouse entrepreneur	Dummy
own	Own house	Dummy
m11	Number of years living in the slum	Continuous
kids	Number of children at school age	Continuous
occupfor	Occupation and formality	Categorical
informal	Informal sector worker	Dummy
inside	Job location inside the slum	Dummy
partime	Works part time (less than 20 hours per week)	Dummy
sector1	Industry	Dummy
sector2	Commerce	Dummy
sector3	Service	Dummy
sector4	Construction	Dummy
sector5	Transport	Dummy
time1	Number of hours per week (less than 20)	Dummy
time2	Number of hours per week (+20 to 40)	Dummy
time3	Number of hours per week (+40 to 44)	Dummy
time4	Number of hours per week (+44)	Dummy
renda	Neighbourhood average income	Continuous
dist	Slum: average distance to downtown Rio	Continuous

Table 7A.2 Selected coefficients of the segmented wage equations (males and females)

	Formal wage earner	Informal wage earner	Formal entrepreneur	Informal entrepreneur
	(1)	(2)	(3)	(4)
Males				
Education	0.048	0.044	0.034	0.009
	(0.000)**	(0.001)**	(0.001)**	(0.002)**
Experience	0.023	0.019	0.002	−0.005
	(0.000)**	(0.000)**	(0.001)*	(0.002)*
Experience sqr	−0.000	−0.000	−0.000	−0.000
	(0.000)**	(0.000)**	(0.000)	(0.000)
Females				
Education	0.052	0.058	0.029	0.028
	(0.000)**	(0.001)**	(0.001)**	(0.002)**
Experience	0.012	0.027	0.014	0.001
	(0.000)**	(0.001)**	(0.001)**	(0.002)
Experience sqr	−0.000	−0.000	−0.000	−0.000
	(0.000)**	(0.000)**	(0.000)**	(0.000)**

Notes:
1 Other covariates: marital; mig; hhouse; sector2; sector3; sector4; sector5; time2; time3; time4; renda; dist; and inside.
2 Robust standard errors in parentheses.
3 *: significant at 5%; **: significant at 1%.

Table 7A.3 Hausman tests of 'independence of irrelevant alternatives' assumption

Omitted category	Chi2	df	*H0*
Informal wage earner	−3.099	26	Accept
Informal wage earner	20.68	26	Accept
Informal wage earner	−0.997	26	Accept

The suggested statistic is distributed as a chi square distribution and has the form:

$$H = (B_c - B_e)'(V_c - V_e)^{-1}(B_c - B_e)$$

where
β_c is the coefficient vector from the consistent estimator,
β_e is the coefficient vector from the efficient estimator,
V_c is the covariance matrix of the coefficients from the consistent estimator,
V_e is the covariance matrix of the coefficients from the efficient estimator.

Table 7A.4 Summary of Cramer–Ridder test for the valid number of sort types

	log *L*	**LR**	***H*0**
Informal wage earner: formal entrepreneur	−1.92e+04	566.581	Reject
Informal wage earner: informal entrepreneur	−1.93e+04	847.944	Reject
Informal wage earner: formal wage earner	−1.92e+04	601.163	Reject
Formal entrepreneur: informal entrepreneur	−1.94e+04	1023.121	Reject
Formal entrepreneur: formal wage earner	−1.93e+04	819.487	Reject
Formal entrepreneur: Informal wage earner	−1.90e+04	270.769	Reject

In this test statistic the covariance matrix is guaranteed to be positive definite only asymptotically and no assurance can be made about the diagonal elements. Negative values along the diagonal are possible. Such a situation would cause the test statistics H to be negative. In this case, the results provide strong evidence that the IIA is justified.

Testing how many sort type regimes there should be

Testing the valid number of sort types can be assessed using the Cramer–Ridder test sequentially. Assuming that there are s_j individuals in j'th alternative and that the total number of individuals n in the sample is denoted by s, Cramer and Ridder (1991; 1992; 2001) showed that a valid likelihood ratio test could be constructed:

$$LR = 2\{\log \hat{L} - \log \hat{L}_r\}$$

where

$$\log \hat{L} = \sum_j n_{sj} \log n_{sj} - n_s \log n_s$$

is the maximum log-likelihood if the estimates are constrained to satisfy $\beta_{s1} = \beta_{s2} = \beta_s$ and $\log \hat{L}$ is the maximum log-likelihood of the original unconstrained model. Clearly, the most appropriate way to proceed is to test the alternative of having three sets of separate coefficients – one set for the reference group and one set each for the two sort types treated. (Note: for identification, it only actually estimates two sets relative to the reference group.) The next step is to reduce the number of alternative sort types by grouping them and testing them until a preferred number of alternatives using this test is found.[13]

Notes

I thank the seminar and conference participants from Newcastle, Durham, Seville (EALE 2003), Helsinki (EGDI-WIDER), and Brasília (UNDP International Poverty

Centre), with special thanks for helpful comments and suggestions to Nauro Campos, Peter Dolton, Simon Parker, Fábio Veras and Nanak Kakwani. I also thank the UK Department for Education and Skills for research support under the ORSAS, Award no. 2002029001. The usual disclaimer applies.

1 Models of occupational choice and entrepreneurship have also received great attention from economists, often taking self-employment as a working definition of entrepreneurship (see Parker (2004) for a comprehensive survey on this subject). The development literature has also produced a family of models to shed light on the process of occupational choice, income inequality and economic development (for more details see Banerjee and Newman, 1993 and Ghatak and Jiang, 2002).

2 The role of educational qualifications has been incorporated into many empirical studies, being a key determinant of success in the labour market. Educational attainment may act as a proxy for ability – individuals of higher ability may make better managers, which in turn may enhance their probability of becoming self-employed. Van Der Sluis *et al.* (2004) have recently produced a comprehensive survey of the effects of education on entrepreneurship in developing countries.

3 An individual's age may also affect his/her propensity to become self-employed via a number of different channels (Lucas, 1978; Calvo and Wellisz, 1980). For instance, age may act as a proxy to capture the effect of an individual's awareness, knowledge and experience in the labour market, thereby reflecting general human capital. Alternatively, as an individual becomes older, he/she may have accumulated the financial resources required for self-employment; hence, age may capture effects related to financial, as well as human capital.

4 Often, marital status has been incorporated into many empirical studies, since it is assumed to represent stability and, as such, may provide a suitable background for 'risk' self-employment. Moreover, Bernhardt (1994) and Blanchflower and Oswald (1990) find that having a working spouse enhances the probability of self-employment. Similarly, Schiller and Crewson (1997) find evidence of intra-coupling risk-pooling with a husband's primary employment increasing the probability that a wife will be observed in self-employment.

5 Of course, the $(\hat{P}_j)$s and $(m(\hat{P}_j))$s depend on all (z_j)s and incorporates all the information behind the multinomial logit model. Their combination on the right hand side of Model (7.10) yields a consistent estimate of the conditional expected value of the residual term in the original outcome Equation (7.4).

6 According to the 1991 Census, there are 462 slums or *favelas* in the city of Rio de Janeiro, with a total population of 882,667 in 224,350 households, or 16 per cent of the total population of the city of Rio de Janeiro. The data from the 2000 census only seems to reinforce this trend. Moreover, the population living in these conditions has grown 23 per cent from 1980 to 1991, which represents a threefold increase in comparison to the citywide population growth average.

7 Following common practice, domestic servants are excluded, since they receive an unknown portion of their pay in kind (see Telles, 1993: 234, and Marcouiller *et al.*, 1997: 3).

8 The fourth possible category (that is, wage-earner from the formal sector) is used as the control category.
9 Error term representing unobservable determinants of earnings.
10 This test was later reintroduced by Cramer and Ridder (1991).
11 Although both variables were statistically significant at the first stage regression neither of them was statistically significant at the second stage.
12 Note that this is an imprecise test because it ignores the variance from the first stage estimates.
13 Stata ado file CRTEST was used to implement this test (Azevedo, 2003).

References

Acioly, C., Jr, (2001) 'Reviewing Urban Revitalization Strategies in Rio de Janeiro: From Urban Project to Urban Management Approaches', *Geoforum*, 32: 509–20.

Azevedo, J.P. (2003) 'CRTEST: Stata Module to Perform Cramer–Ridder Test for Pooling States in a Multinomial Logit', *Statistical Software Components, S433202*, Boston College, Department of Economics, revised 03 Dec.

Banerjee, A.V. and A.F. Newman (1993) 'Occupational Choice and the Process of Development', *Journal of Political Economy*, 101(2): 274–98.

Becker, G.S. (1964) *Human Capital: A Theoretical and Empirical Analysis, with Special Reference to Education* (New York: Columbia University Press for National Bureau of Economic Research).

Becker, G.S. and B. Chiswick (1966) 'Education and the Distribution of Earnings', *American Economic Review*, 56: 358–9.

Bernhardt, I. (1994) 'Comparative Advantage in Self-Employment and Paid Work', *Canadian Journal of Economics*, 27(2): 273–89.

Blanchflower, D.G. and A.J. Oswald (1990) 'What Makes a Young Entrepreneur?', National Bureau of Economic Research Working Paper no. 3252: 29 (NBER: Cambridge, MA).

Blau, D.M. (1985) 'Self-Employment and Self-Selection in Developing Country Labor Markets', *Southern Economic Journal*, 52(2): 351–63.

Bourguignon, F., M. Fournier and M. Gurgand (2002) 'Selection Bias Correction based on the Multinomial Logit Model', CREST Working Paper no. 2002–04 (CREST: Paris).

Cain, G.G. (1976) 'The Challenge of Segmented Labor Market Theories to Orthodox Theory: A Survey', *Journal of Economic Literature*, 14(4): 1215–57.

Calvo, G.A. and S. Wellisz (1980) 'Technology, Entrepreneurs, and Firm Size', *Quarterly Journal of Economics*, 95(4): 663–77.

Cira, D.A. (2002) 'Urban Upgrading in Latin America and the Caribbean', *En Breve*, (3) (Washington, DC: World Bank).

Cohen, B. and W.J. House (1996) 'Labor Market Choices, Earnings, and Informal Networks in Khartoum, Sudan', *Economic Development and Cultural Change*, 44(3): 589–618.

Cramer, J.S. and G. Ridder (1991) 'Pooling States in the Multinomial Logit Model', *Journal of Econometrics*, 47(2/3): 267–72.

Cramer, J.S. and G. Ridder (1992) 'Erratum: Pooling States in the Multinomial Logit Model', *Journal of Econometrics*, 51(1/2): 285.

Cramer, J.S. and G. Ridder (2001) 'Pooling States in the Multinomial Logit Model: Degrees of Freedom: A Correction', *Statistical Papers*, 42(1): 97–9.
De Soto, H. (1989) *The Other Path: The Invisible Revolution in the Third World* (New York: Harper & Row).
De Soto, H. (2000) *The Mystery of Capital: Why Capitalism Triumphs in the West and Fails Everywhere Else* (New York: Basic Books).
Dubin, J.A. and D.L. McFadden (1984) 'An Econometric Analysis of Residential Electric Appliance Holdings and Consumption', *Econometrica*, 52(2): 345–62.
Fei, J.C.H. and G. Ranis (1964) *Development of the Labor Surplus Economy: Theory and Policy* (Homewood, IL: Irwin).
Ghatak, M. and N. Jiang (2002) 'A Simple Model of Inequality, Occupational Choice, and Development', *Journal of Development Economics*, 69: 205–26.
Gill, I., S. Yusuf, J. von Amsberg, W. Dillinger, B. Menezes and M. Neri (1999) *Rio de Janeiro: A City Study* (Washington, DC: World Bank).
Harris, J.R. and M.P. Todaro (1970) 'Migration, Unemployment and Development: A Two-Sector Analysis', *American Economic Review*, 60(1): 126–42.
Hausman, J. and D. McFadden (1984) 'Specification Tests for the Multinomial Logit Model', *Econometrica*, 52(5): 1219–40.
Heckman, J.J. (1979) 'Sample Selection Bias as a Specification Error', *Econometrica*, 47(1): 153–61.
Heckman, J.J. and V.J. Hotz (1986) 'An Investigation of the Labor Market Earnings of Panamanian Males: Evaluating the Sources of Inequality', *Journal of Human Resources*, 21(4): 507–42.
Hill, M.A. (1983) 'Female Labor Force Participation in Developing and Developed Countries – Consideration of the Informal Sector', *Review of Economics and Statistics*, 65(3): 459–68.
IBGE (2000) 'Brazilian Census', Technical Report, Brazilian National Office of Statistics.
International Labour Office (1972) *Employment, Incomes and Equality: A Strategy for Increasing Productive Employment in Kenya* (Geneva: International Labour Office).
LabGeo (1996) 'Mapa Digital das Favelas do Municipio do Rio de Janeiro' (Rio de Janeiro: FioCruz).
Le, A.T. (1999) 'Empirical Studies of Self-Employment', *Journal of Economic Surveys*, 13(4): 381–416.
Lee, L.-F. (1983) 'Generalized Econometric Models with Selectivity', *Econometrica*, 51(2): 507–12.
Lewis, W.A. (1954) 'Economic Development with Unlimited Supplies of Labour', *The Manchester School*: 139–91.
Lucas, R.E., Jr, (1978) 'On the Size Distribution of Business Firms', *Bell Journal of Economics*, 9(2): 508–23.
Magnac, T. (1991) 'Segmented or Competitive Labor Markets', *Econometrica*, 59(1): 165–87.
Marcouiller, D., V. Ruiz de Castilla and C. Woodruff (1997) 'Formal Measures of the Informal-Sector Wage Gap in Mexico, El Salvador, and Peru', *Economic Development and Cultural Change*, 45(2): 367–92.
Mincer, J. (1958) 'Investment in Human Capital and Personal Income Distribution', *Journal of Political Economy*, 56: 281–302.
Mincer, J. (1974) *Schooling, Experience and Earnings* (New York: National Bureau of Economics Research).

Parker, S.C. (2004) *The Economics of Self-Employment and Entrepreneurship* (Cambridge: Cambridge University Press).

Riley, E., J. Fiori and R. Ramirez (2001) 'Favela Bairro and a New Generation of Housing Programmes', *Geoforum*, 32: 521–31.

Saavedra, J. and A. Chong (1999) 'Structural Reform, Institutions and Earnings: Evidence from the Formal and Informal Sectors in Urban Peru', *Journal of Development Studies*, 35(4): 95–116.

Schiller, B.R. and P.E. Crewson (1997) 'Entrepreneurial Origins: A Longitudinal Inquiry', *Economic Inquiry*, 35(3): 523–31.

Schmertmann, C.P. (1994) 'Selectivity Bias Correction Methods in Polychotomous Sample Selection Models', *Journal of Econometrics*, 60(1/2): 101–32.

Silva, D.B., J.M. Lima and P.L. Quintslr (1998) 'A Socio-economics survey for job and income development in Rio de Janeiro slums', Proceedings of the Joint IASS/IAOS Conference: Statistics for Economics and Social Development, Aguascalientes, Mexico. 1–4 September.

Telles, E.E. (1993) 'Urban Labor Market Segmentation and Income in Brazil', *Economic Development and Cultural Change*, 41(2): 231–49.

UN-HABITAT (2003) *The Challenge of Slums – Global Report on Human Settlements 2003* (London and Sterling, VA: Earthscan).

Van Der Sluis, J., M. Van Praag and W. Vijverberg (2004) 'Entrepreneurship Selection and Performance: A Meta-analysis of the Impact of Education in Less Developed Countries', Tinbergen Institute Discussion Papers 03-046/3.

8

Urban Informal Sector and Networks: A Case Study of Delhi Slum Dwellers

Arup Mitra

Introduction

The term 'informal sector' has been used extensively, particularly in the empirical literature, in spite of the difficulties involved in defining the term. The informal sector in India is seen to absorb surplus labour residually in low-productivity activities resulting from the sluggish growth of employment in high-productivity activities. As the poor cannot afford to remain unemployed for long, the phenomenon of 'working poor' is prevalent. Meagre earnings reduce their accessibility to decent living conditions. In other words, there are considerable overlaps among informal sector employment, poverty and slum-dwelling (Mitra, 1994). The inter-linkages among the formal and informal sectors exist but they are not necessarily favourable to the informal-sector workers (see Shaw, 1990; Mitra, 1994). Also, the possibility of graduating to the formal sector is quite remote (see Papola, 1981; Banerjee, 1986; Gupta and Mitra, 2002; Mitra, 2003).

However, the informal sector workers form their own strategies to cope with poverty and overcome uncertainties relating to employment, consumption, health and housing. Informal institutions and networks have been developed by them over the decades to access information pertaining to the job market, enhance earnings and help experience upward occupational mobility over time. Based on a micro survey of slum households in Delhi, this chapter highlights the role of networks in accessing employment. The organization of the chapter is as follows. The next section presents the analytical framework. In the subsequent section, we focus on the empirical analysis and the chapter closes with a summary of major findings and policy issues.

The database of the study is drawn from the 1999–2000 survey carried out over a period of six months for 802 households in 30 slum clusters in

Delhi. The slums considered in our study are of one particular type; the *jhuggi-jhopdi* colonies given in the list prepared by Delhi Development Authority (DDA). In order to select a sample of 802 households, we have used a three-stage stratified random sampling framework.

Analytical framework

Studies on the urban labour market have confirmed extensively the role of contact in accessing information pertaining to jobs in both formal and informal sectors, bringing out the importance of rural-based search for urban jobs through contacts (Banerjee, 1986). These contacts operate through relatives, friends, members of own caste groups and co-villagers. It is interesting to note that migrants whose contact persons are engaged in unskilled manual occupations are informed about the same job more frequently than those whose contacts work in non-manual and skilled manual occupations. Furthermore, migration motivated by the suggestion of contacts appears to be important among those who are uneducated or are non-matriculates; that is, below secondary level (Banerjee and Bucci, 1994). However, one missing area of research is the segmented nature of the urban labour market due to specialization of activities in different areas (zones) within a city. Segmentation along the lines of caste, skill and education has of course drawn adequate attention from scholars, but the physical segmentation of the labour market needs to be explored further.

By physical segmentation, we mean inaccessibility to certain kinds of jobs to certain groups of individuals, primarily because of the distance factor within a city. High-income jobs may be available in a particular locality, but their physical distance from a specific group of migrants' place of residence in the city could be so remote that such jobs may remain inaccessible to them. Even inexpensive (intra-city) transport for commutation does not necessarily eliminate these labour-market barriers, especially in developing countries. Hence, occupational choice is greatly determined by the narrow spectrum of jobs available within the geographic location where the migrants reside, rather than by what they are capable of pursuing. Contact-based migration tends to end up providing jobs in close neighbourhoods of groups' residence: the early settlers help their relatives, friends, members of the same caste groups and co-villagers to migrate to the city by providing information on jobs and spaces to settle down, which is often in the same gamut of space and activities to which they themselves have access. This is particularly true in the case of manual and unskilled jobs (Banerjee, 1986). With wide regional diversities in the cultural background of the migrants in the face of their difficulties to adapt themselves to an urban cosmopolitan culture of upper-income groups, their urge to stay alive and enjoy their cultural identity in the city induces them to reside in close proximity to each other. In India, the multilingual and multiethnic identities of its citizens make such a phenomenon even more important. Besides the activities of the contact persons (early entrants) and the late entrants being mostly similar, sharing of family or individual endowment in their pursuit of economic goals becomes almost inevitable. Efforts to delay demolition programmes planned by the city administrators, and attainment of quasi-permanent residential rights in the city are realized only through collective efforts that help secure political patronage in exchange for their promise to operate as vote banks.

As a result, occupational choice is more or less supply-driven, though from the macro point of view – keeping the entire city in the perspective – the equilibrium choice of occupation would be the outcome of both demand- and supply-side factors. It is also in sharp contrast to the popular interpretation of informal sector employment; namely, the supply (of labour) push phenomenon. This perception gets further substantiated by the fact that intra-city differences (across space) in terms of development, infrastructure and activities are too significant to be ignored. As the literature on agglomeration (particularly the localization) economies suggests, firms conducting similar activities tend to locate close to each other so as to reap economies of scale (Henderson, 1988). Extending this argument – usually made at the inter-city level to explain the differences in activities that cities specialize in – to the intra-city level, the heterogeneity across space even within a specific city can be noted. In other words, not all areas would conduct all activities – each would be responsible for the growth of a predominant activity depending upon the availability of resources required for its generation. Thus, different centres within a city would have specialized activities (Dupont and Mitra, 1995), though from the overall city point of view, all activities would appear to exist within its territory, thus creating the myth of a vast labour market.

Given the importance of contact in securing jobs and the urge to reside in groups formed on the basis of caste-kinship-co-villager bonds, and given the preference of the low-income migrant-households to locate near the workplace in an attempt to minimize transport costs and to carry on multiple jobs, the development of various nodes (centres) within the city – each characterized by specialized activities – explains the physical segmentation of the labour market. This chapter aims at capturing part of this aspect while analyzing the occupational pattern of the low-income households in the city of Delhi.

Empirical analysis

The questionnaire with which the survey was conducted contained information pertaining to the nature of employment (such as self-employment, casual employment and regular salaried employment) and also the exact description of occupations that the respondents are engaged in. Based on this detailed description, eleven categories of occupations have been formed (see Table 8.1).

It may be noted that construction and manufacturing account for more than 30 per cent of the total workers from slum households. Trade, sales and services (both personal and commercial) account for around 50 per cent of total workers (Table 8.1). About 40 per cent of the workers are found to be illiterate, and a large majority of them are engaged in construction, personal services, sales and trade. Those who studied between educational classes 6 to 9 form the second largest group. The occupational structure of these workers does not seem to be much different from that of illiterate workers, except for the fact that commercial services engage a slightly larger percentage of workers in this group than illiterate workers. Though only 7 per cent of the workers seem to have acquired an education of more than secondary level, their occupational pattern appears to be very different from those of the illiterate workers. Professional, sales and trade activities account for more than 80 per cent of the workers who attained an education higher than secondary level.

It is noted that the incidence of all-duration migration in the total number of workers in our sample is more than 70 per cent. Around 55 per cent of the workers are reported to be long-duration migrants (longer than 10 years); short-duration migrants (up to 3 years) comprise only 3 per cent of the workers. Employment in certain activities seems to change significantly with duration of residence. Manufacturing, for example, does not employ any of those who migrated in the preceding year or so. Its share shoots up to around 14 per cent among those who migrated in the last two to three years. Thereafter, it varies more or less between 7 to 9 per cent. This is indicative of the fact that jobs in activities such as manufacturing are available only when migrants develop access to information after continued residence in the urban areas. On the other hand, trading attracts both very short- and very long-duration migrants (20 years and above), but for different reasons, however. Those who migrated in the preceding year or so are employed in trading possibly because of the lack of entry barrier and the low-skill requirement. On the other hand, those who have worked in this sector for a considerable period of time have possibly moved up the ladder by operating and expanding their own enterprises.

Table 8.1 Occupational distribution and educational background of slum workers

Occupation groups	Illiterate	Literate	Studied up to Class 3	Class 4 and 5	Class 6 and 9	Secondary	Above secondary	Total
Professional	2.8	0.0	6.3	3.4	5.5	8.6	21.3	5.5
Sales	14.5	12.0	10.9	12.9	12.5	9.3	11.2	12.8
Trade	11.7	28.0	14.1	14.3	15.1	16.4	21.3	14.7
Personal services	19.9	14.0	23.4	10.2	9.6	2.1	4.5	13.4
Manufacturing	8.0	8.0	9.4	15.6	8.7	12.9	4.5	9.3
Commercial services	9.9	6.0	9.8	9.5	13.3	13.6	12.4	10.9
Transport	2.4		1.6	2.7	4.1	5.0	2.2	3.2
Tailoring, knitting	1.0	6.0	3.1	2.7	3.0	7.9	1.1	2.7
Construction	27.6	12.0	20.3	25.2	20.7	19.3	13.5	22.9
Security	0.0	2.0	0.0	0.7	1.5	0.7	3.4	0.8
Repair	2.2	6.0	3.1	2.7	6.6	4.3	4.5	3.8
Total	100 (39.5)	100 (4.00)	100 (5.11)	100 (11.7)	100 (21.5)	100 (11.1)	100 (7.1)	100

Hence, in understanding the occupational choice of the slum workers, the duration of their migration needs to be considered as an important variable.

The distribution of workers by employment categories reveals that more than 40 per cent of them are engaged as casual labour; the proportion of self-employed workers is also quite high (more than 27 per cent). This implies that a large number of slum households are susceptible to uncertainties in the job market and, therefore, fluctuations in income. Those who are self-employed may not face labour market uncertainties but, in terms of earnings, they experience instability due to climatic, seasonal and other kinds of variation in demand for their products.

The sample of 30 clusters taken from different zones in Delhi – (i) South, (ii) central, (iii) north-west, (iv) west, (v) east, (vi) north-east, and (vii) north – suggests that different areas specialize in different activities. For example, in east and north-east Delhi, commercial services account for about 23 and 24 per cent of the workers in these zones. Manufacturing is significant in north and north-west Delhi. The southern zone shows a larger share of personal services than any of the other zones. Trade is almost uniformly spread out in all zones. The percentage of workers engaged in this activity is typically between 15 and 18 per cent, except in the southern and northern zones. The share of construction is highest in west Delhi (31 per cent) followed by the central, south and north-west zones. Some of these patterns provide an insight with which to model the occupational choice.

Econometric modelling of occupational choice

In this chapter, we examine specifically the role of informal networks used in accessing employment, together with the geographical disparity within a city in terms of the availability and the nature of employment propounded by the workers' choice factor. In the preceding discussion, based on bivariate tables, we have tried to bring out certain patterns relating to the level of education, duration of migration, and the zoned location of the workers in different occupations. This is now followed by a multinomial logit model, which relates variations in occupations to the differences in the nature of accessing information and their geographic presence, other than several household/individual-specific variables.

As mentioned above, we have considered eleven occupational groups, $j = 0, \ldots 10$. The multinomial logit model for occupational choice is

$$\text{Prob}\,(Y = j) = \frac{e^{\beta_j' x}}{\sum_{k=0}^{10} e^{\beta_k' x}} \qquad (8.1)$$

The set of parameters β reflect the impact of changes in $\boldsymbol{x}$ on the probability.

However, there is an indeterminacy problem in the multinomial logit model and, to overcome this problem, the parameters of one group ($j = 0$, for example) are set equal to 0. The probabilities are, therefore:

$$\text{Prob}\ (Y = j) = \frac{e^{\beta_j' x}}{1 + \sum_{k=0}^{10} e^{\beta_k' x}} \tag{8.2}$$

$$\text{Prob}\ (y = 0) = \frac{1}{1 + \sum_{k=0}^{10} e^{\beta_k' x}} \tag{8.3}$$

As the parameters of one group are set equal to 0, the coefficients for the remaining groups are difficult to interpret. Since the coefficients are conditional upon the fact that for one group they are 0, they reveal the relative impact rather than the absolute effect. Therefore, we need to calculate the marginal effects of the regressors on the probabilities:

$$\frac{\partial P_j}{\partial X_j} = P_j(1 - P_j)\beta \tag{8.4}$$

$$\frac{\partial P_j}{\partial X_k} = -P_j P_k \beta \tag{8.5}$$

We noted large variations in occupations across zones, age groups, sexes, levels of education attained and migration status. These variables are therefore included in specifying the model for occupational choice. As previously mentioned, the appropriate specification in this context is a multinomial logit model, as the dependent variable is qualitative. As parameters for all the subgroups cannot be estimated, the occupation group 8 has been used as the reference category; that is, parameters for this group have been set to 0.

Other variables introduced in the model are caste, household size, asset and network. Variables such as age (AGE), household size (HHSZ) and duration of migration (DMIG) are taken in terms of their actual values. The remaining variables are taken mostly in the form of dummies. GEND is the gender dummy, representing 0 for males and 1 for females. There are seven zones for which six zone dummies (zone 1 to zone 6) have been introduced. CAST1 takes a value of 1 for the scheduled caste (low caste) population, and for the rest, 0. The dummy for education (EDUC1) makes a distinction between illiterate workers (0) and literate workers (1) including those who have attained higher levels of education. The dummy, ASSET represents whether households have land for cultivation and/or a house, with a value of 1, 0 otherwise.

In order to capture the impact of networks, we have introduced three dummies. NETWORK1 takes a value of 1 for individuals who received help from relatives (immediate relatives, spouse's relatives and general relatives) and 0 for the rest; NETWORK2 captures the impact of help received from co-villagers, members of the same caste groups, community fellows and friends, taking a value of 1 for them and 0 for the rest; NETWORK3 makes a distinction between individuals who received help from employers, NGOs, private companies and leaders (1) and the rest (0). Those who did not receive any help from anyone and mostly depended on their personal efforts to find employment are taken as the reference category in specifying these network dummies.

It may be noted from Table 8.2, that for professionals (OCCPO) both household size and the duration of migration have a negative effect. Workers from larger-size households (HHSZ) are perhaps less endowed with the skills required to graduate to better jobs. The coefficient of EDUC is positive and highly significant, implying that literate and educated workers are more likely to find professional employment. Incidentally, women have a higher probability of gaining this type of work. NETWORK1 and NETWORK3 (representing the impact of relatives, and NGOs and so on respectively) are highly significant, indicating the existence of both informal and formal flows of information pertaining to the job market. Interestingly, scheduled caste (low caste) workers are less likely to be found in these jobs. Zones 2, 3 and 4 are less likely to conduct such activities or, in other words, these zones are less likely to have slum-dwellers working as professionals.

Among sales workers (OCCP1), CAST shows a negative impact and only NETWORK1 plays a significant role in accessing jobs. Zones 2 and 4 show a lower probability of having sales workers. Women have a higher probability of joining trading activities (OCCP2). Age plays a negative role, meaning that older workers are less likely to participate in this type of work. CAST, again, takes a negative coefficient and EDUC turns out to be positive and highly significant. Relatives again provide an important support in accessing jobs (that is, NETWORK1) and, among various zones, zone 4 shows a lower probability of locating workers in these activities.

It is incorrect to believe that illiterate workers are more likely to be engaged in personal services (OCCP3). Similarly, it is not correct to suggest that workers from larger households are hard-pressed to find a job and therefore land up in personal services employment because entry barriers

Table 8.2 Occupational choice function (estimate: maximum likelihood estimator) multinomial logit model

	OCCP0	OCCP1	OCCP2	OCCP3	OCCP4	OCCP5	OCCP6	OCCP7	OCCP9	OCCP10
EDUC1	1.37	0.05	0.85	0.62	0.72	0.80	0.65	1.82	20.76	1.02
	(4.02)*	(0.25)	(4.00)*	(2.29)**	(2.88)*	(3.25)*	(1.69)***	(3.51)*	(0.004)	(2.70)*
HHSZ	−0.14	0.08	0.07	−0.18	0.02	−0.007	0.14	0.04	−0.01	−0.06
	(−1.87)**	(1.47)***	(1.33)***	(−2.67)*	(0.39)	(−0.13)	(1.74)***	(0.39)	(−0.44)	(−0.70)
DMIG	−0.13	−0.05	0.02	−0.08	−0.01	−0.07	−0.06	0.13	0.004	−0.02
	(−2.58)*	(−1.36)***	(0.58)	(−1.84)**	(−0.24)	(−1.75)***	(−0.90)	(1.65)***	(0.03)	(−0.29)
CAST	−0.50	−0.94	−0.76	−0.12	−0.37	0.55	−1.16	1.24	0.16	−0.37
	(−1.76)**	(−4.41)*	(−3.74)*	(−0.46)	(−1.58)**	(2.19)*	(−3.14)*	(−3.14)*	(0.24)	(−1.12)
GEND	1.34	0.17	0.73	4.40	1.40	1.70	−0.65	1.46	−30.09	0.10
	(2.78)*	(0.39)	(1.90)**	(12.77)*	(3.68)*	(4.69)*	(−0.62)	(2.34)*	(0.001)	(0.13)
AGE	0.005	−0.01	0.03	0.03	0.003	0.05	0.004	0.001	0.06	−0.02
	(0.28)	(−0.83)	(2.96)*	(2.57)*	(0.23)	(3.93)*	(0.18)	(0.03)	(1.52)***	(−1.20)
ASSET	0.68	0.23	0.15	0.04	−0.13	−0.23	−0.21	1.07	18.63	−0.70
	(1.60)***	(0.79)	(0.55)	(0.13)	(−0.43)	(−0.84)	(−0.48)	(1.64)***	(0.003)	(−1.72)***
NETWORK1	1.31	1.19	1.32	1.61	1.45	1.63	0.90	0.69	1.19	1.87
	(3.59)*	(4.34)*	(5.05)*	(4.68)*	(4.60)*	(5.28)*	(2.04)*	(1.42)***	(1.29)	(4.69)*
NETWORK2	−1.13	0.29	−0.18	0.89	0.69	0.72	−0.03	−32.09	1.78	0.22
	(−1.47)***	(0.92)	(−0.54)	(2.44)*	(1.97)*	(1.90)**	(−0.05)	(0.0001)	(2.28)	(0.39)
NETWORK3	1.20	0.04	−0.27	0.61	1.26	1.56	0.17	0.29	−30.55	0.72
	(3.19)*	(0.11)	(−0.76)	(1.59)***	(3.87)*	(5.06)*	(0.32)	(0.51)	(0.0001)	(1.38)***

ZONE1	−0.75	−0.67	−0.53	0.89	−1.66	0.73	−0.43	−0.45	0.85	−1.73
	(−1.38)***	(−1.64)***	(−1.24)	(1.48)***	(−3.81)*	(0.92)	(−0.59)	(−0.62)	(−0.68)	(−2.83)*
ZONE2	−2.01	−0.95	−0.73	−0.05	−1.84	0.82	0.06	−1.17	−0.46	−1.70
	(−2.54)*	(−1.90)**	(−1.43)***	(−0.07)	(−3.32)*	(0.96)	(0.08)	(−1.18)	(−0.35)	(−2.31)*
ZONE3	−1.11	−0.59	−0.45	0.08	−0.74	0.58	−0.87	−32.57	−1.52	−1.18
	(−1.81)**	(−1.34)***	(−1.00)	(0.12)	(−1.71)***	(0.69)	(−1.04)	(0.0001)	(−1.02)	(−1.89)**
ZONE4	−1.53	−1.04	−0.85	0.16	−1.95	0.60	−0.97	−0.65	−0.78	−0.74
	(−2.49)*	(−2.41)*	(−1.88)**	(0.25)	(−4.08)*	(0.73)	(−1.22)	(−0.84)	(−0.63)	(−1.32)
ZONE5	0.03	−0.88	−0.16	0.70	−1.37	1.89	0.21	0.62	−31.53	−1.62
	(0.06)	(−1.79)**	(−0.33)	(1.04)	(−2.71)*	(2.31)*	(0.28)	(0.79)	(0.0001)	(−2.20)*
ZONE6	−0.34	−0.35	0.05	−0.001	−1.06	1.92	−0.88	−0.03	−31.53	−2.04
	(−0.43)	(−0.58)	(0.09)	(−0.001)	(−1.65)***	(2.18)*	(−0.71)	(−0.03)	(0.0001)	(−1.76)**
CONSTANT	−1.25	0.22	−2.02	−3.20	−0.64	−4.56	−2.08	−4.32	−43.20	−0.02
	(−1.34)***	(0.34)	(−3.09)*	(−3.55)*	(−0.89)	(−4.60)*	(−1.90)**	(−3.24)*	(0.0001)	(−0.02)

Notes: OCCP8 is the comparison group.
Figures in parentheses are *t*-ratios.
*, **, and *** represent significant at 5,10 and 20 per cent levels respectively.
Chi-square value is 905.38, which is significant at 1 per cent level.
Pseudo R-square is 0.17.
No. of observations = 1258.

are mostly absent in these activities. Women, as expected, have a higher probability of being engaged in these jobs. Corresponding to manufacturing (OCCP4), women workers and literate relative to illiterate workers show a higher probability of finding employment in this area. All three network dummies are highly significant. Zones 1, 2, 4 and 5 are less likely to have workers in the manufacturing sector.

In the case of commercial services (OCCP5) EDUC, CAST, GEND and AGE, all have a positive impact. Relatives represented by NETWORK1 and NGOs and so on represented by NETWORK3 are highly significant. Zones 5 and 6 seem to have a higher probability of locating these workers. It is interesting to note that jobs in activities such as personal services are usually not available to lower-caste individuals, whereas commercial services are less affected by such factors.

In transport (OCCP6), scheduled castes are less likely to be employed. The role of relatives in obtaining these jobs again turns out to be significant. Tailoring and knitting (OCCP7) have a higher probability of employing women rather than men. Scheduled castes are less likely to be engaged in these jobs too, possibly because of the lack of skill. Literate workers have an edge over illiterate workers in joining these occupations. Security workers (OCCP9) mostly access jobs through friends and co-villagers, and repairing workers (OCCP10) through relatives. Being literate offers a higher probability of finding a job in repairing activities. Zones 1, 2 and 5 are less likely to house the repairing workers.

As already mentioned, the parameters in a multinominal logit model are estimated with reference to parameters of a particular category being set to 0. Hence, interpretation is not invariably unambiguous. Therefore, marginal effects have been calculated to confirm the interpretation made on the basis of the estimate of the parameters (see Table 8.3). For construction activity (OCCP8), for which parameters were set to 0, observations can be made on the basis of the marginal effects. Illiterate workers seem to have a high probability of joining these occupations. NETWORK2 plays a positive role, whereas help from relatives shows a negative marginal effect. Zones 2 and 3 seem to have a greater concentration of construction workers.

Apart from the eleven occupational groups, three employment categories have also been considered to run the multinominal logit model. Self-employment (EMP2) category is the comparison group. With an increase in household size, the probability of joining casual employment falls. Long-duration migrants are less likely to be in casual employment – with a rise in the duration of stay they manage to acquire more information on the job market, and hence shift to more stable jobs. Scheduled castes show a larger probability of joining casual employment as compared

Table 8.3 Marginal effects: occupational choice model

Exp. variables	P0	P1	P2	P3	P4	P5	P6	P7	P8	P9	P10
EDUC	0.035886	−0.0852	0.0197	−0.0128	0.0002	0.0090	−0.0022	0.0298	−0.1664	0.1603	0.0115
HHSZ	−0.007237	0.0110	0.0111	−0.0234	0.0029	0.0002	0.0049	0.0012	0.0020	−0.0007	−0.0020
DMIG	−0.005652	−0.0027	0.0075	−0.0074	0.0018	−0.0045	−0.0009	0.0044	0.0067	0.0003	0.0003
CAST	−0.00939	−0.0770	−0.0624	0.0284	−0.0036	0.0962	−0.0265	−0.0246	0.0762	0.0040	−0.0026
GEND	0.076909	0.0296	0.1172	0.5982	0.1365	0.1927	−0.0187	0.0411	0.0147	−0.2402	0.0062
AGE	−0.00047	−0.0030	0.0026	0.0028	−0.0010	0.0037	−0.0003	−0.0003	−0.0031	0.0004	−0.0013
ASSET	0.026218	0.0037	−0.0075	−0.0212	−0.0307	−0.0470	−0.0129	0.0235	−0.0455	0.1474	−0.0342
NETWORK1	0.012734	0.0147	0.0367	0.0720	0.0352	0.0605	−0.0056	−0.0105	−0.2463	0.0009	0.0302
NETWORK2	−0.026897	0.1178	0.0667	0.2042	0.1230	0.1478	0.0194	−0.8490	0.1456	0.0193	0.0325
NETWORK3	0.054753	−0.0206	−0.0692	0.0547	0.0985	0.1485	−0.0008	0.0024	−0.0453	−0.2460	0.0198
ZONE1	−0.026978	−0.0531	−0.0400	0.1538	−0.1303	0.1084	−0.0054	−0.0053	0.0593	−0.0047	−0.0559
ZONE2	−0.081616	−0.0543	−0.0295	0.0638	−0.1222	0.1464	0.0188	−0.0174	0.1204	0.0005	−0.0446
ZONE3	0.002806	0.0737	0.1042	0.1663	0.0728	0.1898	0.0093	−0.8480	0.2659	−0.0029	−0.0007
ZONE4	−0.05571	−0.0670	−0.0482	0.0910	−0.1327	0.1216	−0.0144	−0.0035	0.1189	−0.0021	−0.0084
ZONE5	0.015582	−0.0805	0.0136	0.1270	−0.1039	0.2325	0.0149	0.0234	0.0569	−0.2503	−0.0525
ZONE6	−0.00241	−0.0064	0.0520	0.0400	−0.0711	0.2420	−0.0186	0.0073	0.0685	−0.2484	−0.0662
CONSTANT	0.032736	0.2643	−0.0255	−0.1819	0.1124	−0.2956	−0.0075	−0.0670	0.4229	−0.3308	0.0694

Note: P0 to P10 stands for probabilities for each of the occupations OCCP0 to OCCP10.

to the non-scheduled class. Similarly, women workers show a higher probability of taking up these jobs compared to men. Both NETWORK2 and NETWORK3 play a positive role in accessing this category of employment. All the six zone specific dummies have positive coefficients and they are significant.

In the case of regular wage/salaried employment (EMP1), it is surprising to note that literate workers have a lower probability of gaining such employment. This is possibly because these jobs are in the lower spectrum of the income ladder, and hence literate/educated workers have a lower preference for these jobs. Women are less likely to find regular-wage employment. The age factor also reduces its probability. Scheduled castes show a greater likelihood of finding regular employment. NETWORK1 is highly significant but it is negatively related to EMP1. NETWORK3 takes a positive coefficient, though it is significant only at 20 per cent. Across space, Zone 1 and Zone 2 are indicative of a higher probability of holding these salaried or regular-wage jobs.

Having assets in terms of cultivable land and/or their own house is also an important determinant of occupational/employment choice. For example, in the equations for OCCP0 and OCCP7, ASSET takes a positive coefficient, though it is not highly significant. However, people with assets are less likely to join the repair work sector. In the equation for EMP0, ASSET is again positive and significant, indicating that people with assets prefer the risk of taking up employment of an unstable type.

On the whole, findings tend to support our hypothesis that the urban labour market is highly segmented in nature and that a great deal of information on the urban job market flows through informal channels. Different regions within the city offer different work opportunities and workers, depending upon their location and information base, access these jobs through various networks. In this sense, a mismatch between supply of and demand for labour does exist across activities and across regions: though jobs at a higher wage may be available in a specific area, job-seekers may not seek them out if their contacts do not happen to be employed in these regions (and activities). However, the brighter side of the story is that, in the absence of informal networks, the outcome would have been much worse than the existing situation. The informal networks in the face of the diverse economic structure of the city are indeed the coping mechanisms for the low-income households.

Earnings

Earnings per month vary considerably across occupations and employment categories with large gender differentials (Table 8.4). The average

Table 8.4 Average earnings (Rs/-) per month by occupation and employment type

Occupation groups	Male	Female	Persons
Professional	2873.8	2250	2801.0
	(1912.9)	(975.04)	(1834.97)
Sales	2110.5	1295	2039.5
	(1233.9)	(842.1)	(1227.2)
Trade	2767	1616.1	2679.1
	(2802.4)	(828.7)	(2718.9)
Personal service	1955.2	952.7	1178.1
	(2468.7)	(4615.5)	(1297.4)
Manufacturing	2201.8	1745.8	2131
	(1743.5)	(1391.4)	(1696.4)
Commercial service	3441.3	2862.4	3331.4
	(2160.9)	(1882.0)	(2116.5)
Transport	2653.8	2750	2656.3
	(1087.4)		(1073.5)
Tailoring, knitting	2472.5	1200	2322.5
	(1302.5)	(697.6)	(1307.0)
Construction	2127.9	1466.2	2088.9
	(774.5)	(467.2)	(775.2)
Security	2254.8	–	2254.8
	(649.5)		(649.5)
Repair	2381.9	2000	2366
	(1306.3)	(1414.2)	(1297.1)
Employment category			
Casual employment	2597	1360	2214
	(1545.0)	(1204.5)	(1556.3)
Regular wage/salaried	2164	1357	2090
	(1384.8)	(571.8)	(1350.9)
Self-employment	2620	1583	2529
	(2372.5)	(796.6)	(2296.9)

Note: Figures in parentheses are standard deviations.

income of self-employed workers is highest among both males and females. While among male workers, earnings from self-employment are only marginally higher than their counterparts in casual jobs, for women workers the differences are quite significant. As women tend to combine household activity with income-yielding activity, self-employed women workers are better off. It is interesting to note that in casual jobs the average earnings of women are almost half those of male earnings. Across occupations, male workers in commercial services, professional jobs, trade and transport are relatively better off. Differences in female–male earnings corresponding to professionals, sales workers, trading, personal services and tailoring are noteworthy.

The earnings function estimated in Table 8.4 includes age, $(age)^2$, education, caste, networks, zones, duration of migration and occupational classes (alternatively, employment categories). EDUC1 is positively significant. Both age and $(age)^2$ have positive and negative signs respectively, implying that earnings increase with age up to a threshold level. Network dummies, unlike in the equation for occupational choice, do not turn out to be significant in the earnings function. But this is understandable because networks help secure jobs rather than decide the level of income. Women receive a lower wage as compared with males, and it is statistically significant. Several of the occupation dummies and the zone specific dummies do not turn out to be significant. Possibilities of similar earnings in different occupation categories at the individual level cannot be ruled out as low-productivity activities exist across occupations and zones.

Conclusion

In this chapter we have focused on questions relating to occupational choice, networks and physical segmentation of the labour market. Our analysis is indicative of associations among occupation categories (employment categories) and several individual attributes, such as education, migration status, assets, networks and the preference to reside near the workplace. Certain occupations (or employment categories) are typically characterized by the presence of certain groups of individuals, indicating the significance of factors such as gender and/or caste in the urban labour market. Two important findings relate to the significance of network dummies and zone specific dummies in the equations for occupational choice.

The interconnections between networks (and the nature of the network) and types of occupation are noteworthy. While certain occupations are accessed through relatives (NETWORK1), certain others are acquired through co-villagers, friends and so on. (NETWORK2) and certain other occupations are secured through more formal contacts such as NGOs and so on (NETWORK3), though in certain occupations multiple networks do operate simultaneously. On the whole, occupation and network are all in a relationship governed by factors such as caste, gender, migration status and education, depending on which the nature of contacts and the access to information pertaining to the job market is determined. However, in our analysis the networks are treated as exogenously given. Although it is not uncommon to note that the informal networks play a major role in securing employment in the urban informal sector, the intricacies and the subtle forms of mechanism that operate in the urban labour market are of significant interest – without an understanding of these existing modes of operation policy, suggestions for the betterment of the urban poor would be incomplete, and possibly also misleading. In suggesting policies for the urban poor or the informal sector workers, the importance of the informal institutions, which have been in operation as a matter of social and cultural practices, needs to be recognized. By recognizing these coping mechanisms, policy interventions can be suggested that would be supportive in nature, such policies being more cost effective compared with direct interventions.

The contours of associations as mentioned above, however, need to be understood in the perspective of the diverse nature of activities across space, reflecting the heterogeneity of the socio-economic structure of the city. In other words, interconnections between individual endowment, preference for type of occupation and its ultimate selection reflect themselves in the intra-city variation in population concentration, dwelling structure and congestion, given the spatial variation in the nature of economic activities conducted within the city. Our second finding relating to the zone specific dummies is suggestive of such tendencies. That workers in certain activities are located in certain areas rather than in all areas is indicative of strong differences in the city's socio-economic structure across space, broad overlaps between the place of work and the place of residence of these low-income households, and thus the physical segmentation of the urban labour market. That not all slums are of the same type, and hence the problems they face could be quite diverse in nature, is borne out by such patterns. Policy measures for the improvement of slum dwellers' lives do not however seem to have considered these aspects. Next, we offer a brief review of the government-sponsored programmes in urban slums.

The earliest attempt made in the context of public housing was the social housing scheme introduced in the First Plan, followed by the integrated subsidized housing sector for industrial workers and economically-weaker sections in 1952 and the low-income group housing scheme in 1954. In the context of the growth of slums, the first attack was made in 1956 – the Slum Clearance Scheme or Slum Area Act, 1956, which, due to its failure, had to follow a different line from clearance to improvement. The scheme for the environmental improvement of slums was formulated in 1972 – extending its scope in 1978 to cover all urban areas. Amenities provided under the scheme were water supply, sewerage, community baths and latrines, streetlights and widening and paving of lanes.

In the Fifth Five-Year Plan, the Integrated Urban Development Programme, along with the Integrated Development of Small and Medium Towns, was introduced to implement land acquisition, development and disposal programmes, urban renewal and redevelopment projects and provision of urban infrastructure, though it was never evaluated seriously. The Sixth Five-Year Plan also recognized the poor environmental conditions and lack of sanitation in the slums, and attached considerable importance to the programmes concerning the provision of basic amenities and purification of slum areas, endorsing the United Nations organization and UN General Assembly proclamation of 1987 as being the International Year of Shelter for the Homeless.

On the whole, most of the policies and programmes formulated up until the Sixth Five Year Plan at the earliest revolved solely around the issue of housing shortage or the scarcity of shelter-cum-basic amenities. But, even then, they suffered several major difficulties due to faulty land policy, shortage of resources and, moreover, poor performance in implementing the objectives. After the Sixth Five-Year Plan, government measures may broadly be divided into two categories: (a) policies designed to improve the condition of housing and basic amenities in the slums; and (b) employment programmes. The Seventh Five-Year Plan attached importance to (a) provision of gainful employment to women and youth; (b) raising the earnings of those in low-paid jobs; and (c) stepping up the productivity and earnings of self-employed workers, though not much was pursued at that point. The Nehru Rozgar Yojana with its three components – Micro Enterprises, Wage Employment, and Shelter Upgrading – was not initiated until 1989. The first Central Government scheme was not formulated until September 1986 – that is, the Self-Employment Programme for the Urban Poor (SEPUP); however, this only offered limited coverage. The National Commission on Urbanisation (1988) came up with two sets of policy suggestions for improving the conditions of the urban poor and slum dwellers: (a) the Programme for Enhancement of Income and Employment Opportunities; and (b) the Extension of Basic Services. Although the suggestions were mainly aimed at augmenting the earnings of the informal sector workers, no mention was made about raising the demand for informal activities either directly or through the intersectoral linkages.

The Eighth Five-Year Plan also laid considerable emphasis on the generation of adequate employment, containment of population growth through the active cooperation of people, and provision of safe drinking water and primary health care facilities. Considerable emphasis was laid on the Nehru Rozgar Yojana, and the existing schemes of SEPUP. It was proposed to implement Self-Employment for Educated Unemployed Youth on a large scale. Another aim was to introduce a wage policy in the urban informal sector to reduce the differences between formal–informal sector earnings. However, enforcement of minimum wage legislation was difficult to implement in the informal sector, partly because of the heterogeneous nature of this sector. Besides, it was feared that such a policy would reduce the waged employment in this sector.

The Nineth Five Year Plan also noted that the problem of urban poverty was due to the lack of productive employment and thus income, a high rate of inflation and the inadequacy of the social infrastructure, which affect both the quality of life of individuals and their employability. Some of the programmes that have been launched relatively recently, or have been given a new orientation to provide more opportunities to involve the poor in the economic process, include the urban poverty-alleviation programmes such as Nehru Rozgar Yojana, Urban Basic Services for the Poor and the Prime Minister's Integrated Urban Poverty Eradication Programme, included in Swarna Jayanti Shahari Rozgar Yojana, launched in December 1997.

Although the issue of employment in the urban context has been given importance in recent years, much more needs to be done at ground level. The share of urban informal sector employment is on the rise, and employment schemes have not been implemented on a large scale in all types of cities and towns. To define the framework of policy for dealing with this sector, one has to recognize its vast heterogeneity. The growing needs of skill development, technology transfer and marketing of products are to be given priority in order to upgrade this sector. This, however, needs to be done without trying to convert it into the formal sector; the elements of informality, which often encourage employment growth in this sector, need to be retained while trying to improve productivity levels. An important feature that follows on from our analysis is that low-income households themselves are actively involved in improving their conditions, and in their attempt to do so they try to take advantage of all resources and networks that are available to them. Even the biggest investors in low-income housing are the poor themselves, as noted by the Global Report on Human Settlements (2001): they manage to find land in the city with their limited resources, invest in housing, negotiate for services and secure land tenure. Policy directives need to recognize some of these efforts, which not only would reduce the burden on the public exchequer but also deal with the problems of slums, basic amenities and poverty more efficiently. Instead of the government always being directly involved in the process of generating employment on a large scale in the informal sector, measures that are protective of and supportive to the efforts made by the low income households can be pursued to enable them to attain their goals. The social capital that individuals in the low income strata have evolved holds prospects for them to receive the beneficial effects of growth, even when the possibility of graduating from the informal to the formal sector is remote.

Note

With the financial support from the Development Economics Research Group (V. Rao and M. Woolcock), World Bank, Washington, DC, the survey was carried out in Delhi slum households by the Institute of Economic Growth under the World Bank-sponsored project Urban Poverty, Social Capital and Risk Management. The author is grateful to the editors of this volume for their constructive comments.

References

Banerjee, B. (1986) *Rural to Urban Migration and the Urban Labour Market* (Bombay: Himalaya Publishing House).

Banerjee, B. and G.A. Bucci (1994) 'On the Job Search after Entering Urban Employment: An Analysis Based on Indian Migrants', *Oxford Bulletin of Economics and Statistics*, 56(1): 33–47.

Dupont, V. and A. Mitra (1995) 'Population Distribution, Growth and Socio-Economic Spatial Patterns in Delhi: Findings from the 1991 Census Data', *Demography India*, 24(1): 101–32.

Global Report on Human Settlements (2001) *Cities in a Globalizing World, United Centres for Human Settlements (Habitat)* (London: Earthscan).

Gupta, I. and A. Mitra (2002) 'Rural Migrants and Labour Segmentation: Micro-Level Evidence from Delhi Slums', *Economic and Political Weekly*, 37(2): 163–8.

Henderson, J.V. (1988) *Urban Development: Theory, Fact and Illusion* (New York: Oxford University Press).

Mitra, A. (1994) *Urbanisation, Slums, Informal Sector Employment and Poverty: An Exploratory Study* (Delhi: B.R. Publishing).

Mitra, A. (2003) *Occupational Choices, Networks and Transfers: An Exegesis Based on Micro Data from Delhi Slums* (New Delhi: Manohar).

National Commission on Urbanisation (1988) 'Report of the National Commission on Urbanisation' (Government of India).

Papola, T.S. (1981) *Urban Informal Sector in a Developing Economy* (Delhi: Vikas).

Shaw, A. (1990) 'Linkages of Large-Scale, Small Scale and Informal Sector Industries: A Study of Thana-Belapur', *Economic and Political Weekly*, 25(7/8): M-17–M-23.

9

Inter- and Intra-household Linkages between the Informal and Formal Sectors: A Case Study for Urban Burkina Faso

Michael Grimm and Isabel Günther

Introduction

The role of the informal sector in the process of economic development was quite a popular question throughout the 1970s when, among others, the International Labour Office started to undertake studies focused specifically on this segment of the labour market (ILO, 1972). Given the current focus of international development policy on pro-poor growth, and given the fact that the informal sector is generally being considered as the economy of the poor, a key question is whether pro-poor growth policies have to address the informal sector specifically or if the informal sector evolves as does the rest of the economy and, therefore, good growth policies are also good informal sector policies. To answer this question, it is important to understand the linkages between the informal sector and the rest of the economy. The importance of understanding such linkages has been emphasized by various authors (see, for example, Tokman, 1978; Hemmer and Mannel, 1989; Harriss, 1990; Xaba *et al.*, 2002) but, so far, not much empirical research has been undertaken.

Here, we limit our analysis to linkages between the informal and the formal sectors in the urban economy. In the empirical element of this chapter, we examine Burkina Faso, one of the poorest countries in the world. Real GDP per capita was estimated at only US$ 384 in 2004. On the basis of its Human Development Index, the country was ranked 175 out of 177 countries (UNDP, 2004). In terms of household expenditure per capita, 47.2 per cent of the rural and 20.3 per cent of the urban population could be considered as poor in 2003 (Grimm and Günther, 2006). Although Burkina Faso knew considerable economic growth throughout the 1990s, with a rather moderate increase of the urban population, Burkina Faso had to support a strong increase in urban poverty. The question is whether we can explain part of this development with the relationship that exists between informal and formal sector earnings. During this period, real formal earnings stagnated, and in some cases even decreased, as wages in the formal sector were not indexed to inflation after the devaluation of the CFA Franc in 1994. If linkages between the formal and informal sector exist, these decreasing real earnings in the formal sector might have driven down wages in the informal sector and, as a result, increased urban poverty. We argue that such linkages between the formal and informal sectors can exist on a macro (market) as well as on a micro (household) level. How formal and informal sector earnings are linked on macro and micro levels, can be determined by both the product market and the factor market.

This chapter is organized as follows. In the next section, we briefly review the literature on linkages between the formal and informal sector in developing economies and, based on this, develop some research hypotheses. The subsequent section presents our data sources. We then analyze whether, and to what magnitude, formal and informal sector earnings are linked on a macro level by looking at inter-household linkages. This is followed by a section in which we consider intra-household linkages. The chapter closes with a conclusion in which we draw some policy implications with respect to pro-poor growth.

Linkages between the formal and informal sectors

There has been much controversy as to how the informal sector should be defined, or whether it can be defined at all, given its heterogeneity. For the following discussion it is, however, sufficient to keep a rather simple definition in mind, which considers economic activities as informal whenever they cannot be classified under the organizational standards of industrialized countries.

The theoretical concept of the informal sector can be seen as an expansion of the dual economy or dichotomy literature originating in Lewis (1954) and Todaro (1969), with the informal sector traditionally being considered as the 'residual sector' of a segmented urban labour market (Fields, 1974; Mazumdar, 1976). The reasons given for this dualism or segmentation of urban labour markets, with apparently homogenous workers being paid different wages depending on the sector of the economy in which they are employed, basically fall into two explanatory categories; institutional and market (Stiglitz, 1974) explanations, of which the former dominates most writings and discussions. As a result, for a long time empirical research on the informal sector, with the ILO Kenya mission report (ILO, 1972) and Hart (1973) probably being the first prominent works, has focused on static comparisons of earnings differentials (Maloney, 1997), which tended to support the theory of segmented labour markets and considered the informal sector more or less as an isolated segment of the economy.

Hence, the first linkages that were analyzed were top-down relationships within the labour market (formal to informal). Here, it is usually assumed that formal sector size and wages are exogenously fixed, and that a function of both determines the extent of rural–urban migration. Informal sector size is then defined as the labour surplus that cannot be absorbed by the urban formal economy (Fields, 1974). Hence, the size of the informal sector expands with the size (and wages) of the formal sector. But given that informal sector income is shared among an 'ever growing' informal sector labour force competing in the same market, this leads to ever diminishing informal sector earnings (Mazumdar, 1976). Besides this relationship, sector dichotomy is assumed, with the informal sector being a more or less autonomous segment with few linkages to the rest of the economy. Evidently this also means that, most of the time, these early writings assumed strict dualism in the product market (Livingstone, 1971; Harriss, 1990), where the formal and informal sectors produce and offer similar goods but at different price levels, serving different markets, segmented by different income categories. With the demand for informal products mainly coming from the informal sector, one of the reasons given for the low potential of the informal sector is its poor 'informal' customer base (Harriss, 1990).

However, today there seems to be broad consensus that the informal and formal product markets are densely interlinked on various levels. A useful framework for analysis seems to be the distinction between complementary, competitive and indifferent markets (Van Dijk, 1980) on the one hand, and between final product and intermediate product markets (Harriss, 1990) or forward and backward linkages (Xaba *et al.*, 2002) on the other hand. A good example for complementary markets is commercial subcontracting, where the informal sector is selling products created in the formal sector. Competitive markets occur in the case where the two sectors compete within the same product market, their respective market share being determined by sector product prices (Hemmer and Mannel, 1989) and/or real sector wages (Cogneau *et al.*, 1996). Finally, markets might be neither complementary nor competitive (Sethuraman, 1997), with the two sectors coexisting in different product markets (but with an overlapping formal–informal customer base).

In sub-Saharan Africa (SSA) there seem to be strong inter-linkages in the final product market, with each sector being a strong supply as well as demand base of the other sector (Charmes, 1996; Xaba *et al.*, 2002), with rising wages leading to a lower propensity to consume informal sector goods (Lachaud, 1990). However, whereas forward linkages (markets beyond the borders of the respective sectors) are strong for both sectors, backward linkages (inputs from beyond the respective sectors) only seem to be significant from the informal to the formal sector; that is, the informal sector buys many of its inputs from the formal sector, but backward linkages from the formal to the informal sector are of little importance (Harriss, 1990). As a result, linkages on the product market seem to be very strong between formal and informal households but rather weak between formal and informal enterprises.

With this new understanding of the linkages on the product market, a new light is shed on the relationship between formal and informal labour markets. The traditional view suggests that informal employment, absorbing rural–urban migration surplus and off-setting economic shocks, would show a counter-cyclical pattern (that is, expanding in size in economic downturns and contracting in economic up-swings), with average informal earnings being negatively related to informal sector size (Charmes, 1990). Also, earlier writings, which explain at least part of the existence of the informal sector as a result of institutions setting formal wages above market clearing prices, would support the argument that higher formal wages generally lead to a larger informal sector with lower informal wages. However, taking the complementary as well as competitive product linkages into account, the described theory does not necessarily have to be true. In fact, Maloney (2003) shows, that informal sector size, depending on the country studied, might react both pro- as well as anti-cyclical, with average informal earnings diminishing or growing.

In addition, recent empirical evidence of urban labour markets in developing countries has also contradicted the earlier concepts of the informal sector labour size and earnings; and hence, also, its relationship to the formal sector. The most important criticism of earlier studies is that the heterogeneity of the informal sector is not appropriately taken into account. Earnings of the informal sector workers are lower on average than earnings in the formal sector, but a considerable overlap of the two distributions still exists. Charmes (1990) therefore distinguishes between the low wage or 'lower-tiers' and high wage or 'upper-tiers' informal sector.

This distinction has some similarities with the 'involuntary entry' and 'voluntary entry' informal sector concept of Maloney (2003), and the primary and secondary (in relation to the structure of household income) informal activity concept mentioned by Lachaud (1990). This heterogeneity might also imply that the various informal sector subgroups are linked to the formal sector quite differently (Blunch *et al.*, 2001; Charmes, 1996).

There has also been criticism that most of the empirical work analyzing the nature of the informal sector and its inter-linkages with the formal sector used enterprises or individuals as the observation unit. However, as Lachaud (1990) states, in the context of SSA, households would be a much more useful unit of observation by which to understand the functioning of urban labour markets. Many households in SSA are engaged in both the formal and informal sectors (Blunch *et al.*, 2001), and the sector of employment of the head of the household may have considerable influence on the labour supply and sector choice of other household members (Lachaud, 1990; Pradhan and Soest, 1997). Charmes (1990) also emphasizes the importance of intra-household transfers. For the case of west Africa, Azam (2004) finds evidence for high investment by formal sector employees into informal enterprises. He also claims that, on average, 40 people are supported by one formal sector income.

In sum, drawing on this literature, our hypothesis is that urban informal and formal sector earnings are linked on a macro (market) level as well as on a micro (household) level. The observed linkage effect can be determined by both the product and factor market. However, in this study we only focus on analyzing whether, and to what magnitude, informal and formal labour earnings are linked. We leave a more detailed empirical analysis of the driving forces behind the observed linkage effects for future research. Given our primary interest in propoor growth, we argue that households and not enterprises or individuals should be used as an observation unit for both the macro as well as the micro level and therefore analyze inter- as well as intra-household linkages.

Data sources

We use three household surveys undertaken by the Burkinabé Institut National de la Statistique et de la Démographie (INSD) and the World Bank in 1994 (EPI), 1998 (EPII) and 2003 (EPIII). The respective sample sizes are 8642 (2718), 8478 (2593) and 8500 (2600) households (the figures given in parentheses indicate the number of urban households).

These surveys contain socio-economic information about households and their members, data on employment, wages, agricultural and non-agricultural activity and profits, housing, expenditures, and certain assets possessed by the households. For a detailed description of the data, see Grimm and Günther (2006). (EP = *enquête prioritorie*: priority survey.)

In order to identify workers in the informal sector, we proceed in three steps. First, we limit the potentially active population to individuals older than 14 years. This seems a reasonable and practical assumption for urban areas. Children below that age working occasionally, or even regularly, present a very heterogeneous group. The inclusion of children in our study would mix our research focus with issues regarding child labour. Second, we determine occupational status (that is, 'occupied', 'unemployed' (self-declared), 'student' and 'inactive'), using the corresponding questions in the surveys. Third, we determine for the occupied individuals the type of activity they carry out. We distinguish between 'wage-earners in the public sector', 'wage earners in the private formal sector', 'informal workers', 'individuals working as family help' and 'other non-remunerated workers and trainees'. The last two groups can, to a large extent, be seen as a subgroup of the informal sector.

Whether somebody works in the public sector or as a family help, trainee or non-remunerated worker is directly observed in all three surveys. To separate wage-earners in the private formal sector from informal workers, we proceed as follows. In 1994 and 1998, we classify declared 'wage-earners in the private sector' as 'wage-earners in the private formal sector' and declared 'independent workers' and 'employers' as 'informal workers'. Of course, the risk here is classifying informal dependent workers as formal workers and, vice versa, formal employers as informal workers. We checked our classification using information on social security, labour contracts and the existence of firms and non-farm profits in the households involved. It turns out that our procedure works quite well and that there should be very few misclassifications. For 2003, we know whether the employer of an occupied person is a 'private enterprise' or 'a single individual or household'. In addition, we know whether this individual is a 'white collar', 'skilled blue collar', 'unskilled blue collar' or 'independent worker'. To achieve consistency with 1994 and 1998, we define 'independent working individuals' in 'private firms' or 'households' as 'informal workers'. The remainder is defined as 'wage-earners in the formal sector'. Table 9.1 describes the resulting occupation and employment structure of the urban population for the three years covered by the household surveys.

Table 9.1 Occupation and employment of the urban adult population (15 years and older), in percentages

	1994	1998	2003
Occupied	53.2	58.7	58.2
of whom:			
(1) Public wage earner	12.8	12.3	12.7
(2) Private formal wage earner	13.6	16.8	17.0
(3) Independent (informal)	41.3	(37.5)	40.6
(4) Family help	25.6	(29.0)	21.7
(5) Non-remunerated (outside family)	6.8	4.4	8.1
of whom (*only categories 1–3*):			
Permanent contract	85.9	91.2	75.5
Seasonal	6.3	3.5	13.8
Daily	1.8	0.9	8.8
Other temporary	6.0	4.5	1.9
Unemployed (open)	8.9	9.4	12.8
Enrolled in school/university	14.3	14.5	13.5
Inactive	23.7	17.4	15.5

Source: EPI, EPII and EPIII; computations by the authors.
Notes: Occupation and activity concerns those carried out the seven days before the survey. However, we computed the same statistics for the main activity over the preceding 12 months; the results were not significantly different. Numbers in parentheses signify that we presume strong measurement error.
The dependency ratio is computed over households; it is defined as the number of inactive and unemployed persons divided by the household size.

Inter-household linkages between informal and formal earnings

Research hypotheses and methodology

In a first step, we try to analyze whether, and to what extent, informal and formal earnings are linked on a macro level. We therefore try to test whether higher formal earnings lead to higher informal earnings. It could be thought that such causal relationships would be specific to some local markets, especially in a country like Burkina Faso, where one can observe a relatively high spatial segmentation of the economy with relatively low spill over effects across regions (see Grimm and Günther, 2006). This means, that such linkages could be examined on the basis of spatially defined clusters: villages, provinces or regions. However, when pursuing such a spatial analysis, the problem arises as to how one can disentangle the effect of formal earnings from the effects of local characteristics. More precisely, in case we find a spatial correlation between formal and informal earnings, we should test between three competing hypotheses:[1]

1 Formal and informal earnings are correlated because linkages exist between formal and informal earnings;
2 Formal and informal earnings are correlated because both depend on unobserved household characteristics, and people with similar characteristics concentrate spatially (free household mobility assumed). Under this circumstance, formal and informal earnings can be correlated, but there is no direct causal link between them; both depend on third variables; that is, the local socio-economic population structure;
3 Formal and informal earnings are correlated because both depend, first of all, on geographic endowments such as ecological conditions, or the supply of local public goods and infrastructure determining both formal and informal earnings. Again, under these circumstances formal and informal earnings can be correlated, but there is no direct causal link between them: both depend on third variables.

Empirically, it is not easy to distinguish between these three competing hypotheses. In a first step, therefore, we simply regress household-specific informal earnings, Π_h^{IF}, on observed individual and household characteristics, X_h, including the number of persons involved in the informal activity, L_h, and the 'local' level of formal earnings, Π_P^F. As 'local', we define here the average within provinces. Urban households are clustered in 16 provinces in 1994, and 19 in 1998. Unfortunately, for 2003 the province of residence cannot be identified; therefore we have to take region specific variables. The equation to estimate reads in logarithmic form as follows:

$$\log \Pi_h^{IF} = \alpha \log L_h + \beta X_h + \gamma \log \Pi_P^F + u_h \qquad (9.1)$$

where u_h is the unexplained residual. This regression involves the problem that the OLS estimates of the coefficient γ of formal earnings can be biased due to the two issues discussed above: (i) unobserved heterogeneity in individual and province specific household characteristics correlated with formal earnings; and (ii) unobserved local endowments correlated with formal earnings. To solve this problem, we would need panel data. This would allow us to make an estimation in differences cancelling out the effect of local population patterns and geographic endowments, supposing that they are more or less constant over a ten year period.

Given the absence of panel data for Burkina Faso, the best we can do is to control as far as possible for province-specific characteristics, and to compare the coefficient γ with the coefficient we obtain if, instead of the province average of formal earnings, we use the province average of non-labour income or total income less informal earnings.[2] Given that it may not be assumed that the sample of households involved in the informal sector is representative for the whole sample of households, we control for this potential selection bias using a selection model in the spirit of Heckman (1979), but estimated via the maximization of the full likelihood. As the dependent variable, we use the log of household informal earnings per capita. We include in the estimation equation the gender, age and education of the head of the household, the log of the declared number of employed persons, and dummy variables indicating whether there is a person in the household working in the public or private formal sector.

Results

All control variables in our estimation have the expected sign and are relatively stable over time (see Table 9.2). An increase of the labour force employed in the household's informal business by 100 per cent increases the per capita informal earnings by 45–60 per cent. Households headed by a man have, on average, higher earnings. The age of the household head is not significant, but age effects are partly captured by the household size and education variables. The log of household size has, as expected, a negative sign. Whereas some, or completed, primary education has no significant effect on earnings, lower and higher secondary education, as well as some technical education, has a significant and positive impact. Knowledge of French also enters positively in the estimation equation. The dummy variables indicating whether there is a person in the household working in the public or private formal sector are both negative, showing that households drawing income from the formal economy are less involved in the informal economy and therefore have lower per capita informal earnings.

The effect of the log of the province-specific average of formal earnings (per capita) has a significant and positive effect on informal earnings. However, the 'linkage coefficient' is smaller than 1, and if we put the average of non-labour income (mainly income from certain agricultural activity and transfers) or of total household income less informal earnings in the estimation equation, we also find a positive impact and an even higher regression coefficient. More precisely, whereas a 1 per cent increase in formal earnings increases informal earnings by 0.16–0.20

Table 9.2 Estimation of informal earning functions (urban areas only, selection model (full maximum likelihood estimator), 1994, 1998, 2003)

Dependent variable log of household informal earnings per capita	(1)		(2)		(3)		(4)		(5)		(6)	
1994												
Log # workers[a]	0.506	***	0.509	***	0.509	***	0.508	***	0.548	***	0.518	***
Head male	0.235	**	0.241	**	0.235	**	0.238	**	0.194	*	0.225	**
Age of head	−0.003		−0.005		−0.004		−0.004		−0.003		−0.006	
Squared age of head	0.123		0.272		0.180		0.248		0.101		0.398	
Log household-size	−0.759	***	−0.753	***	−0.756	***	−0.755	***	−0.754	***	−0.746	***
Education level of household head												
No schooling	Ref.		Ref.		Ref.		Ref.		Ref.		Ref.	
Some primary education	−0.033		−0.041		−0.034		−0.036		−0.025		−0.024	
Primary education completed	−0.021		−0.037		−0.026		−0.032		−0.045		−0.041	
Some or completed low secondary	0.517	***	0.499	***	0.510	***	0.505	***	0.527	***	0.513	***
Some or completed high secondary	1.497	***	1.480	***	1.488	***	1.483	***	1.462	***	1.473	***
Technical education	0.416	*	0.363		0.415	*	0.382		0.447	*	0.374	
Head speaks/writes French	0.675	***	0.689	***	0.675	***	0.681	***	0.686	***	0.688	***
Public worker in household	−0.867	***	−0.863	***	−0.871	***	−0.867	***	−0.886	***	−0.873	***
Private formal worker in household	−0.518	***	−0.537	***	−0.529	***	−0.535	***	−0.574	***	−0.553	***
Province average log formal earnings[b]	0.178	***					0.069		−0.180	**	0.014	

Province average log non-labour income[(b)]			0.483	***			0.329	**				
Province av. log total non-informal income[(b)]					0.310	***						
Province share of formal workers[(b)]									7.382	***		
Province share of informal workers[(b)]											2.902	***
Intercept	10.648	***	7.449	***	8.967	***	8.334	***	13.856	***	12.068	***
rho[(c)]	−0.910	***	−0.903	***	−0.907	***	−0.905	***	−0.893	***	−0.900	***
# of observations	2706		2706		2706		2706		2706		2706	
# of non-censored observations[(d)]	1249		1249		1249		1249		1249		1249	
-Log-likelihood	3808		3806		3805		3805		3794		3802	
1998												
Log # workers[(a)]	0.583	***	0.601	***	0.581	***	0.590	***	0.583	***	0.585	***
Head male	0.502	***	0.474	***	0.498	***	0.481	***	0.502	***	0.499	***
Age of head	0.010		0.007		0.009		0.008		0.010		0.009	
Squared age of head	−1.476		−1.285		−1.388		−1.284		−1.467		−1.395	
Log household-size	−0.933	***	−0.929	***	−0.930	***	−0.926	***	−0.933	***	−0.925	***
Education level household head												
No schooling	Ref.		Ref.		Ref.		Ref.		Ref.		Ref.	
Some primary education	−0.098		−0.115		−0.102		−0.106		−0.098		−0.087	
Primary education completed	−0.228		−0.234		−0.222		−0.227		−0.228		−0.218	

(*Continued*)

Table 9.2 (*Continued*)

Dependent variable log of household informal earnings per capita	(1)		(2)		(3)		(4)		(5)		(6)	
Some or completed low secondary	0.136		0.137		0.141		0.138		0.137		0.147	
Some or completed high secondary	1.007	***	1.042	***	1.012	***	1.024	***	1.006	***	1.017	***
Technical education	0.922	***	0.929	***	0.926	***	0.941	***	0.921	***	0.918	***
Head speaks/writes French	0.490	***	0.520	***	0.490	***	0.496	***	0.490	***	0.486	***
Public worker in household	−1.057	***	−1.061	***	−1.055	***	−1.063	***	−1.057	***	−1.054	***
Private formal worker in household	−0.460	***	−0.420	***	−0.461	***	−0.454	***	−0.461	***	−0.465	***
Province average log formal earnings[(b)]	0.168	***					0.100	***	0.161	**	0.080	
Province average log non-labour income[(b)]			0.785	***			0.568	***				
Province av. log total non-informal income[(b)]					0.355	***						
Province share of formal workers[(b)]									0.096			
Province share of informal workers[(b)]											1.844	*
Intercept	10.388	***	3.994	***	8.106	***	5.171	***	10.453	***	11.165	***
rho[(c)]	−0.897	***	−0.903	***	−0.900	***	−0.901	***	−0.897	***	−0.897	***
# of observations	2583		2583		2583		2583		2583		2583	
# of non-censored observations[(d)]	1300		1300		1300		1300		1300		1300	
-Log-likelihood	3533		3530		3532		3527		3533		3532	

2003												
Log # workers[(a)]	0.456	***	0.449	***	0.455	***	0.453	***	0.454	***	0.450	***
Head male	0.188	*	0.205	*	0.194	**	0.191	**	0.190	**	0.192	**
Age of head	−0.011		−0.009		−0.010		−0.011		−0.011		−0.012	
Squared age of head	0.186		0.076		0.106		0.160		0.199		0.228	
Log household size	−0.803	***	−0.794	***	−0.803	***	−0.801	***	−0.801	***	−0.799	***
Education level household head												
No schooling	Ref.		Ref.		Ref.		Ref.		Ref.		Ref.	
Some primary education	−0.237		−0.226		−0.235		−0.235		−0.238		−0.237	
Head primary completed	−0.001		0.021		0.014		0.005		0.000		−0.002	
Some or completed low secondary	0.214		0.216		0.216		0.214		0.212		0.210	
Some or completed high secondary	1.163	***	1.203	***	1.181	***	1.169	***	1.161	***	1.158	***
Technical education	0.732	**	0.816	***	0.742	**	0.746	**	0.730	**	0.737	**
Head speaks/writes French	0.405	**	0.417	**	0.409	**	0.410	**	0.408	**	0.408	**
Public worker in household	−0.572	***	−0.605	***	−0.581	***	−0.580	***	−0.572	***	−0.578	***
Private formal worker in household	−0.304	***	−0.296	***	−0.310	***	−0.308	***	−0.307	***	−0.306	***
Regional average log formal earnings[(b)]	0.201	***					0.162	***	0.144		0.134	**
Regional average log non-labour income[(b)]			0.528	***			0.156					
Regional av. log total non-informal income[(b)]					0.440	***						
Regional share of formal workers[(b)]									0.934			

(*Continued*)

Table 9.2 (*Continued*)

Dependent variable log of household informal earnings per capita	(1)		(2)		(3)		(4)		(5)		(6)	
Regional share of informal workers[b]											1.281	
Intercept	10.727	***	7.168	***	7.719	***	9.458	***	11.256	***	11.323	***
rho[c]	−0.852	***	−0.863	***	−0.861	***	−0.856	***	−0.853		−0.853	***
# of observations	2556		2556		2556		2556		2556		2556	
# of non-censored observations[d]	1341		1341		1341		1341		1341		1341	
-Log-likelihood	3268		3274		3266		3267		3267		3267	

Source: EPI, EPII and EPIII; estimations by the authors.
Notes: * Coefficient significant at the 10% level.
** Coefficient significant at the 5% level.
*** Coefficient significant at the 1% level.
(a) log of the number of employed workers from inside and outside the household in the informal activity of the household.
(b) The province specific variables are computed without considering the household itself.
(c) *rho* is the correlation coefficient between the residuals of the earnings regression and the selection function. As explanatory variables in the selection function, we use variables for the age and gender composition of the household, knowledge of French, education and age of the head of the household.
(d) Censored households are those who declared not to have had earnings from informal activity.

per cent, a 1 per cent increase in non-labour income increases informal earnings by 0.48–0.79 per cent. If we put formal income and non-labour income together in the estimation equation, we find that the return to the province average of non-labour income is higher in 1994 and 1998. In 2003, the coefficient of non-labour income is not significant. Both income sources are, of course, correlated. The correlation coefficient amounts to 0.77 in 1994, 0.33 in 1998 and 0.46 in 2003.

If, in addition, we control for the province-specific share of workers involved in the formal sector, we find no uniform result across years. In 1994, this share has a huge positive impact on informal earnings; in 1998, the effect of this variable is not significant; and in 2003 both variables, formal earnings and the share of formal workers, are not significant when they enter together in the equation. Likewise, it is not very conclusive if we put the province-specific share of informal workers in the equation. For 1994 and 1998, its effect is strongly positive and outweighs the effect of formal earnings, but for 2003 this variable is not significant.

All this might suggest that the inter-household linkages between informal and formal earnings are positive but rather weak, and it seems that it is the province-specific income level in general that matters most. However, it is also possible that higher formal earnings have a twofold effect on informal earnings. A positive income effect and a negative substitution effect; that is, informal goods are substituted through formal, and often imported, goods. As a result, we might observe a weak positive net effect of formal earnings on informal earnings, although there might indeed be strong linkages but working in different directions. Finally, it should again be emphasized that we have to be very careful with the interpretation of these estimations, given that we cannot appropriately control for the effects of unobserved province specific household characteristics and geographic endowments. We tried to create some variables reflecting features of the provinces such as, for instance, the province-specific age, education and employment structure, and the share of households connected to electricity or modern water facilities, but consideration of these variables in the estimation equation did not yield any reliable results.

Intra-household linkages between the informal and formal sector

Research hypotheses and methodology

In this section, we analyze whether, and to what magnitude, intra-household linkages exist between the informal and formal sectors. Taking into account the socio-economic importance of household units in the SSA context, we consider households as the centre of labour supply decisions and earnings. Our hypothesis is that other household members' activity and earnings have a high impact on individuals' labour participation and earnings in the informal sector. For simplicity, we only distinguish between the head of the household, which we determine by taking the individual with the highest earnings within a household. The 'second order position' is given to all other household members older than 14 years. Concerning the sector of employment, we distinguish only between formal (which includes the private formal, as well as the public sector), informal (which includes self-employment, as well as family help and other non-remunerated work) and non-occupied (which includes unemployed as well as inactive persons).

We start, with a purely descriptive analysis, to determine the working force affected by intra-household linkages; that is, we look how many sectoral 'mixed' households (households where members of that household work in the formal as well as informal sectors) can be found. We then examine how the welfare of people involved in the informal sectors is linked to formal sector earnings (approximated by household expenditure per capita). Given that individuals normally pool their earnings within households and decide jointly on expenditures (the usual unitary model is here assumed), a simple labour-market analysis (only taking into account active individuals) cannot examine this link.

In a second step, we then examine how labour supply and earnings of the formal and informal sectors are linked within those households drawing income from several sources. First, we examine the extent to which labour supply and sector choice are determined by the household head's sector of occupation and earnings. Our hypothesis is that other household members will increase their labour-market participation with decreasing earnings of the household head to maintain the overall household income level – the buffer function of the informal sector via intra-household linkages. In addition, we analyze the impact of the sector of employment of the household head on the sector choice of other household members. Thus, we estimate the following multinomial logit model:

$$\text{Prob}(L_i = j) = [\exp(\lambda_{jX}X_i + \lambda_{jS}S_i^{Head} + \lambda_{jW}\log W_i^{Head})] / [\textstyle\sum_j \exp(\lambda_{jX}X_i + \lambda_{jS}S_i^{Head} + \lambda_{jW}\log W_i^{Head})] \quad (9.2)$$

which gives the empirical probability that individual i takes the occupational choice $L_i = j$, where X_i is a vector of individual and household characteristics, such as age, education and gender. S^{Head} is a vector of dummy variables indicating the sector of employment of the household head and log W^{Head} is the log of monthly earnings of the household head.

In a third step, we analyze the impact of the individual's position in the household and the household head's sector of employment and earnings on other household members' earnings. Evidently, since we define household members with the highest earnings as being the household head, individuals with a secondary household position will have lower earnings. However, the objective is to estimate to what magnitude informal earnings can differ (controlled for observable socio-economic characteristics) if undertaken as a main activity (first household position) or to supplement the main household income (second household position). Further, we test the impact of the household head's sector of employment and earnings on secondary members' earnings. If intra-household investments indeed take place, secondary household members' informal earnings should be higher (controlled for education and experience) if the household head is occupied in the formal sector and can therefore invest more in the informal business of other household members than household heads who are themselves engaged in the informal sector.[3] Hence, we estimate:

$$\log W_i = \beta X_i + \psi C_i + \alpha S_i^{Head} + \gamma \log W_i^{Head} + u_i \qquad (9.3)$$

where log W_i is the log of monthly earnings of person i, X_i are observable individual and household characteristics as before but also include dummy variables for the sector of employment. C_i is a dummy variable taking the value 1 if individual i is not the earner of the main income in his or her household and u_i is the residual. We again control for selection in the group of occupied persons using a selection model. However, we cannot control for unobserved household characteristics that might influence all household members' occupational choices as well as earnings.

Results

Table 9.3 shows that approximately 40 per cent of the total urban population older than 14 years lives in households where the main income comes from the formal sector (public or private). Comparing this figure with the 25 per cent of the active urban population employed in the formal sector suggests that formal sector earnings might play a much more important role in urban household incomes, or well-being, than the sectoral employment structure suggests. In addition, the 25 per cent of urban households that receive labour income from both the formal as well as informal sectors indicates that linkages between the formal and informal sectors in terms of individual well-being might play an important role.

Table 9.3 Sectoral composition of household labour, urban population (15 years and older) in percentages

	1994	1998	2003
Labour income of active population			
Formal wage earner	26.4	29.1	29.7
Informal wage earner	73.6	70.9	70.3
Labour income of household head[(a)]			
Formal wage earner	41.1	41.2	41.6
Informal wage earner	58.9	58.8	58.4
Income structure[(b)]			
Formal wages only	19.4	22.4	19.9
Informal wages only	53.8	52.7	54.5
Mixed (formal and informal)	26.8	24.8	25.6

Source: EPI, EPII and EPIII; computations by the authors.
Notes: (a) Percentage of urban population living in households where the main (highest) labour income comes from the respective sector.
(b) Percentage of population living in households with only formal, only informal and 'mixed' sector income.

Table 9.4 and Table 9.5 show the estimation results for the analysis of intra-household linkages between the informal and formal sectors. All control variables have the expected sign and are more or less stable over time. Age has a positive impact on overall labour-market participation but a negative impact on informal labour market participation; that is, with increasing age a person is more likely to be occupied and more likely to be found in the formal sector (Table 9.4). The same is true for education, with higher education leading to both higher labour market participation and a greater chance of finding a job in the formal sector. Concerning wage rates (Table 9.5), secondary as well as technical education has a significant and positive impact on wage levels in both the formal and the informal sectors, but primary education has no significant impact on wage rates.

Table 9.4 assesses the impact of the household head's occupation and earnings on the labour-market participation of other household members. The estimated multinomial logit model suggests that formal sector occupation as well as higher earnings of the head of the household lead to lower labour-market participation of other household members, but also to a higher probability that they will be found in the formal labour market rather than in the informal labour market. The corresponding coefficients are highly significant over all three years and approximately equal in magnitude.

In Table 9.5, we assess the impact of an individual's position within the household and the household head's sector of occupation and earnings

Table 9.4 Occupational choice, urban population (15 years and older) without heads of household, multinomial logit model, inactivity is reference choice

Dependent variable occupational choice	**Worker in the informal sector**						**Worker in the formal sector**					
	1994		**1998**		**2003**		**1994**		**1998**		**2003**	
Age	0.182	***	0.184	***	0.221	***	0.327	***	0.402	***	0.467	***
Squared age	−0.002	***	−0.002	***	−0.003	***	−0.004	***	−0.005	***	−0.006	***
Female	−0.765	***	−0.530	***	−0.613	***	−1.050	***	−1.760	***	−1.372	***
Highest education level												
No schooling	Ref.		Ref.		Ref.		Ref.		Ref.		Ref.	
Some primary education	0.795	***	0.806	***	0.101		1.051	***	1.327	***	0.516	***
Primary completed	0.348	***	0.789	***	−0.097		0.929	***	1.378	***	0.788	***
Some or compl. low sec.	0.071		0.647	***	−1.145	***	1.570	***	1.741	***	0.219	***
Some or compl. high sec.	0.176		0.428		−2.057	***	2.467	***	2.593	***	0.617	***
Technical education	0.158		0.509		−1.235	***	2.475	***	2.150	***	1.010	***
HH head labour income												
Informal earnings	Ref.		Ref.		Ref.		Ref.		Ref.		Ref.	
Formal earnings	−0.596	***	−0.691	***	−0.785	***	0.367	***	0.285	**	0.417	***
Log monthly earnings (head)	−0.125	***	−0.176	***	−0.145	***	0.145	***	0.197	***	0.112	**
# of observations	5233		4711		5540		5233		4711		5540	
Pseudo R square	0.169		0.214		0.224		0.169		0.214		0.224	

Source: EPI, EPII and EPIII; estimations by the authors.
Notes: * Coefficient significant at the 10% level.
** Coefficient significant at the 5% level.
*** Coefficient significant at the 1% level.
The model only includes individuals who are not specified as heads of the household (that is, individuals not accounting for the main labour earnings of a household); besides the variables noted in the table, the model includes the following explicative variable: city of residence, household size, percentage of occupied household members (without accounting for the individuals themselves) and transfers received.

Table 9.5 Estimation of monthly earning functions, urban population (15 years and older), selection model (full maximum likelihood estimator)

Dependent variable log monthly earnings	1994				1998				2003			
	(1)		(2)		(1)		(2)		(1)		(2)	
Age	0.089	***	0.015		0.131	***	−0.061	***	0.098	***	−0.065	***
Squared age	−0.001	***	0.000	**	−0.002	***	0.001	***	−0.001	***	0.001	**
Female	−0.516	***	−0.917	***	−0.168	***	−1.206	***	−0.344	***	−0.792	***
Highest education achieved												
No schooling	Ref.		Ref.		Ref.		Ref.		Ref.		Ref.	
Some primary	0.076		−0.042		0.108		−0.191		0.113		0.157	
Completed primary	0.356	***	0.368	**	0.273	***	0.161		0.137		0.234	
Some or completed junior high	0.870	***	0.468	**	0.385	***	0.232		0.206	***	0.085	
Some or completed senior high	1.627	***	1.516	***	0.794	***	0.484		0.734	***	−0.027	
Technical	1.418	***	1.638	***	0.628	***	0.147		0.746	***	0.795	
Informal sector	Ref.		Ref.		Ref.							
Formal sector	0.635	***			0.370	***			0.429	***		
Second order labour income (dummy)	−0.582	***	−1.584	***	−0.066		−0.901	***	−0.563	***	−0.643	***

	Secondary household labour earnings only											
Household head labour income												
Informal income	Ref.		Ref.		Ref.		Ref.		Ref.		Ref.	
Formal income	0.023		−0.373	***	−0.504	***	−1.019	***	0.103		−0.529	***
Log monthly earnings (head)	0.324	***	0.311	***	0.570	***	0.603	***	0.431	***	0.516	***
Intercept	3.886	***	7.467	***	7.926	***	7..586	***	2.836	***	7.816	***
rho[(a)]	0.430		−0.374		−0.957	***	−0.902	***	0.190		−0.919	***
# of observations	7263		2702		6203		2371		6338		2312	
# non-censored estimations	944		639		920		536		1167		704	
-Log-likelihood	3913		2127		3409		1652		4082		2091	

Source: EPI, EPII and EPIII; estimations by the authors.
Notes: * Coefficient significant at the 10% level.
** Coefficient significant at the 5% level.
*** Coefficient significant at the 1% level.
The model only includes individuals who are not specified as heads of household (that is, individuals not accounting for the main labour earnings of a household); col. (1) total urban labour force; col. (2) informal urban labour force, only.
Besides the variables noted in the table, the model includes the following explicative variable: city of residence and sector of employment. As explanatory variables in the selection function, we use variables for the age and gender composition of the household, for the age, gender and education of the individual, for percentage of occupied household members (without accounting for the individual itself), for the sector of employment of the head of the household and for transfers received.
rho[(a)] is the correlation coefficient between the residuals of the earnings regression and the selection function.

on household members' wage earnings. It is, of course, evident that the secondary household position has a negative impact on labour earnings, since we set first and second household members endogenously according to their respective wages. However, we can observe that this coefficient is much higher if we only consider informal earnings (Table 9.5 (2)). Hence, the earnings differential between informal first income and informal secondary income is much higher than the wage differential between formal first and formal secondary income, supporting the hypothesis of 'upper-tiers' or 'first income' and 'lower-tiers' or 'second-income' informal earnings.

Concerning the impact of the head of the household's earnings and sector occupation on the earnings of other household members, we observe a strong positive impact of the head of the household's earnings on other household members' earnings (Table 9.5 (1)), which is slightly larger if we only examine the impact of the main income on second order informal earnings (Table 9.5 (2)). This could indicate that 'intra-household investments' of household members employed in the formal sector in informal sector enterprises do indeed take place, but 'unobserved heterogeneity' could, of course, also play an important role. However, besides the generally-higher wage level of formal wage-earners, the additional fact that the head of the household generates this higher wage from the formal sector has no impact (Table 9.5 (1)), or even a negative impact (Table 9.5 (2)) on earnings of other household members. This implies that the positive linkages that exist between formal and informal earnings within households are only established via the generally-higher formal income.

To sum up, we have shown that a considerable proportion of urban households in Burkina Faso receive income from both the formal as well as the informal sectors. Hence, intra-household linkages are evidently important in terms of formal and informal workers' well-being. However, in addition, formal- and informal-sector participation and earnings are also linked via intra-household linkages. We have also shown that one should distinguish between informal income that constitutes the principal income of a household and informal income that only complements the principal income of a household.

Conclusion

Although much has been written on the possible linkages between the formal and informal sectors and their importance for informal sector policy recommendations, to our knowledge not much empirical analysis on those linkages exists so far. In this study, we undertook a first attempt to analyze the linkages between formal and informal sector earnings on a macro- as well as on a micro-level for the case of Burkina Faso. We showed that informal sector earnings are indeed positively linked to formal sector earnings on both levels. However, this linkage coefficient turns out to be much stronger within households than between households. The analysis also shows that when analyzing the informal sector and its linkages to the formal sector of the economy, it is important to distinguish between informal sector earnings that constitute the main income source of households and informal sector earnings that only complement the main (informal or formal) income of households. However, our analysis is mainly descriptive, and better data, especially panel data and detailed data on the formal and informal sectors, would be necessary to identify the existing linkages and causalities.

Regarding pro-poor growth policies, and in particular if we see the informal sector as the 'economy of the poor', our results suggest that good (formal) growth policies are also good pro-poor growth policies. But, given that in SSA those linkages mainly exist between or within households through labour earnings and less between formal and informal enterprises, this is only the case if formal economic growth comes along with increasing formal wages and does not only benefit formal enterprises' profits. This might explain why, in Burkina Faso, we observed stagnating informal labour earnings despite formal economic growth, which was however accompanied by stagnating or decreasing formal sector wages.

However, this study has also shown that the linkage coefficient for both inter- as well as intra-household linkages is smaller than 1 and, therefore, good formal growth policies might be insufficient for informal sectoral growth. Also, this analysis has shown that formal sector growth policies will be more beneficial for workers in the informal sector that are linked to the formal sector via intra-household linkages, and less to workers in the informal sector that are only linked to the formal sector via the market. As a result, pure 'informal' households might be left out of overall economic growth, and we should therefore start to think more about a dichotomy of 'formal and informal' households rather than of informal and formal wage-earners when considering poverty analysis.

Notes

We thank participants at the 17–18 September 2004 EGDI-WIDER Conference on 'Unlocking Human Potential: Linking the Informal and Formal Sectors' for useful comments and suggestions.

1 The theoretical framework has some similarities with that used in the literature on poverty traps. See, for example, De Vreyer *et al.* (2003) or Jalan and Ravallion (2002).
2 Alternatively, we could also try to find an instrument for formal earnings; that is, a variable explaining formal earnings but being uncorrelated with geographical variables and with province-specific household characteristics. However, in our data we could not find such an instrument.
3 Most of the informal sector activity in Burkina Faso is independent and self-employed, and does not constitute wage earnings. Hence, we can assume that intra-household investments can easily take place.

References

Azam, J.P. (2004) 'Poverty and Growth in the WAEMU after the 1994 Devaluation', WIDER Research Paper 2004/19 (Helsinki: UNU-WIDER).

Blunch, N.H., S. Canagarajah and D. Raju (2001) 'The Informal Sector Revisited: A Synthesis Across Space and Time', Social Protection Discussion Paper Series 0119 (Washington, DC: World Bank).

Charmes, J. (1990) 'A Critical Review of Concepts Definitions and Studies in the Informal Sector', in D. Turnham, B. Salomé and A. Schwarz (eds), *The Informal Sector Revisited* (Paris: OECD) 10–48.

Charmes, J. (1996) 'Le secteur informel au Burkina Faso: Evolution sur longue période et suivi conjoncturel', Report prepared for the GTZ and the Ministère de l'Economie des Finances, Ouagadougou.

Cogneau, D., M. Razafindrakoto and F. Roubaud (1996) 'Le secteur informel urbain et l'ajustement au Cameroun', *Revue d'économie du developpement*, 3: 27–63.

De Vreyer, P., J. Herrera and S. Mesplé-Somps (2003) 'Consumption Growth and Spatial Poverty Traps: An Analysis of the Effects of Social Services and Community Infrastructures on Living Standards in Rural Peru', DIAL Working Paper DT/2002/17 (Paris: DIAL).

Fields, G.S. (1974) 'Rural–Urban Migration, Urban Unemployment and Underemployment, and Job-search Activity in LDCs', *Journal of Development Economics*, 2: 165–87.

Grimm, M. and I. Günther (2006) 'Pro-Poor Growth in Burkina Faso. The Role of Price Fluctuations in a Highly Segmented Rural Economy', in M. Grimm, A. McKay and S. Klasen (eds), *Determinants of Pro-Poor Growth: Analytical Issues and Findings from 14 Country Case Studies* (Basingstoke: Palgrave Macmillan).

Harriss, J.C. (1990) 'Linkages between the Formal and the Informal Sectors in Developing Countries: A Review of Literature', World Development Programme Research Working Paper (Geneva: ILO).

Hart, K. (1973) 'Informal Income Opportunities and Urban Employment in Ghana', *Journal of Modern African Studies,* 11 (2): 61–89.

Heckman, J. (1979) 'Sample Selection Bias as a Specification Error', *Econometrica,* 47 (1): 153–61.

Hemmer, H.-R. and C. Mannel (1989) 'On the Economic Analysis of the Urban Informal Sector', *World Development,* 17 (10): 1543–52.

Jalan, J. and M. Ravallion (2002) 'Geographic Poverty Traps? A Micro Model of Consumption Growth in Rural China', *Journal of Applied Econometrics*, 17: 329–46.

INSD (2000) 'Analyse des résultats du Recensement Général de la Population et de l'habitation de 1996', 1, Institut National de la Statistique et de la Démographie, Burkina Faso.

International Labour Office (1972) 'Employment, Incomes and Equality: A Strategy for Increasing Productive Employment in Kenya' (Geneva: ILO).

Lachaud, J.-P. (1990) 'The Urban Informal Sector and the Labour Market in sub-Saharan Africa', in D. Turnham, B. Salomé and A. Schwarz (eds), *The Informal Sector Revisited* (Paris: OECD) 111–30.

Lewis, W.A. (1954) 'Economic Development with Unlimited Supplies of Labour', *The Manchester School*, 28: 139–91.

Livingstone, I. (1971) 'A Reassessment of Kenya's Rural and Urban Informal Sector', *World Development*, 19 (6): 651–70.

Maloney, W.F. (1997) 'Labour Market Structure in LDC. Time Series Evidence on Competing Views', Mimeo (Washington, DC: World Bank).

Maloney, W.F. (2003) 'Informality Revisited', *World Development*, 32 (7): 1159–78.

Mazumdar, D. (1976) 'The Urban Informal Sector', *World Development*, 4 (8): 655–79.

Pradhan, M. and A. Soest (1997) 'Household Labour Supply in Urban Areas of Bolivia', *Review of Economics and Statistics*, 79 (2): 300–10.

Sethuraman, S.V. (1997) 'Urban Poverty and the Informal Sector. A Critical Assessment of Current Strategies', Mimeo (New York: UNDP).

Stiglitz, J.E. (1974) 'Alternative Theories of Wage Determination and Unemployment in LDCs: The Labour Turnover Model', *Quarterly Journal of Economics*, 88: 194–227.

Todaro, M.P. (1969) 'A Model of Labour Migration and Urban Unemployment in Less Developed Countries', *American Economic Review*, 59: 138–48.

Tokman, V.E. (1978) 'An Exploration into the Nature of Informal–Formal Sector Relationships', *World Development*, 6 (9/10): 1065–75.

UNDP (2004) 'Cultural Liberty in Today's Diverse World', *The Human Development Report 2004* (New York: UNDP).

Van Dijk, M.P. (1980) 'De informele sector van Ouagadougdou en Dakar', Doctoral dissertation, Free University of Amsterdam.

Xaba, J., P. Horn and S. Motala (2002) 'The Informal Sector in Sub-Saharan Africa', Working Paper on the Informal Economy 2002/10 (Geneva: ILO).

10

Skill Requirements, Earnings and Labour Demand in Nigeria's Urban Informal Sector

Sam O. Olofin and Abiodun O. Folawewo

Introduction

The informal sector plays an important role in the process of economic development in most developing countries. It has served as a means of cushioning some of the unemployment effects of the Structural Adjustment Programme (SAP) in Nigeria, for example.[1] In spite of its importance however, this sector, compared to the formal sector, has attracted very little policy-oriented research. It is customary to assume low-level skill requirements in the informal sector. Similarly, policies concerning employment planning in this sector are often based on the notion of unrestricted entry and self-employment. This has led to policy circles not focusing attention on waged employment in the sector. However, apart from the training and apprenticeship required for successful self-employment, it is often assumed that there are certain factors that serve as obstacles to the securing of waged employment in the privately owned small and medium-size enterprises found in the informal sector. Furthermore, despite the frequently made assumption of minimum skill requirements in the informal sector, the role of skill level in the employment process and earnings determination in this sector remains largely unclear.

In most developing countries, and especially in Nigeria, emphasis has always been on self-employment activities in the informal sector, while little is known about the nature of waged labour in small and medium-size enterprises. This has limited our understanding of the nature of the informal sector. The resultant effect of this has been government policies that have been inappropriate for the stimulation of the sector's capacity for the creation of waged employment. On the whole, this has hindered the efficacy of manpower planning and employment-boosting programmes. For example, Celestin (1983) identifies lack of information on the labour market as one of the factors that often makes it impossible for many countries to draw up a successful employment forecast at the occupational level. Specifically, the lack of adequate information on the urban informal sector labour market has resulted in the inability of government to identify the skill requirements within the sector, and also has constrained economic planning (see Sanusi, 2001). In addition, it has also made determining the extent of labour mobility in the informal sector subject to guesswork.

If the informal sector is to live up to policy-makers' expectations of providing meaningful contribution to the success of employment-creation-related macroeconomic policies, there is need to understand properly the nature of its labour demand function and skill requirements. As noted by Celestin (1983) and House (1992), the various employment-boosting strategies embarked upon by developing countries could only have meaningful impact on the informal sector if there were appropriate information on what determines new workers' absorption into the sector. Therefore, in this chapter, an empirical examination of the factors affecting labour demand, with particular reference to wage-earning labour in the urban informal sector is undertaken. Furthermore, the nature of urban informal sector employees' skills and how these, along with other employees' characteristics, impact on their earnings are analyzed.

The rest of this chapter is divided into five sections. In the next section, a working definition of the informal sector is provided, as a means of drawing an appropriate demarcation between it and the formal sector. The subsequent section focuses on the empirical model and estimation issues, and data sources. We then present the results of the empirical analysis of skill requirements, earnings and labour demand in the Nigerian urban informal sector, and a conclusion closes the chapter.

Concept of the informal sector

Several criteria have been used to differentiate between formal and informal sectors. Among such factors are wages, productivity, employment, legal status, capital, size, and technology (Hugon, 1977; Bromley, 1978; Mazumdar, 1981; Charmes, 1990; Cole and Fayissa, 1991). With regard to these factors, it is assumed that informal sector firms are characterized by low wages, low productivity, self-employment, extralegal status, modest investment/capital base, small size, and labour-intensive technology compared with formal sector firms. Some studies have also used other criteria to distinguish between informal and formal sector activities (for example, Udall, 1976; Fields, 1990), where ease of entry is used. The informal sector has equally been regarded as one where there is absence of institutional safeguards, which is as a result of a lack of official coverage and government regulation (see Weeks, 1975; Sethuraman, 1981; Folawewo, 2004).

However, given the fact that the concept of the informal sector is 'an extremely fuzzy' one (Peattie, 1987) and that the sector is neither disconnected nor distinctly different from the formal sector (Mazumdar, 1981), this necessitates a clear conceptualization. For the purposes of our study, we view regulation as the key distinguishing factor, and the extent to which such regulation is effective. Thus, if there exists a set of regulations put up by a recognized formal institution (government) to guide the activities of firms, the degree of compliance by firms would serve as a criterion for classifying production units as being formal or informal.

According to Ajakaiye and Akerele (1996), a formal production unit is one that operates under binding, official regulations that compel the installation of a set of rules to govern its behaviour both internally and externally, as well as in all markets and in its production process. Scherer (1980), states that such official regulation may include price determination, control of entry into the sector, product quality, disclosure of information, labour–management relations, and health and safety standards and/or effects on the environment, among others. On the other hand, an informal production unit is one that operates under certain official regulations that do not compel it to abide by a set of rules to govern its behaviour in all markets, as well as in its production process. Such official regulations that this type of firm operates under may include simple licensing permits, registered business names, and registered premises. This framework not only recognizes the heterogeneity of firms; with regard to level of regulation, especially in the informal sector, it also brings out the connection between the formal and informal sector firms.

Given the above, our classification scheme for identifying informal sector activities is provided in Figure 10.1. In this figure, four different classifications of informal production units can be identified. The first are the informal sector production units operating under binding official regulations, but with their own autonomous internal regulations ($IFPU_1$). The second category of informal sector units comprises those production units operating under binding official regulations, but without any internal regulations ($IFPU_2$). Third, is the informal production unit operating without binding official regulations, but with autonomous internal regulations ($IFPU_3$). Lastly, there are the informal production units operating without binding official regulations and without any autonomous internal regulations ($IFPU_4$). The first two categories can be said to comprise those privately owned small and medium-size firms with officially registered

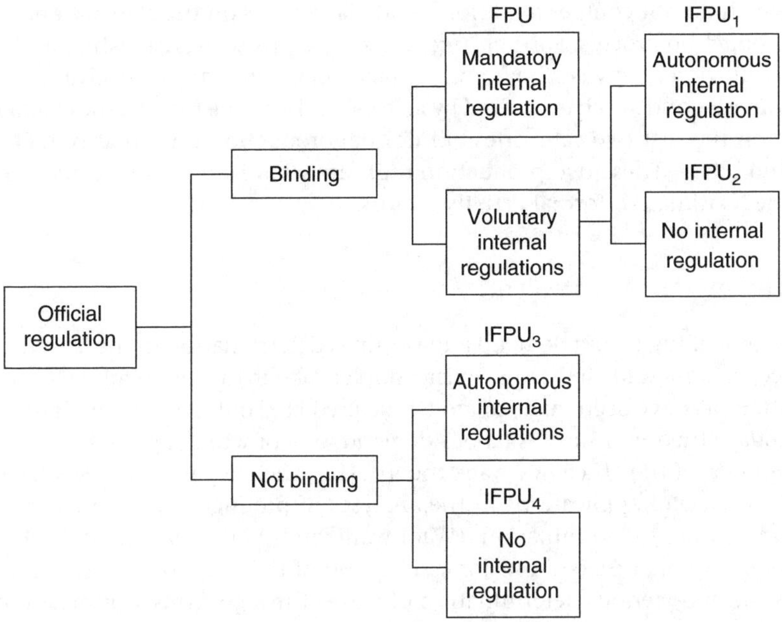

Figure 10.1 Framework for classification of informal sector production units
Source: Ajakaiye and Akerele (1996).
FPU = Formal production unit operating under binding official regulations with mandatory internal regulations
IFPU$_1$ = Informal production unit operating under binding official regulations with autonomous internal regulations
IFPU$_2$ = Informal production unit operating under binding official regulations without internal regulations
IFPU$_3$ = Informal production unit operating without binding official regulations with autonomous internal regulations
IFPU$_4$ = Informal production unit operating without binding official regulation and with no internal regulations

business names and premises, but which do not have any binding official regulations on their internal relations. All the petty traders, store owners, street hawkers/bazaars, carpenters, vulcanizers and cobblers, among others, would fall under the last two categories of informal production units.

In this chapter, the informal sector is defined to include the privately owned small and medium-size enterprises that are officially registered to undertake business activities. However, these enterprises operate under limited official regulations that only cover their operations permit, business names and premises registration, but do not cover their internal relations; that is, enterprises that are operating under official regulations which do not compel rendition of official returns on their operations or production process. Furthermore, these enterprises engage mainly in the production of services, have low capital requirements, are relatively labour-intensive and are characterized by low wages. Thus, the focus of the chapter is on the first two categories of informal production unit; that is, $IFPU_1$ and $IFPU_2$. These two production units are what Hart (1973) refers to as the legitimate informal activity sectors.

The model

In modelling labour demand and earnings determination in the informal sector, we found the Harris–Todaro surplus labour theory useful. Different attempts have been made to model the predicted outcomes of the Harris–Todaro theory of surplus labour demand, one of which led to the development of the efficiency wage theory. The efficiency wage models have found useful applications in the analyses of productivity, earnings and employment-determination (Wadhwani and Wall, 1991 and Levine 1992, among others). A major assumption of the efficiency wage theory is the endogenous determination of wages through firms' optimization behaviour. The variant of the efficiency wage model adopted in this chapter follows that of Riveros and Bouton (1991), which was built upon by Teal (1995). Thus, the empirical specification here draws heavily from Teal (1995). As a starting point, a constant returns to scale, Cobb–Douglas production function with two inputs – effective labour, (e^aL), and capital, K – specified as:

$$Y = (e^aL)^bK^{(1-b)}f\varepsilon \tag{10.1}$$

This specification includes a firm-specific productivity factor (f) that is time-invariant, and independently identically distributed (i.i.d.); shocks to the production function ε, which is assumed to be uncorrelated with changes in a, L or K. Under the efficiency wage hypothesis, if the production function is expressed in labour–output terms and firms' fixed effects are allowed for by differencing, we have:

$$\Delta \ln Y/L = b\Delta \ln Rel(w) + (1 - b)\Delta \ln K/L + \Delta\varepsilon \tag{10.2}$$

where $Rel(w)$ is the relative wage in the firm.

The implication of this hypothesis, as shown by Levine (1992), is that the coefficient on the relative wage term should be equal to the labour share parameter. The relative wage, $Rel(w)$, could be estimated by considering the actual firm wage, relative to the wage predicted by the human capital characteristics of the workers in the firm. This is equivalent to assuming that firms would pay the predicted wage to employees of a given skill level in a competitive market. Insofar as the actual wage is higher than the predicted wage in some firms than in others, then the question becomes whether this is due to the productivity effect of higher wages or higher profits, which are a reflection of higher productivity, leading to higher wages from rent-sharing.

Nickell and Wadhwani (1990), Christofides and Oswald (1992) and Blanchflower *et al.* (1993) have shown that wage-determination can be understood as a process in which workers and firms bargain, and that one element in the game is a measure of a firm's performance. Thus, to capture the effect of rent-sharing, firm's profit and the inherent human capital of the employees is allowed to determine the nominal wage; that is:

$$\ln w = \beta_0 + \beta_1 \pi/L + \beta_2 w^e + \beta_3 H + \textit{controls} \tag{10.3}$$

where π/L is profit per employee; w^e is the exogenously-available wage, and H is the human capital variable, which allows controls for different levels of education and skills.

Since we assume a Cobb–Douglas production function, this gives the share of labour in output as $b = wL/Y$. If profits per employee are defined as value-added less wages, then we have:

$$\pi/L = Y/L - w = (1 - b)\, Y/L \tag{10.4}$$

If we rewrite Equation (10.4) in logs, in order to make the comparison more direct, we have:

$$\ln w = \beta_0 + \beta_1 \ln \pi/L + \beta_2 \ln w^e + \beta_3 H + \textit{controls} \tag{10.5}$$

and using the definition of profits per employee, this equation can be written, as:

$$\ln w = \beta_0 + \beta_1 \ln Y/L + \beta_2 \ln w^e + \beta_3 H + \textit{controls} \tag{10.6}$$

In order to set up a comparison between rent-sharing and efficiency theories, Equation (10.6) is transformed so that it becomes an equation for the relative wage of the firm. We write:

$$\ln[w/(\textit{Predicted wage})] = \beta_0 + \beta_1 \ln Y/L + \beta_2 \ln w^e + \textit{controls} \tag{10.7}$$

where the predicted wage is estimated simply from the human capital term in the earnings Equation (10.6).

Writing Equation (10.7) as one that explains productivity, and differencing to allow for firm fixed effect, we have:

$$\Delta \ln Y/L = \beta_0/\beta_1 + (1/\beta_1)\Delta \ln \textit{Rel}(w) - \beta_2/\beta_1 \Delta \ln w^e \tag{10.8}$$

where *Rel*(*w*) stands for actual to predicted wage.

Two important issues arise from Equation (10.8); the first is the measure of output, and the second is the availability of relative wage. This is because in the informal sector productivity is hardly measurable (Maloney, 1998). In order to apply the efficiency wage model to what obtains in the informal sector, Equation (10.8) is transformed into a form that yields labour demand, which is conditioned on the actual wage in the firm and returns to capital.

Following Teal (1995; 1997), a labour demand function, where employment is determined by wage rate and cost of capital, is specified as:

$$L_i^d = \alpha W_i + \beta r K_i \qquad (10.9)$$

where L^d, W and rK are labour demand, wage rate and returns to capital respectively, and i stands for the typical firm. However, given the informal nature of the activities of firms being investigated, rK is proxied by three different factors: cost of capital/borrowing, level of investment (size of firm), and profit level. The replacement of rK by these variables can be explained in two ways. First, in the informal sector, firms do not have access to a formal credit market, where an official interest rate is charged on borrowings; rather, they often resort to the informal financial market where it is usually difficult to keep formal records of charges on loans. Second, the higher the informal cost of borrowing (capital), the lower will be the opportunity to borrow/invest and this will in turn affect the level of profits. Ultimately, this will affect productivity and employment.

The estimable labour demand function can be written as:

$$L_i^d = \alpha W_i + \beta_1 ck_i + \beta_2 I_i + \beta_3 \pi_i \qquad (10.10)$$

where ck is cost of capital, I is investment and π stands for profit. Oswald (1995), Teal (1995; 1997) and Carneiro and Henley (1998) have shown that these variables affect employees' earnings and the determination of labour demand, particularly in the informal sector.

Given the cross-sectional nature of the data, in order to eliminate any effect of oscillations that may result in heteroscedasticity, and to ensure constant variation across the series, Equation (10.10) is expressed in natural log form as:

$$\ln L_i^d = \alpha \ln W_i + \beta_1 \ln ck_i + \beta_2 \ln I_i + \beta_3 \ln \pi_I + \mu_i \qquad (10.11)$$

Equation (10.11), which is estimated, shows the market-clearing condition, where a single labour demand function holds. First, it relates labour demand to the expectation of the firm, through the dependence on the cost of capital, rate of profit and investment level. Also, since the wage rate is influenced by the demographic and human capital variables of the informal-sector workers, this yields a specification of labour demand function, which depends on price, and the estimation of the determinants of the price, which is captured by wages.

The specification of the above labour demand function raises three major issues. The first issue is methodological, this has to do with the problem of how simultaneously to measure the effects of both firm-level factors and employees' characteristics on employment. In the first case, since one of the determinants of L_i^d given by Equation (10.11) is wage, W_i, which itself is determined by employees' characteristics, the problem of endogeneity surfaces. This implies that wage function should be specified as:

$$\ln W_i = a_0 + a_1 X_{ji} \tag{10.12}$$

where X is a vector of individual employees' characteristics, in terms of productivity (measured by educational level – representing human capital), experience and gender, as well as other characteristics of the employees. Equation (10.12) can be explicitly written as:

$$\begin{aligned}\ln W_i = a_0 &+ a_1 Education_{ji} + a_2 Age + a_3 Age^2 + a_4 Experience \\ &+ a_5 Tenure + a_6 Sex + U_2\end{aligned} \tag{10.13}$$

Education, Age, Experience and Tenure are included to reflect the effects of human capital on wages, which will affect the probability of being employed. Age-squared is included to pick up the possible non-linearity between age and wages. To solve the endogeneity problem, a step-by-step estimation approach is adopted. First, the wage equation (10.13) is estimated, using Ordinary Least Square (OLS). Equation (10.11) is then estimated by the instrumental variable (IV) estimation technique, in which case the determinants of W_i are used as instruments. All the variables are estimated at levels, given the fact that they are primary data and they are not measured over time.

The second issue has to do with variable measurement. The relevant variables of the model are measured as follows: the number of employees in each firm is used as a proxy for labour demand by such a firm. Wage, W_i, is measured by average wage per employee being paid by firm i. Cost of capital, ck_i is proxied by the average prevailing lending rates of cooperative societies. This is because cooperative loans and advances are more readily available to SMEs, especially in the informal sector, than commercial bank credit facilities. Investment, I_i, is measured as the total amount of capital invested by firm i in the business; that is, the capital concept of investment is used for variable I_i. The variable π_i is measured as average annual profit per firm. Employees' skill, proxied by level of educational attainment, is measured in years. Gender difference and other characteristics of the workers such as experience, tenure, and age are captured by discrete values.[2]

The third issue relates to data requirement. The data are drawn from an administered structured questionnaire. Two sets of questionnaires were administered; the first set was administered to firms while the second set was administered to employees. Therefore, earnings and employment determination in the urban informal sector is examined using a matched employee–employer data set. The sample size covers 1,475 enterprises and 2,739 workers in 28 cities, in the six south-western states in Nigeria (Ekiti, Lagos, Ogun, Ondo, Osun and Oyo states). In the selection of enterprises covered by the survey, we used the Federal Office of Statistics (FOS) listing of enterprises. Given the focus of the study (that is, salaried workers), the listing is used to select enterprises that have waged employees in each of the towns covered by the study. Also, the choice of employees was made by the enterprises – employer determined. Therefore, selection of both the enterprises and employees was based on a purposive sampling technique.

Empirical results

Estimation of wage equation

In the analysis of earnings in the informal sector, we used both individual-based and firm-average data. Table 10.1 gives the OLS results of estimating the wage equation (10.13). Model [1] shows that when the wage equation is estimated using individual employee-based data, all the explanatory variables are significant in the determination of wage variation. As expected, Age has a positive effect on wages. An interpretation of this is that as the age of workers increases, the level of their skill acquisition increases and the offered wage goes up. The significance of the squared term is based on the hypothesis of the non-linearity effect of age on wages based on earlier findings. Education, as a variable, has a positive sign, implying that a higher level of education will translate to a higher level of human capital; hence, higher wages. The positive relationship between Wages and Tenure, as well as between Wages and Experience, demonstrates that as a worker keeps on working, skill acquisition will also increase and wages will rise with the increase in their stock of skills. This indicates the critical role of skill in the informal sector. However, the negative sign of the Gender variable can be interpreted as meaning that a predominance of females tends to depress wages. Also,

Table 10.1 OLS estimation of wage equation using individual worker based data and firm averaged data

Dependent variable: ln (wages)	**[1]**	**[2]**
Constant	−4.502	−1.968
	[−6.520]	[−3.861]
Age	2.370	2.186
	[9.750]***	[8.671]***
Age^2	−0.062	−0.041
	[−2.189]**	[−1.965]*
Education	0.433	0.361
	[7.624]***	[8.855]***
Gender	−2.304	−0.115
	[−7.646]***	[−1.344]*
Experience	0.046	0.166
	[2.724]**	[2.845]***
Tenure	0.104	0.254
	[6.780]***	[2.517]**
Age*Education	−0.118	−0.424
	[−6.555]***	[−2.114]***
Age*Gender	0.203	0.185
	[8.417]***	[2.225]**
Gender*Education	−0.253	−0.171
	[−3.988]***	[−2.012]***
Adjusted R^2	0.635	0.596
Std error	0.750	0.862
No. of observations	2,738	1,474

Notes: T-Statistic in brackets.
*, ** and *** indicate 10%, 5% and 1% significance levels respectively.

the negative sign of the interaction between Age and Education indicates that as both the age and education of workers increase, the wage level is likely to fall. The basic reason for this is that as employees become older, though their level of education may rise, their age would have priced them out of waged employment in the informal sector. This is supported by the fact that a majority of workers with a high level of education are young, while most of the older workers have a low level of education.

On the other hand, the positive sign of the interactive term between Gender and Age shows that irrespective of the gender of workers, as the age of a worker increases, the wages offered will equally increase. The negative relationship between Wage and the interactive term of Gender and Education suggests that no matter the level of education, wages tend to fall as the gender dominance of workers changes from male to female. This is particularly so since male workers in the informal sector tend to have higher educational attainments compared to their female counterparts.

Model [2] gives the result of the estimation of the wage equation, using firm-average data. The results obtained are not significantly different from those for Model [1]. Although the Gender variable still retains its negative sign in Model [2], its significant level falls from 1 to 10 per cent. This implies that gender may be more important in the determination of wages at individual employee level rather than at firm level. Also, while still maintaining their respective signs, Tenure and the interactive term of Age and Education become less significant. This shows that these are not as important in the determination of wages at the level of the firm as they are at the level of the individual worker.

Estimation of the labour demand equation

In the estimation of the labour demand equation (10.11), we used both OLS and IV estimation techniques. Table 10.2 presents the results from the estimation of the labour demand equation at aggregate and sectoral levels, using OLS and IV. Models [1] to [4] are estimated using OLS, while Models [5] to [8] give the results obtained when wage is instrumented. All the models depict a positive relationship between labour demand and the year of the establishment of firm, investment and profit. This result implies that an increase in the level of investment and profit-level will lead to an increase in labour demand and that the older a firm is, the greater will be its ability to employ more labour. Also, investment and profits are significant in all the cases, while the year of establishment is only significant at the aggregate data level. However, ownership structure is generally insignificant in all the models.

On the other hand, labour-demand has an overall negative relationship with ownership, wages and the cost of capital. This indicates that increases in wages and cost of capital would discourage labour employment. The negative relationship between labour-demand and ownership can be explained by the fact that as ownership of enterprises moves from one person to partnership and so on, owners are likely to bring their relatives into the business rather than hire more labour from the labour market. Generally, the results show that irrespective of estimation technique, wages are not important in the determination of labour employment in the informal sector.

Table 10.2 OLS and IV estimations of labour demand equation

	OLS				IV			
	[1]	[2]	[3]	[4]	[5]	[6]	[7]	[8]
Variable	Aggregate	Agric.	Manu.	Services	Aggregate	Agric.	Manu.	Services
Constant	−0.13	0.03	−0.38	0.30	1.95	0.22	0.18	−0.55
	[−1.08]	[0.19]	[−0.56]	[3.21]	[−1.08]	[1.21]	[2.10]	[−0.40]
Yestab	0.07	0.02	0.09	0.21	0.03	0.02	0.04	0.08
	[3.26]a	[0.79]	[0.97]	[1.89]b	[2.34]b	[1.20]	[0.36]	[1.09]
Ownship	−0.03	−0.05	−0.33	0.25	−0.01	−0.04	−0.23	−0.01
	[−0.87]	[−1.57]	[−1.37]	[2.07]b	[−0.30]	[−1.94]	[−1.21]	[−0.29]
Ln (Wage)	−0.28	−0.13	0.03	−0.10	−0.11	−0.03	−0.00	0.04
	[−2.07]b	[−1.19]c	[0.63]	[−1.71]	[−1.11]c	[−0.09]	[−0.14]	[0.75]
LN (Investment)	0.19	0.37	0.30	0.54	0.63	0.66	0.68	0.04
	[4.68]a	[3.77]a	[1.16]	[4.71]a	[6.02]a	[5.70]a	[6.56]a	[0.81]
Ln (Profit)	0.22	0.23	0.23	0.55	0.15	0.59	0.52	0.49
	[5.37]a	[2.44]c	[1.30]	[5.11]a	[1.75]b	[4.40]a	[4.88]a	[2.19]b
Ln (Cost_cap)	−0.32	−0.11	−0.45	−0.03	−0.06	−0.01	−0.31	−0.02
	[5.36]a	[−1.99]c	[−2.81]c	[−1.30]	[−1.81]b	[−0.84]	[−2.28]b	[−1.10]c
Adjusted R^2	0.60	0.55	0.52	0.58	0.66	0.59	0.51	0.60
Std error	0.81	0.96	0.98	0.91	0.34	0.82	0.98	0.80
No. of observations	1472	216	104	1152	1472	216	104	1152

Notes: Dependent variable in all models is log of labour size.
T-Statistic in brackets.
a, b, c indicate 1%, 5% and 10% significance levels.
Instruments: Age, Age^2, Education, Gender, Experience, Tenure, Age*Education, and Gender*Age.

Conclusion

This chapter has attempted an analysis of skill requirements and the determinants of earnings and labour demand in the urban informal sector of south-western Nigerian. The importance of Education, Tenure and Experience variables in earnings-determination shows that high levels of skill are critical in the informal sector. This is contrary to the expectation of a prevalence of low-skilled labour in the sector, as is often assumed in the literature. From a policy point of view, this is an indication that skill requirements in the informal sector, with regard to waged employment, may not be different from what obtains in the formal sector.

The study has shown that profits, investment and cost of capital are crucial factors affecting the labour-demand of urban informal enterprises. The significance of investment in the determination of labour-demand suggests the need for government to ensure that there is adequate provision of capital for the informal sector operators. The government could provide direct loans for the privately-owned small and medium-size enterprises, and limit such provision to the officially-registered firms as a means of hedging against default. This could also be achieved by involving the Community and Peoples' banks, as well as various trade associations. It is, however, important that such credit and loans be provided at relatively low cost, since the study has shown that a high cost of borrowing discourages investment and employment: were this to be undertaken, there would be a positive spill over effect on profits and, hence, labour employment. That is, the informal sector would be able to live up to policy-makers' expectations of the sector contributing meaningfully and significantly to government's employment-boosting programmes.

It is important to note that the results and conclusion of this chapter are directly relevant to the SMEs within the informal sector. However, the results may not be generally applicable to all the production units within the informal sector, especially with regard to $IFPU_3$ and $IFPU_4$.

Appendix I

Variable definitions

Human capital variable definition:

Age	The age of the worker
Age^2	The age of the worker squared, used to capture possible non-linearity between age and wages
Education	The years of education of the worker. This was constructed based on the answers to the question on the final stage of

	education completed. It is treated as a continuous variable representing average years spent to complete a particular level of education. The different levels of education are defined as: Primary = 6 years Secondary = 12 years NCE/ND/Technical = 14 years HND/University = 16 years It must however be stated that years of education cannot be precisely measured.
Experience	Previous work experience of a worker before joining current job (number of years of previous) experience
Tenure	Number of years a worker has spent in current organization

Demographic variable

Gender	Gender of the worker 1 = Male, 0 = Female

Firm characteristics

Labour	Measure of size (the number of full-time employees in the firm). Employees that are paid monthly wages.
Yestab	Year of establishment (this is taken to measure the age of the urban informal enterprises)
Ownship	Ownership structure of firms: sole proprietorship = 1; partnership = 2; family = 3; cooperative = 4
Investment	Total amount of capital invested by the firm, measured in total stock
Profit	Average annual profit of the firm in the past three years
Cost_cap	This is the measure of cost of capital and it is calculated as the prevailing average lending rate of cooperative societies as at the time of survey multiplied by the level of investment of firms. The average lending rate used is 18.0 per cent.

Notes

1 SAP was adopted by the Federal Government of Nigeria in August 1986, as a comprehensive economic reform programme, aimed to correct the structural imbalance in the economy and serve as an elixir to the economic crisis brought about by the fall in the international prices of petroleum in the early 1980s.

2 See the Appendix of variable definitions for detailed descriptions of all the variables used in the present study.

References

Ajakaiye, O. and W.O. Akerele (1996) 'Overview of Conceptual and Methodological Issues in Informal Sector Research', in E.U. Olisadebe and O. Ajakaiye (eds), *Conceptual and Methodological Framework for Informal Sector Research in Nigeria*, CBN/NISER Informal Sector Study (Lagos: CBN) 7–25.

Blanchflower, D.G., A.J. Oswald and P. Sanfey (1993) 'Wages, Profits and Rent-Sharing', Mimeo, IES (Oxford: Oxford University Press).

Bromley, R. (1978) 'Organisation, Regulation and Exploitation in the So-Called Urban Informal Sector: The Street Traders of Cali, Columbia', *World Development*, 6: 1161–71.

Carneiro, F.G. and A. Henley (1998) 'Wage Determination in Brazil: The Growth of Union Bargaining Power and Informal Employment', *Journal of Development Studies*, 34, 4: 117–38.

Celestin, J.-B. (1983) 'Manpower Planning Information in French-Speaking Africa', *International Labour Review*, 122, 4: 78–96.

Charmes, J. (1990) 'A Critical Review of Concepts, Definitions and Studies in the Informal Sector', in D. Turnham, B. Salome and A. Schwartz (eds), *The Informal Sector Revisited* (Paris: OECD) 112–36.

Christofides, L.N. and A.J. Oswald (1992) 'Real Wage Determination and Rent-Sharing in Collective Bargaining Agreements', *Quarterly Journal of Economics*, August: 985–1002.

Cole, W.E. and B. Fayissa (1991) 'The Urban Subsistence Labour Force: Toward A Policy-Oriented and Empirically Accessible Taxonomy', *World Development*, 19, 7: 779–89.

Fields, G.S. (1990) 'Labour Market Modelling and the Urban Informal Sector: Theory and Evidence', in S. Turnham and Schwartz (eds), *The Informal Sector Revisited* (Paris: OECD) 26–42.

Folawewo, A.O. (2004) 'Urban Informal Sector Labour Employment: A Case Study of South-Western Nigeria', Unpublished PhD dissertation (Ibadan: University of Ibadan).

Hart, K. (1973) 'Informal Income Opportunities and Urban Employment in Ghana', *Journal of Modern African Studies*, 2: 43–65.

House, W.J. (1992) 'Priorities for Urban Labour Market Research in Anglophone Africa', *Journal of Developing Areas*, 27, 1: 49–68.

Hugon, P. (1977) 'La Petite Production Merchande et L'emploi dans le Secteur Informel', *Le CAS Africain* (Paris: IEDES) 48.

International Labour Organisation (1972) *Employment, Incomes and Inequality: A Strategy for Increasing Productive Employment in Kenya* (Geneva: ILO).

Levine, D. (1992) 'Can Wage Increases Pay for Themselves? Tests with a Production Function', *Economic Journal*, 102: 1102–15.

Maloney, F.W. (1998) 'The Structure of Labour Markets in Developing Countries: Time Series Evidence on Competing Views', Working Paper 1940 (Washington, DC: World Bank).

Mazumdar, D. (1981) *The Urban Labour Market and Income Distribution: A Case Study of Malaysia* (New York: Oxford University Press).

Nickell, S. and S. Wadhwani (1990) 'Insider Forces and Wage Determination', *Economic Journal*, 100: 496–509.

Oswald, A.J. (1995) *Rent-Sharing in the Labour Market*, Mimeo (London: London School of Economics).

Peattie, L. (1987) 'An Idea in Good Currency and How it Grew: The Informal Sector', *World Development*, 15, 7: 851–60.

Riveros, A.L. and L. Bouton (1991) 'Efficiency Wage Theory, Labour Markets, and Adjustment', Working Paper 731 (Washington, DC: World Bank).

Sanusi, J.O. (2001) 'Forward', in *A Study of Nigeria's Informal Sector, Vol. II – In-Depth Study on Nigeria's Informal Manufacturing Sector*, CBN/FOS/NISER (Abuja: Central Bank of Nigeria) 3.

Scherer, F.M. (1980) *Industrial Market Structure and Economic Performance* (Chicago: Rand McNally) 32–8.

Sethuraman, S.V. (1981) *The Urban Informal Sector in Developing Countries: Employment, Poverty and Environment* (Geneva: ILO).

Teal, F. (1995) 'Efficiency Wages and Rent Sharing: A Note and Some Empirical Evidence', Working Paper WPS/95–17 (Oxford: Centre for the Study of African Economies).

Teal, F. (1997) 'Real Wages and the Demand for Skilled and Unskilled Male Labour in Ghana's Manufacturing Sector: 1991–1995', Working Paper WPS/97–10 (Oxford: Centre for the Study of African Economies).

Udall, T.A. (1976) 'The Effects of Rapid Increase in Labour Supply on Service Employment in Developing Countries', *Economic Development and Cultural Change*, 24, 4: 765–85.

Wadhwani, S.B. and M. Wall (1991) 'A Direct Test of the Efficiency Wages and the Employer Size Effect in Zimbabwe', *Journal of Development Economics*, 53: 305–38.

Weeks, John (1975) 'Policies for Expanding Employment in the Informal Urban Sector of Developing Economies', *International Labour Review*, 111, 1: 1–13.

11

Survival Strategy and the Importance of the Informal Sector for Urban Poor Families: A Case Study of Jakarta

Tulus Tambunan

Introduction

Economic growth and the change of economic structure in the last 30 years or more in Indonesia have resulted in large scale urbanization. This has not only happened in Indonesia, it is a global phenomenon and, as economic development and growth continues, people from rural areas will continue to arrive in urban areas and big cities. Economic growth, structural change and globalization are increasingly linked to the urbanization process, to urban expansion, to the movement of people from villages to cities, and to more populous urban settlements than rural development. Metropolitan cities like Jakarta can offer the lure of better employment, education and health care, and contribute disproportionately to the country's economy. However, rapid urban expansion is often associated with poverty, a growth of an urban informal sector, problems of clean water supply and housing, environmental degradation, crime, urban slums and so on. These place social and human development, and even the sustainability of economic development in urban areas, at risk.

Since the economic crisis in 1997, urban poverty has become an obvious phenomenon in Indonesia. This is acute in most cities, including Jakarta, which suffer from serious problems such as a lack of sufficient housing, shortage of energy, chaotic traffic, a severe shortage of clean water, air, water and land pollution and increased open and hidden unemployment. In Jakarta, the problem of poverty has put great pressure on society, which local and central governments are not capable of managing. Governments at all levels are strained beyond their financial capabilities to build the necessary facilities for the cities' citizens. These factors exacerbate the strife of urban poverty. Planning, land allocation, and physical and social infrastructures are all deplorably inadequate and therefore unable to cope with the situation. Thus, an increasing number of the urban population lives in unplanned, often illegal, shanty towns with limited access to basic services and in environmental conditions that threaten health and life.

This chapter is based on a recent study that examined the urban poverty level and the condition in which the urban poor in Indonesia live, identifying their main survival strategies, particularly in coping with the economic crisis in 1997–98. The chapter also assesses the importance of the informal sector for the urban poor. Urban poverty-alleviation policies in Indonesia are also discussed.

Urban poverty in Indonesia

Recent trends

Data from the National Socio-Economic Household Survey (*Survei Sosial Ekonomi Nasional*: SUSENAS) show the numbers and percentage of the population living under the poverty line, by region, in Indonesia. As can be seen, the percentage of poor people in urban areas declined by 15 per cent from 10 million people in 1976 to about 8.5 million people in 2001, or from 38.8 per cent to almost 9.8 per cent of the total population. It rapidly increased again in 2002 to 13.3 million people or 14.5 per cent (Table 11.1).

'Where and how do the poor live?' is probably the most important and frequently asked question in studying the urban poor. To answer this question requires a city poverty profile, which is by definition a spatial tool with which to define the extent and nature of poverty within a given area. Providing an accurate mapping of where the poor live and where they are concentrated within cities is an important input required for targeting appropriate responses. Spatial information, especially on land use patterns, slum location and the physical location of facilities, is also an important input.

The poverty profile in Jakarta as presented in Table 11.2 shows some important aspects of poverty in relation to the type of occupation, employment status, gender and educational attainment. The SMERU (Social Monitoring and Early Response Unit) Research Institute also conducted poverty mapping in Jakarta, which showed that poverty in the city is concentrated in the western and eastern areas, as indicated by their higher poverty headcount ratios than in other parts of the city. These are also the most populated areas of the city, which as a consequence has

Table 11.1 The Indonesian poverty line, number and percentage of poor people, 1976–2002

Year	Poverty line (Rp/capita/month)		Poor people (%)			Number of poor people (million persons)		
	Urban	Rural	Urban	Rural	National	Urban	Rural	National
1976	4,522	2,849	38.8	40.4	40.1	10.0	44.2	54.2
1978	4,969	2,981	30.8	33.4	33.3	8.3	38.9	47.2
1980	6,831	4,449	29.0	28.4	28.6	9.5	32.8	42.3
1981	9,777	5,877	28.1	26.5	26.9	9.3	31.3	40.6
1984	13,731	7,746	23.1	21.2	21.6	9.3	25.7	35.0
1987	17,381	10,294	20.1	16.1	17.4	9.7	20.3	30.0
1990	20,614	13,295	16.8	14.3	15.1	9.4	17.8	27.2
1993	27,905	18,244	13.4	13.8	13.7	8.7	17.2	25.9
1996	42,032	31,366	13.6	19.9	17.7	9.6	24.9	34.5
1998	96,959	72,780	21.9	25.7	24.2	17.6	31.9	49.5
1999	92,409	74,272	19.4	26.0	23.4	15.6	32.3	48.0
2000	91,632	73,648	14.6	22.1	19.0	12.1	25.2	37.3
2001	100,011	80,382	9.8	25.0	18.4	8.5	28.6	37.1
2002	110,230	95,345	14.5	21.1	18.2	13.3	25.1	38.4

a stronger demographic pressure on the informal urban labour market than in other areas of the city.

Survival strategy and the importance of the informal sector for urban poor families: a case study of Jakarta

'What is the nature of urban poverty?' is another important question. While income-based poverty measures provide a fair sense of which part of the urban population may have unmet needs and where they are located, these measures fail to capture the dynamic aspects of urban poverty, in terms of the cause and extent of deprivation, risk factors, and the coping strategies employed. This can include analyzing vulnerability, urban–rural linkages, and perceptions.

In many cases, especially when the poor live in informal settlements, they may not be included in existing administrative data, which are the basic information for the poverty profile of Jakarta as shown in Table 11.2. Table 11.2 also does not provide information on coping strategies employed by urban poor families and their region of origin; yet, these are two important aspects of urban poverty that need to be studied. To cover these two aspects, a general household survey in Jakarta (the capital) was conducted during December 2003 and January 2004 for this study, using a structured

Table 11.2 Poverty profile of Jakarta

Description	1999	2000	2001	2002
Poverty as a percentage of total population in Jakarta	3.99	4.96	2.95	3.42
	(2.43)[1]	(3.38)	(2.88)	(2.15)
	(19.41)[2]	(14.60)	(9.79)	(14.46)
Poverty Gap Index (P1) (%)	0.58	0.82	0.43	0.39
	(4.33)[3]	(3.51)	(3.42)	(3.01)
Distributionally-Sensitive Index (P2) (%)	0.14	0.22	0.09	0.07
	(1.23)[3]	(1.02)	(0.97)	(0.79)
Poverty by gender as a percentage of the total population in Jakarta:				
Male	4.15	0.53	2.98	3.52
	(23.42)[4]	(19.07)	(18.37)	(17.49)
	(0.80)[5]	(1.17)	(0.67)	(0.82)
Female	3.98	4.70	2.91	3.34
	(23.31)	(18.83)	(18.42)	(17.66)
	(0.78)	(1.06)	(0.66)	(0.78)
Poverty by education as a percentage of total poverty in Jakarta:				
No formal education/did not finish elementary school	31.62	21.99	17.38	18.47
	(48.11)[6]	(47.38)	(48.98)	(44.56)
Elementary school graduate	45.58	37.56	25.98	46.32
	(35.69)	(35.78)	(36.83)	(38.84)
Junior high school graduate	14.03	19.27	17.10	16.50
	(8.83)	(9.12)	(7.96)	(9.76)
Senior high school graduate	7.55	19.20	26.60	17.35
	(6.74)	(7.12)	(5.49)	(6.24)
Tertiary/college/university graduate	1.22	1.97	12.94	1.36
	(0.63)	(0.59)	(0.74)	(0.60)
Poverty by occupation/sector as a percentage of total poverty in Jakarta:				
No work	25.19	21.71	14.21	18.02
	(8.47)[7]	(9.26)	(6.33)	(8.61)
Agriculture	1.75	0.32	0.19	1.83
	(54.19)	(51.73)	(62.99)	(57.75)
Industry	9.54	22.09	14.93	15.10
	(12.65)	(13.84)	(11.86)	(12.53)
Service	63.53	55.89	70.68	65.18
	(24.68)	(25.17)	(18.82)	(21.22)
Poverty by employment status as a percentage of total poverty in Jakarta:				
No work	25.19	21.71	14.21	18.02
	(8.37)[8]	(9.26)	(6.28)	(8.54)
Self-employed	43.57	30.09	28.97	30.47
	(27.19)	(28.06)	(18.55)	(23.26)
Employee with family/hired workers	2.77	11.82	11.01	6.17
	(36.07)	(34.78)	(46.34)	(37.75)
Employer/worker	28.48	36.06	45.20	45.47
	(27.56)	(27.03)	(27.89)	(29.99)

(*Continued*)

Table 11.2 (*Continued*)

Description	1999	2000	2001	2002
Family worker	0.00 (0.81)	0.32 (0.87)	0.60 (0.93)	0.00 (0.57)

Notes: Percentage by category in Indonesia: 1 = total urban poverty; 2 = total urban population; 3 = at national level; 4 = total population by sex; 5 = total poverty by sex; 6 = total poverty by education; 7 = total poverty by occupation; 8 = total poverty by employment status.

questionnaire. This survey also aimed to examine the importance of the informal sector for them. Due to time constraints, the sample survey only included 70 households, and the heads of the selected families are the respondents. The selected study area was one subdistrict of the city; namely, Tambora in west Jakarta, which is the poorest district in the city (Suryahadi *et al.*, 2003).

West Jakarta consists of eight subdistricts with 56 villages. Based on the poverty mapping results, the population of this district as of mid-2001 was about 1.5 million people. The population density was 124 people per hectare, and so it is the second most densely populated part of the city after central Jakarta. Of the eight subdistricts in west Jakarta, Tambora is known as being the most densely populated subdistrict, with 493 people per hectare.

The people of Tambora are considered, in general, to be middle- or low-income earners. Most people in this subdistrict work in very low income activities, such as petty traders and *ojek* (motorcycles or bicycles used as informal public transport) drivers. This latter type of low-income activity is common in Tambora. In general, poor people do not have permanent jobs, easily change their jobs and are found in informal low income economic activities. This phenomenon is very evident in Tambora.

Another important characteristic of poverty in Tambora is that this subdistrict has no space available for development of new houses or estates. Shacks occupied by many people, such that they have to take turns to sleep, are common in Tambora. One shack is sometimes occupied by two or three shifts. Due to the limited space, poor households have to arrange the schedule or activities of their family members to determine who stays in the shack.

In Tambora, one *kelurahan* or *kampung* (village) was selected for the survey; namely, Kampung Kalinjar. According to local government officials, this *kampung* is the poorest of a total of 11 *kelurahan* in Tambora. The area is about 33 hectares and about 29,555 people are living there, or almost 90,000 people per km^2. The majority of inhabitants work in the informal sector, as garment-makers, silk-screeners, small shop-owners, food vendors, cigarette vendors, potable water suppliers, workers in car or motorcycle repair workshops, or as *ojek*- and taxi-drivers.

Most of the houses of the families (respondents) were cramped, and many were occupied by more than one family with a total of more than ten persons: father, mother, and their unmarried children, as well as their married children with their own children. Their houses did not meet health and safety standards, and this was a general condition of most of the houses in Kelurahan Kalianjar. Only a small number of houses visited have their own bathroom and laundry facilities. In one of the sample families, the head of the family worked as a security guard for a big company in central Jakarta, and his wife took care of a stall in front of their house, selling basic needs. Of their five children, only two of them were still in school (primary), while the remaining three, aged 10 to 12 years old, were not in education. Instead, they were also family income-earners, selling newspapers/magazines in crowded main roads in the city. The married son is an *ojek* driver, and his wife helps her mother-in-law in managing the shop. Of their four children, aged one to six years old, only the six-year-old girl was in school. But as the mother said, when she finishes at her primary school, she will not continue her education simply because no money is available for that purpose. The mother did not yet have any idea what her daughter would be doing after that.

So, a study of poverty in these two districts reveals the nature of urban poverty in Indonesia. The sample households in the subdistrict covered in the survey were selected by stratified random sampling technique and this was achieved by dividing the population into stratum or sub-population; the household sample was drawn randomly to allow for degree of representativeness.

In general, the findings of the survey are given in table form. First, the characteristics of the respondents with respect to marital status, age and education are presented in Tables 11.3–11.5. In Table 11.3, it is shown that 73 per cent of the respondents are married. The selection of poor families as respondents for this study, with the procedure as explained before in the methodology, has resulted in 19 divorced women/widows in the group. Table 11.4 shows that the majority of the respondents are within the age range of 51–60 years (approximately 32.9 per cent of the total families interviewed) or 26–40 years (31.4 per cent of the total families interviewed). Therefore, the majority of the respondents are middle-aged people. Table 11.5 reveals that the majority of the respondents are only elementary school graduates; many of them never even finished

Table 11.3 Marital status of respondents

	Number of respondents		Total	% Distribution
	Male	**Female**		
Married	51	–	51	73.0
Divorced/widows	–	19	19	27.0
Total	51	19	70	100.0

Source: Survey.

Table 11.4 Age distribution of respondents

Age	Frequency	% Distribution
25 or younger	2	2.9
26–40	22	31.4
41–50	14	20.0
51–60	23	32.9
More than 60	9	12.8
Total	70	100.0

Source: Survey.

Table 11.5 Education of respondents by age category

	Age structure					Total	% Distribution
	≤25	26–40	41–50	51–60	>60		
No education/ elementary schooling uncompleted	–	2	2	5	3	12	17.1
Elementary graduate	2	18	10	18	6	54	77.1
Junior high school graduate	–	2	2	–	–	4	5.7
Senior high school graduate	–	–	–	–	–	–	–
Tertiary	–	–	–	–	–	–	–
Total	2	22	14	23	9	70	100.0

Source: Survey.

Table 11.6 Distribution of respondents by main source of income (occupation)

	Age structure					Total	% Distribution
	≤25	26–40	41–50	51–60	>60		
Formal							
– Company employee	–	2	1	–	–	3	4.3
– Civil servant	–	–	–	2	1*	3	4.3
– Construction daily worker	–	2	1	2	–	5	7.1
– Taxi-driver	–	1	–	–	–	1	1.4
– Public transport driver	1	1	2	–	–	4	5.7
– Factory worker	–	–	–	1	–	1	1.4
– Motor cycle garage worker	–	–	2	–	–	2	2.9
– Shop employee	–	–	1	–	–	1	1.4
– School teacher	–	–	1	–	–	1	1.4
– Other	–	1	–	–	–	1	1.4
Informal							
– Petty traders	–	2	–	3	–	5	7.1
– Small shop/stall owner	–	2	2	2	1	7	10.0
– Household industry	2	7	3	1	–	13	18.6
– Free-lance daily paid worker	–	1	–	1	–	2	2.9
– Food stall owner	–	1	–	1	1	3	4.3
– Other**	–	1	–	2	1	4	5.7
Unemployed	–	1	1	7	5	14	20.0
Total	3	22	14	22	9	70	100.0

Notes: * one respondent is already retired
** such as money lender and dress cleaner.
Source: Survey.

their schooling. So, this may suggest that one main factor behind their poverty is a low level of education.

Tables 11.6 and 11.7 show the economic conditions of the respondents. As can be seen in Table 11.6, half of the respondents have been found to have main sources of income in the formal sector (51.4 per cent), while the other half are employed in informal economic activities (48.6 per cent). In the formal sector, the majority of them work in low income generating jobs such as daily construction workers, public transport, low-paid company employee and civil servant. In the informal sector, most of the

Table 11.7 Distribution of respondents by monthly income (head of the family)*

Rupiah	Frequency	% Distribution
0–100,000	–	–
101,000–200,000	3	5.0
201,000–300,000	23	38.3
301,000–500,000	21	35.0
501,000–1000,000	12	20.0
>1000,000	1	1.7
Total	60	100.0

Note: * Many respondents said that their incomes are not permanent/stable, depending greatly on work/order availability.
Source: Survey.

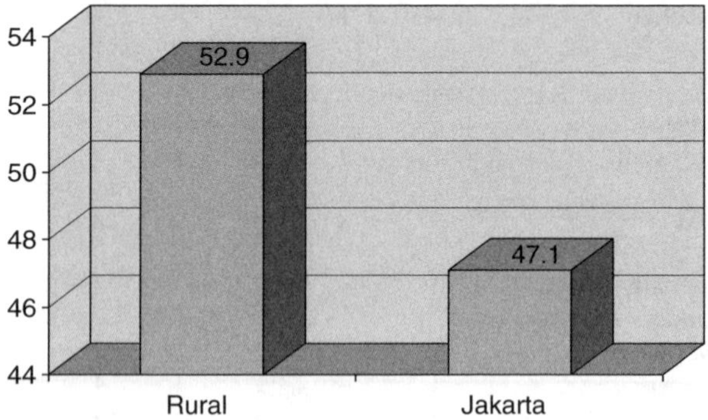

Figure 11.1 Region of origin of respondents

respondents work in home industries producing garments. This does not provide a stable monthly income; it depends on market competition and how creative they are when trying to find customers. From total respondents of 70 families, 14 of them (20 per cent) have been found to have no work (unemployed), whereas Table 11.7 shows that the majority of the respondents fell in the monthly income category of 500,000 *rupiah* or less.

This study has also attempted to discover whether the poor people in Jakarta (or in other urban areas) have come from rural areas and, if so, their main reason for moving to cities. The finding, as shown in Figure 11.1, shows that, indeed, the majority of the respondents (almost 53 per cent) originated from rural areas, mainly from rural Java.

During the survey, the respondents who were born in or originated from outside Jakarta were given three options for their main reason for

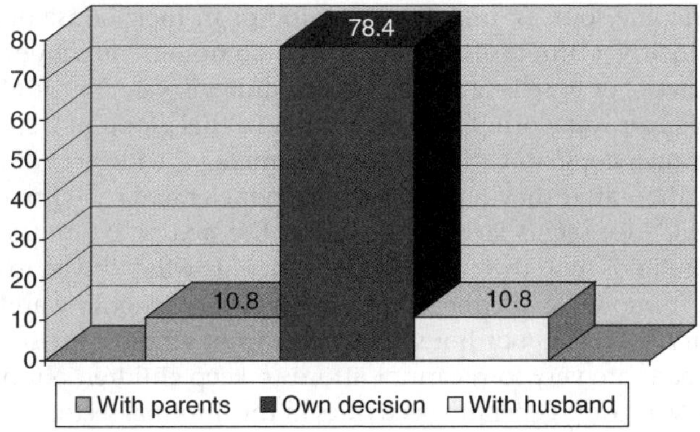

Figure 11.2 Main reasons to come to Jakarta

Table 11.8 Family survival strategy of respondents

	Frequency*	**% Distribution**
Diversification of income sources	16	20.5
Borrow money	23	29.5
Overwork	9	11.5
Sell household items	3	3.9
Reduce monthly expenditure on basic needs	18	23.1
Other**	6	7.7
No response	3	3.9
Total	78	100.0

Notes: * Some respondents gave more than one option.
** e.g. financial support from children or neighbours.
Source: Survey.

moving to the city. As generally might be expected, Figure 11.2 indicates that the reason the majority of them came to Jakarta was to find work or a better living standard. The remaining respondents in the group moved to Jakarta with their parents or came with their husbands to look for work.

Finally, during the survey the respondents were asked about their survival strategy or the main means that they undertake in order to cope with their poverty, especially during the economic crisis in 1997–98. They were asked to respond to various options as given in Table 11.8. The findings show that, for example, borrowing money from neighbours or relatives and/or reducing monthly expenditure are the strategies adopted by the majority of the respondents. Another strategy is diversification of family income sources; mainly letting rooms in their house or sending such of their yet unmarried children who do not attend school to work as *ojek* drivers, or to sell cigarettes, bottled mineral water or the afternoon newspapers or some other freelance work. In this group of respondents, many families could not afford to keep financing the further education of their children after they had graduated from elementary school.

This evidence seems largely to confirm the luxury axiom that asserts that households send their children to work only when driven to do so by poverty. It implies that child non-work (typically schooling and leisure) is a luxury good for poor households. Such households, the incomes of whose heads are very low, cannot afford to keep children out of work – mainly low income generating activities in the informal sector (Tzannatos, 2003). In other words, if parents are too poor to meet the necessary expenditures of the household and cannot borrow against the future earnings of their children, dissavings in the form of child labour may be necessary for survival (Humphries, 2003).[1]

One important implication of the above evidence is that, although many families in the sample depend on the formal sector as their main source of income, there is no doubt that the informal sector is also very important for them. The importance of the informal sector is also supported by SUSENAS data at the national level, showing that in the period 2000–01, the percentage of workers in the informal sector in Indonesia increased from 47.38 to 64.44 per cent (Table 11.9). As shown previously in Table 11.2 (the poverty profile of Jakarta), self-employed workers, who

Table 11.9 Number and percentage of workers in informal and formal sectors by gender, 2000 and 2001

	Male		**Female**		**Total**	
	Number	**%**	**Number**	**%**	**Number**	**%**
Formal						
2000	34,080,017	61.47	13,193,618	38.36	47,273,635	52.62
2001	22,029,568	38.56	10,265,190	30.48	32,294,758	35.56
Informal						
2000	21,359,046	38.53	21,205,049	61.64	42,564,095	47.38
2001	35,101,856	61.44	23,410,803	69.52	58,512,659	64.44
Total						
2000	55,439,063	100.00	34,398,667	100.00	89,837,730	100.00
2001	57,131,424	100.00	33,675,993	100.00	90,807,417	100.00

Source: SUSENAS.

form the most important category in the informal sector, played a crucial role as the main source of income for the urban poor families. As is also found from the survey, the majority of those who undertake activities or work as low-income paid workers in the informal sector are 'pushed' to do that, either as their main source of income because of difficulties in finding better jobs elsewhere, or as their secondary income to complement their low income from formal sectors. Due to its unique characteristics (such as easy entry and exit, very low initial capital outlay and no requirement for a high level of skills, no tax or other duties to be paid, and very flexible in adjusting to changes in the market), the urban informal sector has become the only and the easiest option for urban poor families. Moreover, although it depends on the type of activity or market service, in general, incomes from the informal sector are more secure than formal income sources, even in bad economic circumstances. This is because the market is also secure, as the majority of the population in Indonesia, as in other less developed countries, is poor and can only buy cheap essential goods and services from the informal sector.

Main cause of rural poor families moving to urban areas

Although there are probably many contributing factors, there is no doubt that the most important cause of increasing urban poverty in Indonesia is poverty or economic backwardness in rural areas. But, this is not specifically an Indonesian story; it is a general phenomenon in many other developing countries. Since the economy in rural Indonesia, which is much less developed than in urban areas, is dominated by agriculture, the main source of rural poverty is low productivity/real income per worker in the agricultural sector. Official data on the distribution of poor families by occupation in Indonesia indicate that the vast majority of poor families are in agricultural work, predominantly on farms (Table 11.10).

Table 11.10 Distribution of poor families by occupation, 1999–2002 (number of heads of families in 000s of persons)

	1999	2000	2001	2002
Unemployed	4,063	3,560	2,349	3,072
Agriculture	25,997	20,109	23,375	20,605
Industry	6,069	5,380	4,401	4,471
Services	11,840	9,784	6,984	7,571
Total	47,969	38,833	37,109	35,719

Source: SUSENAS.

Land is the most important store of wealth in agrarian societies, and in Indonesia it is typically distributed very unequally. This fact challenges the common presumption that the majority of urban poverty emerges from the poorest farm households. Data from an agricultural census indicates that Indonesian agriculture is dominated by a large and increasing number of small family farms. An agricultural census undertaken in 2003 indicates that are 25,437 million farmers working the land, 13,663 million (almost 57 per cent) of whom are marginal farmers with less than half of the land under their control. In 1993, the number of households farming the land was 20,518 million (an increase of 1.8 per cent per year during the period 1993–2003), whereas the number of marginal farmers was 10,804 million (an increase of 2.6 per cent per year over this period). In Java, the number of family farms working the land and the marginal farmers increased by 1.5 per cent and 2.4 per cent respectively per year over the same period.

Unfortunately, no official data exist on socioeconomic characteristics of migrants who move from rural areas to urban ones, as the Central Bureau of Statistics (BPS) or Department of Population never conduct surveys or studies on migrants. However, this Jakarta case study may give some support to the view that rural poverty or poverty in agriculture has been the main cause of continuing movement of people from rural to urban areas. As shown before (see Figure 11.1), the majority of the respondents were from rural areas. Most of them came to Jakarta to find work after they finished their primary school; only a few of them have a secondary diploma. The majority of them are from poor farm households without their own land, whose fathers work as daily-paid agricultural labourers. Only some respondents had worked as agricultural workers, local transport-drivers or as daily-paid workers in micro enterprises for several years before they moved to Jakarta.

Urban poverty-alleviation policies

The importance of good policy and initial favourable conditions were identified as the main factors contributing to poverty-reduction in rural as well as urban areas during the pre-crisis period in Indonesia. There were four main important policies and programmes devised by the new order government (1969–98). First, the rice policy, which subsequently led to Indonesia's attainment of 'rice self-sufficiency' in 1984, had a lasting impact on the alleviation of poverty. Second, during the oil boom in the 1970s, the government made substantial allocations to the social and human resource development sectors, as well as to the transport infrastructure. It was during this period that the government implemented the expansion of primary schools (SD INPRES) and health centres (PUSKESMAS) to ensure wide access to these basic social services. Also, during this period the government established the INPRES funding system, which allows direct grants from the centre to the regions. Third, the government ensured that particular social sectors were protected within the development budget, primarily by utilizing the INPRES mechanism. Fourth, labour-intensive projects were put in place; these have long been part of the government's efforts to stimulate employment and income for the low-skilled working population, especially during tough economic times. These low-skilled employment generation projects were aimed mainly at reducing unemployment, and hence poverty, in urban areas. Some projects were also implemented in rural areas.

An extremely high inflation rate, and its severe impact on poverty during the economic crisis in 1997–98, led the Indonesian government to introduce a social protection policy, widely known in Indonesia as the social safety net (SSN) programme. This programme is aimed at minimizing the deterioration of social welfare and sustaining key human-resource investments. Although rural poor households were also targeted, this programme was more focused on the urban poor as urban economic activities – dominated by industry, trade and services – were hit more severely by the crisis than the agricultural based rural economy.

One of the features of the SSN programme was the Special Market Operation (OPK), which aimed to provide cheap rice to poor households, not only in urban but also in rural areas. It was introduced partly in response to the economic crisis and partly in response to the drought that affected many parts of eastern Indonesia in 1997–98. In early 1999, this targeted rice-subsidy programme reached approximately 50 million people, almost equivalent to the entire population officially recorded as poor by the end of 1998 (Dhanani and Islam, 2000). In terms of central government expenditure, data from the National Planning Agency (BAPPENAS) indicate that the OPK programme is the most important of Indonesia's targeted schemes providing rationed benefits in kind. In the first year, the expenditure on this programme was 3.7 per cent of total central government expenditure, and declined to 3.14 and 1.22 per cent respectively in the following two years. As a percentage of total anti-poverty spending, the share of the OPK programme stood at 41.5 per cent during the fiscal years 1998/99–1999/00, and declined to 21.6 per cent in 2000.

The SSN also has a scholarship programme to protect pupils from poor households from dropping out as a result of the negative effects of the economic crisis 1997/98.[2] Other scholarship programmes existed prior to this – such as the *Gerakan Nasional Orang Tua Asuh* (National

Movement of Foster Parents), smaller government programmes and other, mainly private initiatives – but none of these was comparable in size with the SSN scholarship programme (Sparrow, 2003). The SSN scholarship programme provided scholarships or school grants to children thought to be most at risk of dropping out, while schools in poor areas received budgetary support in the form of block grants to help them maintain quality of education. SUSENAS data from 1998 and 1999 indicate that school attendance rates at all three levels were maintained during the crisis. This suggests that the scholarship programme may have prevented a large number of poor school children from dropping out of school.

After the OPK and the scholarship programme, a health care and nutrition programme was also introduced as part of the SSN in 1998, which included a mix of direct funding to individual households and block grants to service-providers, such as hospitals, clinics and family planning services (World Bank, 2000). A separate nutrition programme, which operated from 1998 until 2000, provided supplementary food and vitamins for infants and pregnant women (Daly and Fane, 2002).

The employment programme related to the SSN programme was also introduced during the financial year 1998/99, financed by a World Bank loan. This scheme is aimed at creating jobs for unskilled workers, and comprises two components: the first provides grants for the development of the infrastructure; the second provides loans for business activities. This scheme played an important role in substantially preventing the increase of urban unemployment, and hence poverty, during the crisis. Through this scheme many low-skilled/low-paid workers and those who were laid off from industry, manufacturing, construction and banking (many companies in these sectors were bankrupted by the crisis) were either employed to build or repair the public infrastructure or supported by government grants to start their own small businesses. Daly and Fane (2002) refer to this scheme as being not just labour-intensive (*padat karya*) programmes, but also 'job-creation schemes'.

Overall, none of the respondents in the sample survey agreed that these poverty alleviation programmes are capable of substituting for or reducing the role of the informal sector. For them, informal economic activities, even though they sometimes only generate very low incomes (depending on the type of activity), offer some kind of security for their long-term survival.

Conclusion

This chapter began with an examination of the evidence on the trend towards poverty in Indonesia since the inception of the new order government or the pre-economic crisis and the subsequent period. The evidence shows that sustained rapid economic growth since the 1970s up until the mid-1990s led the incidence of poverty to drop significantly. When the economic crisis occurred in 1997–98, poverty in Indonesia increased again sharply, and when the country's economy rebounded in the subsequent two years, the percentage of the population deemed to be poor declined, but it is still higher than the lowest level it has ever reached; that is, 15.1 per cent in 1990. But, the evidence also shows that, since the crisis, urban poverty has become a serious problem, and this problem is not only a result of the crisis but also an accumulated effect of increasing rural–urban inequality and the continuing underdevelopment of agriculture in the country.

This chapter also gave some important evidence from the results of a survey of poor families in Jakarta, which shows that sending children to work in the informal sector is an important way of diversifying their sources of income. This evidence seems largely to confirm the luxury axiom, which asserts that households send their children to work only when driven to do so by poverty.

Another important implication of this evidence is that, although many families in the sample depend on the formal sector for their main source of income, there is no doubt that the informal sector is very important for them, at least as a secondary or a complementary source of income.

This chapter also tried to examine the main causes of urban poverty in Indonesia. It may be concluded that the most important cause of increasing urban poverty in the country is poverty or economic backwardness in rural areas. Since the rural economy in Indonesia is dominated by agriculture, the main source of rural poverty is in the agricultural sector, as the vast majority of poor families are in agricultural work, predominantly on farms, most of them being marginal farmers. This problem has been aggravated since the Indonesian government has gradually reduced its support for agricultural development since the mid-1980s, and since the economic crisis the government has reduced or stopped its input subsidies (fertilizers, seeds).

The above evidence provides some important policy implications for urban poverty-alleviation in Indonesia. There is no doubt that many factors have contributed to urban poverty but, among these factors, poverty in rural areas has been the main cause, as every year thousands of unemployed or poor people move from rural to urban areas, especially Jakarta. This implies that urban poverty-alleviation policies, including SSN programmes as discussed above, will yield an optimal result only if they are combined with rural poverty-alleviation policies such as the improvement of labour productivity in agriculture and the distribution of agricultural assets (especially land), development of the physical and social infrastructure and non-farm activities in rural areas, and more access for the rural poor to better education and health facilities. In other words, policies fighting urban poverty cannot be considered in isolation; they need to take into account the wider problem of poverty; that is, poverty and its main determinant factors in rural areas.

Notes

1 The role of poverty has been the cornerstone of much of the thinking about child labour, and evidence such as this from the sample study in Jakarta can also be found in many other big cities in Indonesia or in urban areas in other poor countries, where child labour is widespread. Results of a recent study by Nagaraj (2002) of the *beedi* industry in Tamil Nadu and Karnataka, India, show that the number of children aged 5–14 attending school increases as monthly household per capita incomes, presented by consumption expenditures, rise. Further, at a more macro level, country case studies from India and China (ILO, 1996) and Thailand (Tzannatos, 2003), for instance, show a clear relationship between household income and child labour: as nations become richer, the incidence of child labour tends to fall. For more discussion, see, for example, Jayaraj (1993), Grootaert and Patrinos (1999), Ray (2000a; 2000b), Edmonds (2001), Admassie (2002), Nagaraj (2002) and Wahba (2002).

2 The economic recession in the late 1980s had been associated with a decline in school enrolments and there was official concern during the 1998 crisis that this should not be repeated. Therefore, before the beginning of the school year in late August 1998, the government together with the World Bank and the Asian Development Bank (ADB), assisted by other external donors, including the Australian Agency for International Development (AusAID), hastily assembled the Scholarships and School Grants Programme, which was designed to prevent a fall in school enrolments.

References

Admassie, A. (2002) 'Exploring the High Incidence of Child Labor in Sub-Saharan Africa', *African Development Review*, 14: 251–75.

Basu, K. and Z. Tzannatos (2003) 'The Global Child Labor Problem: What Do We Know and What Can We Do?', *World Bank Economic Review*, 17(2): 147–73.

Daly, A. and G. Fane (2002) 'Anti-Poverty Programs in Indonesia', *Bulletin of Indonesian Economic Studies*, 38(3): 309–29.

Dhanani, S. and I. Islam (2000) 'Poverty, Inequality and Social Protection', Working Paper 00/01, April (Jakarta: UNSFIR).

Dhanani, S. and I. Islam (2002) 'Poverty, Vulnerability and Social Protection in a Period of Crisis: The Case of Indonesia', *World Development*, 30(7): 1211–31.

Edmonds, E. (2001) 'Will Child Labor Decline with Improvements in Living Standards?', Working Paper 01-09, Dartmouth College, Department of Economics, Hanover, NH.

Grootaert, C. and H. Patrinos (eds) (1999), *The Policy Analysis of Child Labor* (New York: St Martin's Press).

Humphries, J. (2003) 'Child Labor: Lessons from the Historical Experience of Today's Industrial Economies', *World Bank Economic Review*, 17(2): 175–96.

ILO (1996) *Economically Active Populations: Estimates and Projections, 1950–2010*, (Geneva: ILO).

Jayaraj, D. (1993) 'Labor Force Participation of Children in Rural India', Working Paper 116, Madras Institute of Development Studies, Gandhinagar.

Nagaraj, K. (2002) 'Female and Child Workers in a Household Industry: A Case Study of Beedi Industry in Karnataka and Tamil Nadu', Working Paper, Madras Institute of Development Studies, Gandhinagar.

Ray, R. (2000a) 'Analysis of Child Labor in Peru and Pakistan: A Comparative Study', *Journal of Population Economics*, 13(1): 3–19.

Ray, R. (2000b) 'Child Labor, Child Schooling, and Their Interaction with Adult Labor: Empirical Evidence for Peru and Pakistan', *World Bank Economic Review*, 14(2): 347–67.

Sparrow, R. (2003) 'The JPS Scholarship Program', *SMERU News*, 6, April–June (Jakarta: SMERU).

Suryahadi, A., W. Widyanti, D. Perwira, S. Sumarto and C. Elbers (2003) 'Developing a Poverty Map for Indonesia: An Initiatory Work in Three Provinces', Part I: Technical Report, SMERU Research Report, May (Jakarta: SMERU).

SUSENAS (1963/64–2003) 'National Socio-Economic Household Survey' (Jakarta: Central Bureau of Statistics) http://www.rand.org/labor/bps.data/webdocs/susenas/susenas_main.htm

Tzannatos, Z. (2003) 'Child Labor and School Enrolment in Thailand in the 1990s', *Economics of Education Review*, 22: 523–36.

Wahba, J. (2002) 'The Influence of Market Wages and Parental History on Child Labor and Schooling in Egypt', Working Paper, Department of Economics, University of Southampton.

World Bank (2000) 'Health Strategy in a Post-Crisis, Decentralizing Indonesia', Report 21319-IND, Human Development Sector Unit, East Asia and Pacific Region (Washington, DC: World Bank).

12
Public Policies to Promote Productive Occupation and Increase Formality Among the Moderate Poor: The Mexican Agenda

Eduardo Sojo and Roberto Villarreal[1]

Introduction

Public policies for the alleviation of poverty have been in place in Mexico for a long time. The nature of these policies has varied, from universal consumption subsidies to support for public infrastructure and income transfers and subsidies for human capital accumulation of targeted low-income groups. At present, the federal government pursues a far-reaching strategy for the permanent reduction of poverty, basically at its deepest levels.[2]

Macroeconomic policies have also contributed to poverty-reduction by maintaining price stability and a strong foreign exchange rate, thus preventing real income losses for the population. The combination of stable macroeconomic conditions with active social policies for poverty alleviation has proved effective. As a result, the population under three poverty lines (line A, income just sufficient to buy required food; line B, income roughly sufficient to buy required food plus basic health and education goods and services; and line C, income barely sufficient to acquire said nutrition, health and education items, plus goods and services related with clothing, transportation, housing and other important needs) has decreased steadily. Even if extreme poverty (defined, for the purposes of this chapter, as being indicated by a per capita income below poverty line B) is still unacceptably high, the declining trend indicates that ongoing policies are operating in the right direction. Indeed, the number of individuals in extreme poverty in 2002 was around 26.9 million (26.5 per cent of the total population), 4.2 million less than two years previously.

As the real income of the extreme poor has increased, many have entered into moderate poverty (defined as being indicated by a per capita income between poverty lines B and C). This has brought about important transformations in poverty. First, the number of moderate poor reached 25.6 million by 2002, a magnitude very close to that of the extreme poor (moderate poverty represents almost half the total poverty in the country). And, second, geographically, moderate poverty has become more frequent in urban areas in contrast with extreme poverty, which is more evenly spread in rural and urban localities. In fact, in 2002 moderate poverty represented 16.5 million in urban areas, while there were 10.1 million extreme poor in the same localities. In contrast, rural areas had 16.9 million extreme poor and 9.1 million moderate poor. Therefore, 64 per cent of the moderate poor inhabited urban areas, while 53 per cent of the extreme poor lived in rural areas.

Faced with these trends, public policies for the alleviation of poverty in the country deserve careful consideration. While the strategy already operating for the extreme poor needs to be maintained and the number of households covered by the corresponding programmes must be enlarged, additional new strategies are required for the moderate poor, whose economic and social characteristics are considerably different from those in deeper levels of poverty. Moreover, policies aimed at expanding productive occupation for the moderate poor, in a context of increasing formality,[3] gain an unprecedented importance in the development strategies of Mexico.

These issues are analyzed in this chapter. The next section contrasts several characteristics of the moderate poor against other income groups, in aspects that are relevant to the planning of adequate public policies designed to foster the human and economic development of the moderate poor. The subsequent section shows that informal occupation is not a mere residual when labour-demand is low but is, rather, a permanent or structurally-determined category. Additionally, evidence is presented in the sense that informal jobs, although providing useful income for poor households, offer lower earnings and seldom provide security against risks. The chapter goes on to analyze how informality is largely provoked by the presence of a gap between existing laws and regulations and the actual conditions of occupation in industries where small businesses are very numerous. The penultimate section points out some directions in which laws, regulations and government support programmes should be reformed to reduce informality and to promote the human and economic development of the moderate poor.

Characteristics of the moderate poor and implications for public policies aimed at facilitating their participation in formal economic activities

Household income and expenditure surveys are rich in socio-demographic information, which permits us to distinguish several features of the population in moderate poverty *vis-à-vis* those in extreme poverty and the non-poor. These differences must be taken into consideration in order to design appropriate public policies for the human and economic development of the moderate poor. Based on the survey of 2002, four aspects merit attention.

First, households in moderate poverty have a lower average proportion of members between 0 and 18 years of age and a smaller demographic dependency ratio (that is, the quotient of the number of members in the age ranges under 18 and above 65 relative to those aged 18–65), compared to poorer households. This is of considerable importance, for two reasons. On the one hand, it permits moderately poor households to accumulate capital over time, since such dependency ratio (89.2 per cent) favours a smaller consumption-to-income ratio and some savings potential. In contrast, in extremely poor households, the dependency ratio equals 124.3 per cent, thus resulting in a negligible savings capacity.

On the other hand, the smaller number of members under 18 years of age or above 65 reduces time requirements for family care. In a society in which this role has traditionally been entrusted to women in a disproportionate manner, the lesser number of dependents in moderately poor households facilitates a more frequent participation of women in extra-domestic economic activities. This opens several important avenues for the social and economic development of moderately poor households, since additional income can be provided by a greater number of employed women[4] to expand the family budget (which in many cases will move these households out of moderate poverty) and, at the same time, empowerment of females through income-generation in good jobs would accelerate social change and improve gender equity. The relevance of this as a general strategy is even more remarkable when it is considered, as the survey indicates, that one in every five households in moderate poverty is headed by a woman.

Second, school attendance of household members aged 6–18, although equally frequent among the moderately and extremely poor households

(80 per cent), is still below that observed among the non-poor population (87 per cent). To some extent this is a consequence of early school abandonment by the children and teenagers of poor families who enter the workforce before concluding their basic education,[5] but it is also caused by insufficient or inadequate access to childcare institutions for the poor, so that often small children must stay together with their working mothers in informal jobs. Similar problems occurred in the more distant past, resulting today in 80 per cent of moderately poor household members aged 18–65 not having completed their high school education. Even if this proportion is lower than in extremely poor families, it is still much higher than among the non-poor (63 per cent) and, to the extent that competition for jobs in the formal sector favours workers with a better education, as discussed below, the lower schooling of the poor puts them at disadvantage and influences their need to find jobs in informal activities.

Third, the average rate of economic participation, as well as the average number of employed income-earners, is not very different among the three income groups. Even if these indicators attain slightly larger values among the non-poor population (suggesting fewer restrictions on access to job opportunities or greater work effort) this fact appears of lesser importance than the differentials in average income of employed earners. Indeed, average income per employed earner among the moderate poor is only 39 per cent of that of the non-poor and twice that of the extremely poor. Obviously, these huge differentials are related with equally remarkable differences in productivity, due to factors that are explained later, many of which are associated with informality.

The differences in average income per employed earner, combined with the demographic characteristics previously analyzed, explain the differentials in mean income per capita, as well as the contrasting savings capacity, among the three income groups. Indirect evidence on capital accumulation potential is provided by the survey through statistics on holdings of physical assets. The moderately poor households have better dwellings than the extremely poor, both in terms of size and quality of materials. Similarly, the proportion of households who own motor vehicles and domestic appliances is significantly higher among the moderately poor, although much lower than in non-poor families.[6]

Fourth, on occupational characteristics, the survey shows that employment rates do not vary across income groups (97 per cent). However, the types of occupation more frequent in each case do differ: self-employment is far more common among the poor (23 per cent of employed members in moderately poor households and 35 per cent in extremely poor households, compared to 17 per cent among the non-poor). Self-employment results in considerably lower earnings: the self-employed from moderately and extremely poor households earn 80 per cent and 70 per cent, respectively, of the amount earned on average by all employed workers from the same income groups.[7]

But lower labour earnings are not the only disadvantage for poor households. Protection against risks is also relatively rare for them, as they have less access to health care and pensions from social security. Only 44 per cent of those employed from moderately poor families enjoy social security, compared to two thirds of those from non-poor households.

Differences in schooling among the income groups have been pointed out in preceding paragraphs. However, such differences also exist within each group, according to occupational status. The self-employed stand out as the category with the lowest level of schooling in the three income groups. In poor households, employed members that enjoy more years of schooling are mainly wage-earners, while members with less schooling are self-employed or business-owners. Thus, schooling differentials are found, once more, to be a determinant of participation in activities that exhibit characteristics of informality.

Gender issues influencing occupation in informal activities are also confirmed when examining the survey data. The distribution of employed members of moderately poor households, by occupational status, indicates that a large majority of males are wage-earners (69.3 per cent, excluding agricultural activities), while almost half of the females are self-employed, and about one out of every ten is employed with no wage in a family-owned business. Moreover, self-employment among males from moderately poor families is not negligible: one out of every six men employed is from this income group. Occupation as business-owners is also considerable among males from moderately poor households, yet in economic units of five or less persons employed (6.2 per cent of all men employed are found within this income group) and seldom in units of a larger size (1.5 per cent).

The large proportion of women who are self-employed, as has already been explained, reflects social or institutional factors that restrict women from finding full-time extra-domestic activities and make it difficult for them to be hired in formal businesses. While 75 per cent of males from moderately poor households work more than 40 hours per week, only 45 per cent of females do so. Conversely, 47 per cent of women in this income group work less than 36 hours per week extra-domestically. Restrictions of socio-cultural origin against the full-time participation of women in extra-domestic activities are an important determinant of informality (considering that part-time hours and flexible time schedules are very common in informal jobs), since the alternative for women of not participating at all in productive activities would bring their families into deeper degrees of poverty.

In sum, this section explains how several demographic and social characteristics of the population influence its participation in informal activities. Unless adequate public policies are adopted to cope with or modify those characteristics over time, or the laws and regulations that interact with those characteristics, informality will persist, since informal jobs are a key income alternative for large groups of a disadvantaged population.

Informal and formal occupation: some economic determinants and implications

This section presents an additional view on informality, looking at national aggregates of formal and informal occupation from an economic perspective, based on data from the quarterly National Employment Survey of INEGI.

The simultaneous changes in occupation recorded in the structured and non-structured sectors of the Mexican economy[8] show a very different relationship when measured over different time spans. Looking at quarterly absolute changes of employment in the structured and non-structured sectors, over the period 2000–02, most often they have opposite signs, indicating that informal occupation usually increases in the short run when formal occupation declines, and vice versa. In contrast, absolute changes in formal and informal occupation normally are of the same sign over one-year periods. This reveals that informal jobs appear to be substitutes to formal ones in the short run, while these two types of jobs are complements, in the aggregate, over the medium or long run.[9]

This phenomenon is interesting, since it articulates two apparently different conceptions of informal occupation. Indeed, informal employment grows when labour demand in the formal sector is low, but this mainly reflects short-run economic behaviour: informal jobs may be attractive, but only as an immediate and temporal alternative to formal jobs, for individuals whose characteristics would allow them to get a formal job later on, once demand for labour grows in the formal sector. However, this substitutability between formal and informal jobs does not exist for those who are structurally restricted to access formal jobs, such as many women who are time-constrained and persons with relatively low schooling, as previously explained. Thus, over the medium and long run, even if demand for labour in the formal sector expands, informal occupation continues to grow if labour supply from the structurally disadvantaged population keeps increasing.

Formal and informal jobs are not close substitutes since they have very different characteristics in terms of remuneration and protection against risks such as unemployment and health or death risks. The poor who, because of structural factors, such as those analyzed above, must take informal jobs more frequently than non-poor individuals, suffer noticeably from the lower quality of informal jobs. Among the employed members from moderately poor households, 56 per cent do not have social security, compared to 33 per cent in the case of non-poor families. Similarly, 40 per cent of the moderately poor workers do not have a written labour contract, while this proportion is only 22 per cent among non-poor workers.

The National Employment Survey also reveals that most jobs in the informal sector are found in very small-scale economic units. Actually, 97 per cent of the persons occupied in the informal sector are own-account workers (that is, self-employed) or work in units of two to five individuals. Only 3 per cent are occupied in economic units of six or more individuals.

In economic units so small, value added per employed person is very low. As indicated by quarterly time series, even though some productivity increases have been observed between 1996 and 2001 in the formal and informal sectors, average value added per employed person in informal activities remains close to 40 per cent of that in formal activities. So, income for business-owners or waged employees in informal activities is relatively low. Average profits of owners or the self-employed among moderately poor households are broadly one quarter of those among non-poor households.

Similarly, the survey indicates that in each industry over the period 2000–03, formal occupations paid more than informal ones. In retail commerce, formal jobs resulted in earnings 35 per cent higher than informal ones. This ratio was more remarkable in transport (60 per cent higher) and construction (70 per cent higher).

The lower earnings for individuals who participate in informal economic units are likely to result from a combination of causes. Some are related to production aspects: in general, informal businesses operate with fewer educated workers and the owner-entrepreneurs usually have less human capital; management, marketing and innovation are comparatively more traditional and less competitive; applied knowledge and technology in production processes are generally outdated; capital is significantly lower, as reflected in smaller stocks of machinery, tools and equipment, and small and poor buildings and installations, as well as little working capital. Other causes relate to differential access to markets by micro-firms: financial markets are rarely accessible to them and, in particular, commercial bank credit is unavailable to very small firms or the self-employed, not only due to their low profitability and high risks, but also because of insufficient or inadequate collateral and considerable difficulties in enforcing contracts through the judicial system. Small loans from relatives or friends, or informal credit markets that charge considerably high interest rates, constitute the most frequent sources of finance for micro-businesses. Similarly, their access to product markets is restricted to segments where commercialization without tax receipts or invoices is common, as in informal markets on the streets and in poor neighbourhoods, where sales costs are high because of the limited quantities of goods and services that can be marketed. In these market segments, profit margins are rather low as prices must consider the low purchasing power of their clienteles. So, informality translates into lower earnings because of low productivity, high financial costs and small profit margins for the majority of micro-firms or the self-employed.

If informal jobs result in lower incomes and less protection against economic or health risks, there must be reasons why occupation in informal activities is so numerous. In every year in the period 2001–03, there were roughly 10.6 million individuals occupied in the informal sector, with a minor upward tendency. The view in this chapter is that existing laws and regulations (particularly those on labour and social security, but also on other matters concerning which administrative burdens are too high) are too costly to comply with for most firms. Larger firms deal with these high costs by hiring more productive workers under conditions that help reduce average labour costs, while smaller firms often cannot cope with these costly laws and regulations and operate without compliance with the juridical framework.

This view is supported by data regarding the incidence of informal occupation across different industries. Again, during the period 2001–03, survey data indicate that slightly more than three out of every four individuals occupied in the non-structured sector were employed in retail commerce; services (including a large variety, such as transportation, personal or professional services, and many others); construction; food preparation in the streets; and similar economic activities. Knowledge of these industries tells that larger production units do not evidently result in lower costs per unit of output or, in other words, these are industries where economies of scale are low or insignificant. Therefore, competition in the corresponding product markets does not induce the concentration of total supply in a small number of production units. Rather, total output in these industries is produced by large numbers of small-sized businesses (often thousands of them in every industry, totalling approximately 5 million in aggregate, with one or two workers collaborating with the owner of each firm): a myriad of small productive units, market-efficient and able to survive in a competitive environment.

This setting is propitious for a widespread lack of observance of applicable legislation (in matters such as labour, social security, taxes and so on), for two reasons. From the outside of businesses, it is practically impossible for enforcement authorities to supervise the effective observation of laws and regulations in millions of economic units (many of which do not operate at fixed locations). And, at the same time, from the inside, workers in these firms do not find it convenient to form small unions, which would be very small, in order to oblige the strict observance of those laws and regulations that benefit them; because compliance with those ordinances is costly, they are not put into practice by the vast majority of small units of production. So, informality is observed.[10] Individuals restricted by structural factors from participation in better formal jobs, as explained before, have recourse to occupations in those activities where labour demand is consistent with their own characteristics, in activities that are viable on a very small scale.

Industries in which the costly benefits established by the existing legislation are actually honoured have to be more productive in order to balance those costs with additional revenues. The higher productivity is, in part, the outcome from scale economies. But it is also generated when workers with greater human capital are employed, and when productive activities are organized according to long-run optimized procedures, with higher capital–labour ratios. For these reasons, it is natural that less informality is associated with industries in which scale economies exist, where more capital and better-educated workers are employed and where full-time employment is fundamental in order to optimize production procedures.

Some considerations on the need of an adequate legal framework for micro-firms

The high concentration of informality in industries where scale economies are not significant indicates that existing laws and regulations (basically those on labour and social security matters) are considerably more difficult for small businesses to obey than for large ones, because the economic conditions of micro-businesses limit their productivity and make it very difficult for them to face the costs implied by the existing legal framework.

This gap in compliance with legislation may be explained by the fact that the core of the existing legal framework on these matters was designed and enacted by the mid-1900s, when the future economy was foreseen as consisting almost entirely of productive units large enough so that the laws and regulations could be brought into effect without extraordinary enforcement costs.

However, the subsequent decades demonstrated that economies of scale do not prevail in a considerable part of the economy and, therefore, the enforcement costs of the previously enacted legal framework are not only disproportionately large in many industries but, more importantly, those costs exhibit significant differentials across industries. Therefore, enforcement of the legal framework is viable in industries where large firms are common but seldom in activities where micro-firms dominate.

Two aspects of the existing laws and regulations may be recognized among the main causes of informality. The first consists of administrative burdens imposed by the legal framework that can be borne by relatively large entities but that represent a disproportionate cost for smaller production units and the self-employed. This is the case, for example, in applications for government licences or permits (to open or operate a business, import goods, use registered trademarks and so on); submission of periodical reports to several agencies (including tax declarations,[11] information for statistical purposes, employment data for social security and so on); inspections in situ mandated by different authorities (on labour and fiscal matters, safety of installations, ecology and so on), among many others. This kind of legal burden has received substantial attention from policymakers and thus has lead significant efforts in the deregulation arena.[12]

Another important aspect of the existing legal framework that provokes informality is geared around the regulation of labour relations within the firm. The central laws governing the relationship between firm-owners or managers, on one side, and workers or employees, on the other side, assume as a paradigm the theoretical model of a firm in which large asymmetries are observed between both sides: workers have less physical and financial wealth, as well as less human capital, and derive their income solely from the wages they receive for their participation in the firm's earnings. In contrast, owners are wealthier, more educated and obtain profit incomes from diversified sales of different products in several markets. In this conceptual context, it is efficient and makes sense to distribute risks or uncertainty unevenly among both sides in the labour relationship, making owners take on a larger share of the costs of insurance for social protection (labour contracts impose penalties on owners for unjustified dismissals, contributions to health and life insurance as well as to retirement funds under social security to a considerable extent must be faced by employers and so on). Moreover, the asymmetries in wealth and associated social or political power enjoyed by firm-owners are compensated for in the existing legislation by a set of rights accruing to workers (forming unions, burden of proof in labour suits accrues to owners and so on), so as to equilibrate labour relations and mitigate possible abuses against the labour force.

The paradigm broadly sketched above once more reflects the views of legislators in the earlier decades of the twentieth century. Indeed, worries about the exploitation of labour by capitalistic units of production were shared by most countries worldwide, and laws and regulations were enacted to face those challenges in labour relations, which were key for social, economic and political reasons in that time. Nonetheless, the observed situation in most micro-firms challenges the described paradigm: in very small production units, where an owner-entrepreneur collaborates with two or three workers (possibly including some family members), labour relations usually do not exhibit the antagonistic nature assumed by the general labour legislation, but rather are characterized by collaborative attitudes. Solidarity among participants in very small firms is widely present, bringing important social aspects and not only economic considerations into the relationships of the owner-entrepreneur and workers. In addition, the presumed asymmetries between both sides, as outlined before, are less profound and sometimes do not exist at all among those that collaborate in very small production units. Quite often their wealth is of the same order of magnitude, education gaps are noticeable (as shown by the data presented in the preceding sections) but not as wide as in larger firms, and income diversification is as limited for workers as for the owner-entrepreneur due to the fact that the micro-firm is not as diversified in products and markets as larger firms are.

Faced with this marked contrast between the nature of labour relationships in very small production units and the paradigm underlying existing labour regulation, it is not surprising that those who participate in micro-firms, either as workers or as owner-entrepreneurs, find it more efficient to regulate their relationships by social standards or rules existing in their communities, instead of following those codified in formal laws and regulations.[13] The non-compliance with legal standards and rules on labour and social security matters in most micro-firms reflects the fact that the contents of formal regulations as of today bring about considerable inefficiencies in the organization and operation of productive activities in micro-firms, therefore inducing individuals who participate in them to behave according to their more suitable social (although informal) norms. The income opportunity losses that would be provoked if micro-firms were to behave strictly as mandated by formal or codified laws and regulations just cannot be borne by people living under some degrees of poverty.[14]

Two specific examples illustrate these notions around two of the most critical problems related with moderate poverty and informality: the occupation of women and, in general, of individuals with a comparatively low level of education. Given the costs of compliance with existing labour and social security legislation, formal firms find it inefficient to hire women on part-time arrangements, as employers would have to pay contributions to social security on a full basis. Thus, they require full-time contracts to lower hourly labour costs. But this implies that women from moderately poor households (for the reasons previously given) cannot engage in such terms and consequently are relegated to self-employment or to jobs in micro-firms (where the costly legal conditions are not met; that is, informal jobs). Moreover, over-regulation makes many childcare institutions function with rigid time schedules and be located apart from today's working zones, implying greater constraints on women to commute and meet those time schedules, which magnifies the need for jobs with flexible conditions, seldom found in formal firms.

In the case of less educated males or females, similar constraints make it incompatible for them to continue their education on a part-time basis while at the same time holding a job in a formal firm. This is why many young members from moderately poor households engage in informal occupations (in micro-firms or self-employment), which allow them the flexibility of pursuing their education while contributing to family income.

In sum, different capacities to cope with costly legislation as previously explained, as well as differentials in enforcement costs, result in the legal framework being honoured in one part of the economy, but not in another. So, to the extent that the legal framework does not recognize such differentials, informality persists in certain industries.

The inconvenience of this situation is twofold. On the one hand, in a considerably large part of the economy the state cannot efficiently apply the rules it has enacted. On the other hand, to the extent that the population perceives the legal framework as inequitable (since it poses identical obligations on productive units that are evidently distinct), many individuals feel less compelled to obey what are perceived to be such unfair rules. Thus, both enforcement and compliance of legislation are lowered: the rule of law is weakened, as well as associated political and juridical institutions.

On the other hand, small productive units live in a state of permanent legal uncertainty since, even though existing laws and regulations are not likely to be enforceable on them, the risk exists that this might happen, implying potentially large sanctions. Under this uncertainty, the self-employed, as well as entrepreneurs and owners of micro-firms, are discouraged from committing greater effort and more resources to their productive activities, which results in no productivity improvements and stagnating incomes.

In conclusion, there are strong reasons to propose a legal reform to overcome these fundamental problems. To reduce informality and bring all economic units under a common, equitable and efficient set of legal ordinances, the legal framework must be redefined in the case of small productive units, according to the experiences observed during the last decades. The aim would be to promote a dynamic and fair process of social and economic development, based on the productive efforts of the disadvantaged population.

A strategy to overcome moderate poverty and informal occupation

Considering that about one quarter of the Mexican population suffers from moderate poverty and that nearly the same proportion of the occupied labour force works in informal conditions, the country faces the challenge of adopting effective public policies to overcome these problems.

The proposals in this chapter correspond to two categories: first, the improvement of the legal and regulatory framework to induce greater formality of economic units; and second, the establishment of a coherent government programme to provide support for entrepreneurship among moderately poor households, as well as to enhance productivity and the formality of occupation in micro-firms.

An improved legal framework

With regard to the juridical framework applicable to micro-firms, the existing laws and regulations need profound reform in order to address both the need to regulate labour relations in these economic units so that they may realistically meet their specific nature according to the considerations presented above, and the need to reduce the administrative burdens imposed by laws and regulations on micro-firms. The four main objectives of reform would be:

1 To increase profitability among micro-firms, by raising their productivity, facilitating their access to lower cost-input markets as well as to larger and richer product markets. In this respect, two promising areas for reform are the fiscal and financial areas. On the fiscal side, valuable improvements can be made at least to two aspects: efforts are required further to simplify administrative procedures related to tax payments; and tax credits or deductions should stimulate human capital investment in micro-firms. Improvements in these directions would allow micro-firms to increase their sales and profit margins by facilitating their access to larger and more affluent formal product markets, and would also raise their productivity from a more skilful labour force.

   On the financial side, the legal and regulatory framework should continue to foster the sustainable development of competitive private or social financial intermediaries specialized in financial services for the poor. The savings potential of the moderately poor must be stimulated further, since capital accumulation over time would fundamentally change the economic conditions of these families, permitting them permanently to overcome poverty. Legislation must provide the poor with access to formal financial services and intermediaries, adequately regulated, so as to offer positive and secure returns on savings.[15] In addition, further improvements in legislation should promote the prudent expansion of micro-credit, development bank loans for viable productive projects, seed or risk capital for innovative activities considered by low-income entrepreneurs, and public warranties to facilitate access to finance from commercial banking. The capitalization of micro-firms would increase productivity and earnings in these economic units, improving the income of workers from moderate poor households;
2 To provide individuals who are self-employed or occupied in micro-firms with effective access to basic elements of insurance, so as to reduce their vulnerability to the main risks they face (health, accidents, death, retirement and so on). Adequate insurance must be redefined, so that actuarially balanced contributions do not discourage individuals from entering into these schemes. Complementing this, it would be useful to reconsider the convenience of offering increasing levels of protection during the life cycle of individuals instead of requiring protection against all risks from the moment

they enter employment. The matching of different types of insurance to the life cycle would be efficient, since it would reduce individual insurance costs[16] and would help individuals in micro-firms to enjoy renewed instruments of social protection.

In particular, labour legislation needs adequately to address the risk of job loss for individuals employed in micro-firms. So far, all firms are strictly sanctioned for unjustified dismissals by federal labour law. Generally, entrepreneurs consider compensation is too high and, moreover, the law favours workers disproportionately in cases of termination of the labour relationship. To the extent that micro-firms are fragile economic entities and that owner-entrepreneurs of these micro-firms are seldom wealthy individuals, the procedures to end the labour relationship in the case of micro-firms must be revisited in order to provide workers with certain minimal conditions of job security, without discouraging new hiring and firm growth in these small productive units.

3 That labour and social security reform should lead to a significant expansion of employment opportunities for women. In this respect, part-time employment must be facilitated in all firms and childcare institutions should be regulated in new ways so as to make them more accessible for working women. Insurance costs for female workers should also be improved, considering adequate protection for the entire household without requiring redundant contributions from several family members.
4 That the reformed juridical framework should explicitly highlight the fundamental obligations with which micro-firms must comply on key matters. Having these obligations dispersed in innumerable pieces of legislation makes it too difficult for small firms to be well informed, and creates legal uncertainty that discourages their owner-entrepreneurs to invest more over time. A concise catalogue of obligations for small economic units would facilitate their development and growth in a clear context of formality especially defined for micro-businesses.

A coherent government programme to enhance entrepreneurship and productivity of the self-employed and those occupied in micro-firms

At present, the federal government operates a large variety of programmes with diverse characteristics aimed at improving the employment possibilities of the disadvantaged population and enhancing productivity in small firms. These programmes cover aspects such as subsidized education and scholarships at all school levels; technical training; assistance on managerial, marketing and technological matters; finance for productive projects; development of financial intermediaries for low-income groups and so on.

However, these programmes are administered by a variety of ministries and agencies in independent and uncoordinated ways. Building upon existing programmes, a coherent and comprehensive strategy is called for that will make government support to entrepreneurship and the productive occupation of the moderately poor more effective overall. This can be developed along the following lines:

1 Individuals should be provided with information and access to the different programmes in one-stop modalities, and by streamlined applications and procedures. This requires a considerable re-engineering of government to overcome the historical situation in which individuals have personally to come before each ministry or agency in order to apply, to meet diverse eligibility criteria, provide repetitive documentation and follow procedures that are often cumbersome and time-consuming.
2 A common registration database needs to be constructed, with complete records of the benefits each individual receives from all programmes. This is important in order to evaluate the effectiveness overall of government's efforts to provide support, instead of partial evaluations of each programme. Moreover, the database would also permit improvement to the distributional effects of the government programmes by income deciles. In the past, few programmes have pursued this and evidence exists that a large part of the benefits go to members of the population in income levels above those originally considered by the programmes. A well-structured database could also be made publicly available to assure transparency regarding government support programmes.
3 The operation rules by which each government programme is managed must be improved in order to introduce incentives for beneficiaries to enter formality. Otherwise, redefinition of the juridical framework to facilitate compliance with adequate formal norms would be hampered if government programmes did not reinforce the move towards formality.

Conclusion

Laws and regulations are means by which to achieve the determined goals of society by harnessing the conduct of individuals in ways convergent with the attainment of those goals. To eradicate or significantly reduce informality, laws and regulations must consider the specific characteristics of the groups whose informality is to be overcome.

Reducing informality in this fashion is important for several reasons. Reduced informality would improve income and social protection for the moderately poor; integrate sectors that can benefit from trading with each other, in order to increase the competitiveness of the Mexican economy; and improve political governance and consolidate the rule of law. The benefits would be reaped not only on pure juridical grounds but on economic, social and political aspects as well. Thus, public policies to reduce informality belong to the set of development policies required by a modern society permanently to increase the income and protection of its members.

Notes

An earlier version of this chapter was presented at the EGDI-WIDER Conference on 'Unlocking Human Potential: Linking the Informal and Formal Sectors', Helsinki, 17–18 September 2004 and published as Sojo and Villarreal (2005).

1 The authors collaborate in the Office for Public Policies at the Executive Office of the President of Mexico. Their views and statements in this chapter must be considered strictly personal and do not necessarily convey the official position of the Mexican authorities. The authors are grateful to Claudia Guerrero and Marco Antonio Sánchez for excellent research assistance, as well as to the National Institute for Statistics, Geography and Informatics (INEGI) for access to income and employment surveys. Nonetheless, any errors are the sole responsibility of the authors.

2 Since the mid-1990s, a new strategy (*Progresa*) looks for human capital accumulation among the extremely poor, while efforts continue to concentrate subsidies on consumption goods for the poorest. This was maintained during the Fox administration, although with a new name (*Oportunidades*), and its original policy interventions were complemented with new ones: support to education went beyond basic levels to include high school; access to financial services has been widely promoted to stimulate savings among poor households, while government income transfers and private remittances from migrant workers are facilitated through a new network of private and social financial intermediaries; and finance for productive activities of the poor has multiplied through micro-credit. The geographical scope of *Oportunidades* widened to include marginal urban areas, reaching 5 million households by August 2004. Moreover, programmes to build a public infrastructure for the extremely poor were focused on micro-regions where rural poverty is most profound.

3 Informality is understood throughout the chapter as occupation in the non-structured sector, where individuals are not only unprotected by labour and social security laws and regulations, but also seldom pay federal or local

taxes, in most cases performing their economic activities without compliance with regulations on public health, environment, use of space and so on. By far, the largest proportion of employment in these informal conditions comprises individuals whose social, demographic or economic characteristics restrict them from finding good jobs in larger formal firms. In order to meet the economic needs of their families, they engage in the production of goods and services in the informal context just described, mostly self-employed or in very small businesses. Only a minor proportion of total employment in the informal sector constitutes criminal activities (trading in stolen or counterfeited goods, or merchandise illegally introduced into the country). Statistics on occupation in the non-structured sector are generated by INEGI according to definitions given by the ILO. These statistics therefore reflect the total of the self-employed, plus those occupied in economic units of less than 5 persons in service industries or less than 15 in manufacturing (excluding agricultural activities) which do not comply with legislation on labour and social security with regard to business owners, waged-employed or unpaid family members.

4 Employment surveys by INEGI show that practically all men of productive age among moderately poor households already have a job (either formal or informal). Therefore, additional labour income can only be generated by productivity gains or by a larger extra-domestic participation of still economically inactive women.

5 Poverty alleviation programmes in Mexico include grants and scholarships for pupils from poor families and cover education from primary level to high school level. *Oportunidades* stands out in this sense. Yet, the *Programa Nacional de Becas* (PRONABES) has also contributed with over 6 million scholarships for high school or university education.

6 However, the moderately poor often do not have formally-recognized property rights over the assets they own. The potential costs from eventual risky litigation concerning those assets reduce their liquidity and lower their market value. Granting this population efficient means by which clearly to establish their formal property rights is tantamount to giving them considerable capital gains.

7 The opposite is observed among employed individuals from non-poor households: the self-employed on average earn 10 per cent more than the waged employed. Thus, the self-employed from poor families, even if they work in an autonomous way, suffer from conditions that lower their labour productivity compared to individuals otherwise employed. The differences in human capital between the self-employed and the wage-earners are also relevant, as pointed out in the text.

8 The non-structured sector is synonymous with the informal sector in this chapter. See note 4.

9 This can be explained in terms of dynamic adjustment costs. See Villarreal (1986).

10 The marked differences in the incidence of informality by industry (depending on whether scale economies exist or not) make less appealing the notion that informality is simply explained by a lack of will to coerce the application of existing laws and regulations. Differences in cultural aspects across industries, or differential incidence of corruption in distinct activities, are not very convincing.

11 Present Mexican tax law does not impose high levels of taxation in the tax brackets in which micro-firms usually operate. The problem derives more from the administrative burden associated with the payment of taxes. However, complying with fiscal legislation must be considered an important aspect of formality, not just for the revenues that would result for the treasury (which would be small, given the low taxable income and moderate tax rates of the moderately poor population), but for two other basic reasons. First, it would permit micro-firms to access larger and more affluent markets and, second, it conveys the right signals in terms of political culture and citizenship (individuals may claim a number of rights from society and the state, but in balance they must comply with a proportional set of obligations).

12 In the early 1990s, Mexico started a deregulation programme fostered by a specialized authority in order to facilitate businesses and increase efficiency. Nonetheless, emphasis on reducing informality has not been stressed to a comparable extent.

13 The fact that micro-firms seldom comply with labour and social security laws and regulations does not mean that the labour relationships among workers and owner-entrepreneurs are totally open to all kinds of possible abuse from either side. Quite the opposite; participants in very small firms bring into their productive activities a wide array of social norms, standards and values that are commonly accepted in their communities and even solve controversies or conflicts as they occur by means of those social (although informal) rules. It must not be overlooked that, in very small firms, information on the economic conditions of the production unit is more evenly shared by all participants, as compared with what happens in larger firms, thus eliminating or considerably reducing chances of abuse from any participant in the micro-firm against the other.

14 In most cases, participants in micro-firms are aware of the expected costs of the sanctions they would face if detected by the authorities. However, they consider that those expected costs are outweighed by the income opportunities that would be lost if they had to comply strictly with the existing laws and regulations.

15 This is why, in 2001, at the start of the Fox administration, a new law (*Ley de Ahorro y Crédito Popular*) was approved by Congress to guide the gradual transition of financial intermediaries typically serving the poor into more solid, reliable and regulated financial institutions.

16 The aggregate aspects of these proposals have to be investigated as well, considering the age distribution of the population and its foreseeable evolution, so as to warranty the financial sustainability of the new system that could be developed.

References

Edwards, S. and N. Lustig (eds) (1997) *Labor Markets in Latin America: Combining Social Protection with Market Flexibility* (Washington, DC: Brookings Institution Press).

International Labour Organization (ILO) (2002) *Decent Work and the Informal Economy*, Report VI, 90th session (Geneva: ILO).

Kanbur, R. and L. Squire (2000) 'The Evolution of Thinking about Poverty: Exploring the Interactions', in G.M. Meier and J. Stiglitz (eds) *Frontiers in Development Economics: the Future in Perspective*, World Bank (New York: Oxford University Press).

Lay, J. (2002) *Segmentation and Informality in Urban Labour Markets: Evidence from Bolivia and Implications for Poverty Reduction* (Kiel: Kiel Institute of World Economics).

Levenson, A. and W. Maloney (1998) 'The Informal Sector, Firm Dynamics and Institutional Participation', Working Paper (Santa Monica, CA: Milken Institute for Job and Capital Formation).

Lustig, N., O. Arias and J. Rigolini (2002) 'Poverty Reduction and Growth: a Two-way Causality', Sustainable Development Department Technical Paper Series (Washington, DC: Inter-American Development Bank).

Maloney, W. (1999) 'Does Informality Imply Segmentation in Urban Labor Markets? Evidence from Sectoral Transitions in Mexico', *The World Bank Economic Review*, 13, 2, May.

Organization for Economic Cooperation and Development (2004) *OECD Economic Surveys: Mexico* (Paris: OECD).

Piore, M. (1983) 'Labor Market Segmentation: To what Paradigm does it Belong?', *American Economic Review*, 73, 2.

Samaniego, N., A. Hernández and R. Gutiérrez (2000) *Los principales desafíos que enfrenta el mercado de trabajo en México en los inicios del Siglo XXI* (Geneva: ILO).

Sojo, E. and R. Villarreal (2005) 'Public Policies to Promote Productive Occupation and Increase Formality among the Moderately Poor: The Mexican Agenda', WIDER Research Paper 2005/17 (Helsinki: UNU-WIDER).

Villarreal, R. (1986) 'Investment and Financing Interactions at the Firms Level: A Microeconometric Simultaneous Equation Approach', unpublished PhD dissertation, Department of Economics (Cambridge, MA: MIT).

Women in Informal Employment: Globalizing and Organizing (WIEGO) (2004) 'Addressing Informality, Reducing Poverty: A Policy Response to the Informal Economy', Carr Center for Human Rights, Kennedy School of Government, Harvard University.

Index

Notes: f = figure; n = note; t = table; **bold** = extended discussion or heading emphasized in main text.